Incomplete Democracy

A book in the series
Latin America in Translation / en Traducción / em Tradução

Sponsored by the Consortium in Latin American Studies
at the University of North Carolina at Chapel Hill
and Duke University

INCOMPLETE DEMOCRACY

POLITICAL DEMOCRATIZATION
IN CHILE AND LATIN AMERICA

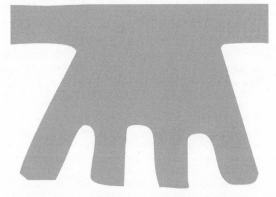

Manuel Antonio Garretón

Translated by R. Kelly Washbourne
with Gregory Horvath

THE UNIVERSITY OF NORTH CAROLINA PRESS
CHAPEL HILL AND LONDON

Designed by Lou Robinson
Set in Minion Type
by Keystone Typesetting, Inc.
Manufactured in the United States of America

This book was published with the assistance of the William R. Kenan Jr. Fund of the University of North Carolina Press.

Translation of the books in the series Latin America in Translation / en Traducción / em Tradução, a collaboration between the Consortium in Latin American Studies at the University of North Carolina at Chapel Hill and Duke University and the university presses of the University of North Carolina and Duke, is supported by a grant from the Andrew W. Mellon Foundation.

The paper in this book meets the guidelines for permanence and durability of the Committee on Production Guidelines for Book Longevity of the Council on Library Resources.

Library of Congress Cataloging-in-Publication Data
Garretón Merino, Manuel A. (Manuel Antonio).
[Política y sociedad entre dos épocas. English]
Incomplete democracy : political democratization in Chile and Latin America / by Manuel Antonio Garretón ; translated by R. Kelly Washbourne with Gregory Horvath.
p. cm. — (Latin America in translation/en traducción/em tradução)
Includes bibliographical references and index.
ISBN 0-8078-2810-6 (cloth: alk. paper)
ISBN 0-8078-5483-2 (pbk.: alk. paper)
1. Latin America—Politics and government—1980– 2. Democracy—Latin America. 3. Democratization—Latin America. 4. Political culture—Latin America. 5. Chile—Politics and government—1973– 6. Democracy—Chile. 7. Democratization—Chile. 8. Political culture—Chile. I. Title. II. Series.
JL966.G37513 2003
320.98—dc21
2003042613

cloth   07 06 05 04 03   5 4 3 2 1
paper   07 06 05 04 03   5 4 3 2 1

Contents

Acknowledgments

This book would not have been possible without the support of the Department of Sociology and the School of Social Sciences at the Universidad de Chile for all my teaching activities and research, and for the research of the school's undergraduate and graduate students. I am grateful for the contribution made by the students at the Universidad de Rosario, whose political science conferences have offered an excellent opportunity for debate, and I thank the Ford Foundation in Chile and all the institutions whose activities created a space to develop the information and ideas contained here. My exchanges with Guillermo O'Donnell, Jonathan Hartlyn, and Peter Cleaves were especially meaningful, as were my collaboration in numerous projects with Tomás Moulián and Marcelo Cavarozzi and the constant intellectual inspiration and friendship of Alain Touraine.

The first part of this volume correlates with my book *Política y sociedad entre dos épocas: América Latina en el cambio de siglo* (Rosario, Argentina: Editorial Homo Sapiens, 2000). In the second part, Chapters 9 and 10 are derived from Chapters 3 and 4 of my book *Hacia una nueva era política: Estudio sobre las democratizaciones* (Santiago: Fondo de Cultura Económica, 1995), and Chapter 11 is a modified and updated version of my article "Balance y Perspectivas de la democratización política chilena" (in A. Menendez and A. Joignant, *La caja de Pandora: El retorno de la transición chilena* [Santiago: Planeta/Ariel, 1999]). Thanks to all the aforementioned for granting permissions for this translation.

Incomplete Democracy

Introduction

The principal phenomenon occurring throughout Latin America in recent decades, with effects that vary from country to country, is the disarticulation of the relations between state and society that have characterized it since the 1930s. This is accompanied by attempts to recompose those relations, and attendant changes in the development model and the way the region is inserted into the world. This breakdown could be permanent, or it could give way to positive recompositions in which the state, the system of representation—especially the party system—civil society actors, and the democratic regime that binds all the elements together, are simultaneously strengthened, made autonomous and complementary to one another. Such a decomposition and likely recomposition are carried out through four processes that are interrelated but that nevertheless have their own dynamics. None of these can be subordinated to another, nor can one be given priority over another, since all of them are immediate concerns.

The first process is to build working political democracies that counteract the de facto powers, guarantee representative majoritarian governments, advance citizenship, and channel social conflicts and demands. In addition to the incomplete tasks of the democratic transitions and the consolidation of institutions to prevent authoritarian regressions, the main challenges that these countries must face are those of the deepening, quality, and relevance of their democracies.

The second process is that of social democratization, which includes the phenomena of participation and overcoming growing inequalities. The main problem to address here, which affects all areas of social life and collective action, is the new nature of exclusion. The world of the excluded, which in some countries constitutes 60 or 70 percent, and which totals hundreds of millions throughout the region, tends to be defined today by their total marginalization and by the disregard with which the mainstream society treats them. Today the organizational and ideological resources that characterized exclusion in the national popular era and the era of so-called inward-oriented development, which prompted populist or revolutionary forms of mobilization, are absent.

The second phenomenon is multidimensional and has to do with the expansion and narrowing of citizenship. The concept of a territorial "polis"—the classic space of citizenship, the polity—seems to be exploding. Citizenship has always been the demand and the recognition of a subject's bearing of rights before power and authority. This was identified early on as civil rights, later was associated with the right to belong to the "polis" (political rights), and was subsequently extended to economic and social rights. Today, gender relations, the media, the environment, and local and transnational systems are among the areas in which there are powers to be opposed and rights to be claimed. Therefore they constitute spaces of citizenship. People want to be citizens, and not merely to have access to justice, a minimum wage, and social and political rights. Yet these new areas are not recognized by the political institutions, a problem that evidently is not unique to Latin America. On the one hand the concept of citizenship is taking off and spreading. On the other hand, it has to contend with new exclusions.

The third process is that of the redefinition, beyond structural adjustment and autonomization of the economy from politics, of the development model. Here markets and international opening are not sufficient to redefine a process of insertion into a transnationalized economy that has to integrate all of society and not merely the "included" part. If the inward-oriented development model seems to have run its course, it is unlikely that inequalities and the problem of exclusion can be resolved within the framework of the new model that is being implemented in the region. Due to economic growth, there seems to have been a reduction in poverty, but not inequality, in several countries. If a process of redistribution is not brought about, however, there is a limit to this growth. One must bear in mind that the redistributive dimensions should be carried out in a democratic, noncoercive framework. To accomplish this, the formation of large political majorities is needed. And today, such redistribution would involve not only economic resources but also information, knowledge, communication, organization, and diversified mechanisms of power. All that entails a strengthening of the role of the state as the fundamental agent of development, social integration, and redistribution in a context of greater autonomy of economic phenomena that must be regulated.

The fourth process—which in a sense encompasses the previous ones yet has its own specificity—is that of defining an alternative model of modernity, in other words, the constitution of social subjects and the generation of collective action. The classic expressions of collective action (populism, clientelism, revolutionary ideologies, antiimperialist nationalism, etc.) are widely challenged today by two models of modernity that are fighting for control. One model involves the marriage of market and technocratic rationality with mass media culture, which wipes out collective identities and memories. The other model is the invocation of historical community and identity (religious, ethnic, or a combination of the two), which brings the risk of new fundamentalisms. Between these models lies a void of subjects and collective action.

Any successful unfolding of these processes will depend on the emergence of political projects that manage to respect diversity without breaking down society into particularisms; incorporate technological and scientific rationality without suppressing the expressive-communicative dimension or historical memory; generate coalition-building capacity without overlooking societal conflicts; and generate capacity for representation without falling into ideological voluntarisms. There is no single social subject or single political actor that can face this task and be the sole bearer of a project of this sort.

The role of intellectuals lies in elaborating and implementing projects that can account for this complexity. The fulfillment of these tasks, always ambiguous and ambivalent, will force them to abandon messianic prophesying and subordination to new forms of technocratic domination. In addition, it will require joining a knowledge of reality and of what it hides with utopian, always partial, visions of the possible and the desirable.

In the Latin American context, the Chilean case has been wrongly judged to be a double transition: a transition to the so-called market economy, considered "successful," and to democracy, considered "exemplary." Neither assessment seems accurate, though they may serve to give undue satisfaction to those who through blood and fire assembled a difficult-to-change economic model that gave rise to profound upheaval and huge inequalities, and who had prepared a transition to a limited democracy riddled with authoritarian inheritances. In this framework, the opposition to the dictatorship had to accept both economic and political determinants and, as a government, later had to become embroiled in a struggle that was not always successful—not to prevent an authoritarian regression, a goal that was already assured, or to consolidate a limited democracy, but to correct the economic model and achieve full democracy.

Transformations of the political system, especially those involving democratizations, and their relations with the whole of society in Latin America and Chile, make up the central topics of this book. This study cannot be understood without the twofold reference to an intellectual and a political trajectory.

This study is heir to the intellectual tradition of Latin American sociology and Chilean social thought and, thus, to the trajectory it has followed. It is also an attempt to move away from ideology and the determinisms permeating that tradition. This search, at once engaged and removed, for an interpretation of situations that have been experienced firsthand and have affected the course of our lives, was begun under the Chilean military dictatorship, though all the chapters of this book were written under the new democratic regime. My ongoing involvement in intellectual debate, the founding of working groups and networks, discussions, seminars, and teaching in Chile and internationally have been instrumental in this search, as have my professional involvement in social science research and ongoing participation in political debate through self-critical polemics, participation in democratic struggles, the renewal of ideological thinking, and programmatic development.

Thus, topics considered over the last ten years, many of which have had preliminary versions published elsewhere, are revisited and reworked here. The reader should not be surprised to have already read some of these studies and should accept the reiteration of certain ideas throughout the chapters, as well as the deliberately cursory treatment they receive in certain sections, since they are developed more fully in others.

The book is divided into two parts. The first concerns Latin America and begins with the elaboration of analytical orientations in the first chapter. In the following two chapters, I reflect on the transformations that are redefining the historical context of Latin America. In that framework I take stock of the theories about and processes of democratization. Subsequent chapters consider the transformation of the state, the meaning of social policies, the crisis of representation, and the role of political parties. I end with some brief reflections on civil society and political culture in the region.

The second part, focused on Chile, is presented in three chapters. First, I examine the fall of democracy; I then look at the struggle for its recovery, and finally, I assess the Chilean political democratization undergone in the last decade. The epilogue is devoted to conclusions on the prospects for Latin American and Chilean democracies.

PART I

Latin America between Two Eras

✳ 1

Analytical Orientations and the Latin American Problématique

Ten Orientations for Sociopolitical Analysis

In what follows one should not seek social or political theory as such, but theoretical and conceptual orientations that have been constructed over time along with the analysis of sociopolitical phenomena.[1] They are therefore provisional but absolutely necessary in order to pass from mere opinion and ideology to study and inquiry. Rather than an in-depth, systematic treatment, we attempt an overview of these orientations, pointing out some of the analytical principles that we deem relevant to the study of particular sociopolitical processes, including those of democratization.

First, this work seeks to overcome a universalist structural determinism in which particular or national histories are mere illustrations of general laws. Similarly, it rejects the essentialist, abstract vision of a correlation, defined once and for all, between economy, politics, culture, and society—that is, the idea that to a given economic system there necessarily corresponds a certain political or cultural form, or vice versa. This is not to deny that determinations between levels or components may take place, but to view such determinations within a flexible scheme of interactions between economic, political, social-organizational, and cultural models. There is no universal determination between these dimensions; rather, these determinations or relations are historical and vary for each national case and each historical moment. They are shaped, moreover, by processes of globalization that, being directly or indirectly ever present, also differ in behavior from case to case.

In today's world, each sphere—cultural, social, economic, and political—"shoots off" in its own direction, to use a vivid turn of phrase; in other words, we inhabit societies in which these spheres do not correspond exactly with one another within a given territorial space. At one time we could speak, for example, of industrial society, where we would find that there was a kind of class structure or type of family organization, a type of ethic, and a type of political system. What is unique to contemporary society is this disruption, this separation, this self-dynamizing of each of the spheres, which are not automatically determined among themselves but which are also not self-regulated either singly or as a whole.

Thus, if there is an instance of "totality," to use the old terminology, it is politics—not as the place in which the content of the other spheres is determined but as the place where the spheres meet, where it is possible somehow to articulate them. Furthermore, for politics to exist, the only requirement is that there be "society," in this case national-state society. The latter, classically called the "polis" (the polity in modern terms), was the place where the people, the nation, the social actors, the citizens, the classes, whatever one wishes to call them, made decisions through a center called a state.

Second, even if one remains in the structural realm, it must be admitted that we are facing a change in the basic referential societal type in contemporary Latin American society as a result of globalization, the expansion of principles of identity and citizenship, and other factors. That means a disarticulation of what, though with widely varying degrees of development in different concrete historical societies, had been the predominant societal type: the national-state industrial society. This was organized around labor and politics, particularly the latter in Latin America, and around processes of social change such as modernization, industrialization, and development. Its fundamental social actors were classes, parties, and the social movements related to them.

This change is not a shift from one societal type to another but rather the amalgam in each concrete historical society of the national-state industrial society with a societal type that we can term "globalized postindustrial." The latter is structured around consumption, information, and communication and has as its main actors the public, the de facto powers, and identitarian actors. In other words, Latin American societies are no longer, in different stages or degrees, a historicoculturally specific expression of the national-state industrial society, but have become a combination, also historicoculturally specific and original, of the former with the globalized postindustrial dimension. This transformation is redefining the role of politics and states, the central actors of social change, and the very concept of development. A model of development is much more than a mode of production, such as industrialization, or a mode of accumulation, such as capitalism. It is not identified with a specific instrument, such as the market or the state, or a specific strategy, such as the open economy, either; rather it implies the particular combination of all these elements in a given historical context. As we will see, all of this has major implications for the future of democracy in our region.

Third, the autonomy of social processes vis-à-vis their "structural base" should be stressed. The task of the social sciences is not to write a natural history of social structures and their dynamics, but to understand their meaning. That cannot be done without bringing in the concept of actor or social subject. The whole problem of sociology and political science lies in describing how a material situation or structural category becomes actor-subject, and how actors are constituted and interact within a historical and institutional context that they themselves help produce and reproduce. Hence, society is not defined starting from a structure or a system of values, but from the particular configuration of relations in each society among state, political regime and parties, and civil society or social base.

Fourth, this historically defined relation is what allows one to speak of a sociopolitical matrix, that is, a constitutive matrix of social actor-subjects that is unique to each society. The concept of sociopolitical matrix or constitutive matrix of society points to the relation between states, or the moment of unity or orientation of society; the system of representation or politico-partisan structure, which is the moment of aggregation of overall demands and of political claims of subjects and social actors; and the socioeconomic and cultural base of the latter, which constitutes the moment of participation and diversity of civil society.

Fifth, the idea of a sociopolitical matrix rests on the concept of actor-subjects (the two dimensions of which we use interchangeably), that is, bearers of individual or collective action, which appeal to principles of structuring, conservation, or transformation of society, which have a certain historical density and become involved in projects and counter-projects, and for which there is a permanent unresolved tension between subject—or constitutive principle of historic action—and the actor who invokes it.

Sixth, the meaning of the struggles and more generally of the social action of actors is not given univocally by the struggle against "the" domination or by a type of society determined ideologically from outside its own policies. The autonomization or interrelation of various social dimensions that hitherto have appeared subsumed mainly under economies and politics gives rise to various conflicts, struggles, and social movements, and therefore to various ends of these struggles, as well as various utopian principles. The system of domination in a society—or, more properly, the systems of domination—is the product of a combination of different axes or systems of action and not the reflection of a single one of them, even when one or more of them may be dominant. In each axis or system of domination in a given society, there is a conflict around the principles and means that define its course and ends. Thus, there is not a single subject of historical action but several; even when, in moments of condensation of the historical problématique of a society around one of the principles or axes of power, a privileged actor-subject may emerge, it always occurs in terms restricted to that specific struggle or conflict. This orientation is characterized by the disappearance of utopia as the model for a kind of society in which history ends (modern, democratic, or socialist society), as that gives way to partial utopias that aim for the provisional fulfillment of only some of the principles that define a society. There is no ideal society around the corner, but neither is the end of history or of collective action at hand; there is always struggle and process.

Seventh, as we refer to political processes of struggle and social change, the issue of social actors is recovered with that of social movements, defined as collective actions with some stability in time and some level of organization, geared toward changing or preserving society or some sphere of it. The idea of the social movement tends to oscillate between two theoretical poles. One is a vision of collective action that responds to specific tensions or contradictions and is oriented to resolving that specific contradiction. The other is the view of the social movement as the bearer of the meaning of history and fundamental agent of social change. These poles can be seen as two dimensions of the social movements. On the one hand, the social movement is oriented toward the "sociohistorical prob-lématique" of a given society and defining its central conflict; on the other, social movements are concrete actors oriented toward specific, problemat-ically related goals, which are defined in each society and moment. In analyzing political processes, one must bear in mind that social move-ments are one kind of collective action, but not the only one, that they should be distinguished from at least two other major forms of collective action in processes of regime change—demands and mobilizations—and that some historical periods may be characterized by the absence of social movements.

The above has consequences for the way in which social scientists study social movements. One must resist two temptations. One is that of becom-ing prophets of "the" central social movement, inventing a concrete social movement that would constitute it and overlooking the true meaning of its action. The other temptation, in the absence of a central social movement, is that of becoming prophets of a particular identity, overlooking its mean-ing to society as a whole. These two opposing types of certitude about social movements should provide the stimulus for more modest efforts to deal with the ambiguity of social life. This means developing new theoret-ical approaches to social change, as well as entailing an attempt at solidarity and identification, simultaneously with the distancing necessary for com-prehension and critique.

Eighth, the political model or system of a society comprises the state, the institutional relations, and the mediations between state and society, that is, the political regime; the actor-subjects that partake in political matters on behalf of social projects that address the historical-structural prob-lématique (what some call the historicity) of each society; and the political culture or particular form of relations between these elements. In this conceptualization, the political regime is the institutional mediation be-tween state and society, called on to resolve the problems of who will govern and how, how the relation of the people with the state (citizenship in the case of democracy) is defined, and how social demands and conflicts are institutionalized.

It is true that between the political regime and the other spheres of society there are conditional, determinant, and structural regularities; in this sense we cannot speak of either total indeterminism or the reduction of society to pure flux or chance or to the whole of its individual strategies.

Yet as we indicated above such determinants are historical and valid only for certain moments and certain societies. The task of social and political analysis is to describe and interpret them without turning them into immutable laws that would make of historical situations mere illustrations. That entails avoiding the idea of the principle of the single, essential determination by one sphere, dimension, or realm of society over the others, where history would already be explained once and for all, but also avoiding the idea of reducing society to a field of individual strategies and behaviors where history cannot be explained or understood.

Ninth, democracy is, strictly speaking, neither more nor less than a political regime characterized by certain principles or ethoses and certain mechanisms: popular sovereignty, universal human rights guaranteed by a state of law, universal suffrage for the free election of leaders, political pluralism expressed primarily although not exclusively through political parties, the principle of rotation of power, and respect for majorities and minorities. That means that democracy in a given society is characterized by a tension between ethical principles and the institutions created to embody them; therefore, it is pointless to speak of minimalist or maximalist definitions of democracy.[2]

The analytical perspective of this book, then, starts from the assumption that political democracy should be analyzed beginning precisely with political factors, understanding that there are factors from other spheres, such as the cultural, economic, and social, that facilitate or hinder political democracies but do not in and of themselves determine their existence, duration, and nature. In other words, there is no one type of family, culture, or economy that "corresponds" to political democracy. Political democracies can exist in very different types of culture, social organization, and economy; however, some of these elements may favor political democracy to a greater or lesser extent.

Tenth, by "modernity" we mean the principle of affirming the capacity of individual and collective subjects for historical action, which is not identified with any specific model of organization or modernization. Modernity is the way in which a society constitutes its individual and collective subjects. The absence of modernity is the absence of subjects. It must be remembered that one cannot speak sociologically of "modernity"; rather, one must speak of "modernities." Each society has its own modernity. Different models of modernity are always a problematic combination of scientific-technological rationality, the expressive and subjective dimension (feelings, emotions, instincts), identities, and the collective historical memory.

In the framework of the above conceptual orientations, I will seek to show the different elements that make it possible to speak of a new problématique of society.

The New Latin American Problématique

Today a new complication has been added to the perennial difficulty of analyzing Latin America as a whole.[3] It is no longer enough to specify a certain situation and note its variations from country to country, establishing general typologies. At present we are no longer in a position—and perhaps never again will be—to define "a" Latin American problématique, as we were when we spoke of "development," "the revolution," "dependency," "the modernization," or "the democratization," using the singular form of the noun. In a way, the concept of "problématique" referred the totality of challenges that societies were facing to one central situation. This allowed the issue of regional diversity to be resolved: All Latin American societies were deemed to have the same problématique, but to varying degrees, and with varying effects and means to solve them.

Today several fundamental processes are developing that are interconnected but whose relationship is neither one of necessity nor of essential causality. Rather, it is empirical and historical, and can be theoretically established if one steers clear of abstract determinism or essentialist reductionism. In other words, one must consider that each of these processes has its own dynamic and its own actors, and that the relationship between them and their results is not inscribed in a hard-and-fast script. There is no longer a single paradigm of relations or determinations, as social analysis sought in decades past, but neither is there total indetermination of social processes.

If we examine the social science literature of the 1990s, we find that generally—with the exception of studies that fall theoretically in the preceding stage and attempt a general theory—the works refer to four different processes. Many aim to relate them, but in general the corpora of literature have fashioned middle-range theories about one or another of these processes.[4] Democracy building, the redefinition of the development model and of international insertion, social integration, and the search for Latin American modernity constitute the foundational processes that define, without reductionisms among them and with variations from country to country, the present problématique, or rather, problématiques, of the region.

Political Democratization

The first process is that of building political democracy, to which we refer in Part II. While I do not deny the existence of unsolved problems arising out of democratic transition and consolidation, it is my view that it is in the deepening, relevance, and quality of the regime that the democratic fate of Latin American societies lies. These are the challenges that will define the stability of the regimes and the likelihood of regressions to new waves of authoritarianism. This will be the subject of other chapters of this book.

Social Democratization

The second process is that of social democratization, which is not to be confused with political democratization and which constitutes one of the ethical principles of the latter in Latin America. At stake here are three different points, to which we will return throughout this book: the issue of social exclusion and cohesion, the phenomenon of the expansion of citizenship, and the topic of participation.

The phenomena of social cohesion and integration are being redefined today in light of the new nature of exclusion. In fact, exclusion/integration and fragmentation/cohesion have proven to be major foundational problématiques for nationalities, identities, and the principle of "stateness" in Latin American societies. Today when we refer to exclusion, we are speaking of the sector—sometimes the majority, and other times half or only a third of the population—made up of people who are left virtually outside of society, merely surviving and reproducing themselves. Those who are "outside" are not necessarily in a relation of exploitation or a relation of necessity with those who are "inside." All social categories, which had been generators of identity, are intersected by the phenomenon of exclusion. This makes collective action more difficult and helps to account for its weakness in Latin America. On the other hand, it does not seem possible to accomplish the integration of excluded sectors, millions of people in different countries, within the framework of the present development models.

The second phenomenon has to do with the expansion and narrowing of citizenship. This is a multidimensional phenomenon. There seems to be an explosion of the concept of territorial "polis," the classic space of citizenship. The latter has always been the demand and the recognition of a subject of rights vis-à-vis a power. It was initially identified with civil rights and then with the right to belong to the "polis" (political rights), and later it was extended to economic and social rights. Today, gender relations, the media, the environment, and local and transnational systems, among others, also constitute fields in which there are powers to oppose and rights to claim. This means that they constitute spaces of citizenship. People want to be citizens, not only to have access to justice, a minimum wage, social rights and political rights. Yet these new fields are not recognized by political institutions, a problem that apparently is not limited to Latin America. Therefore, on the one hand, the notion of citizenship is exploding and expanding. On the other hand, it must address new exclusions.

A third dimension of the phenomenon of social democratization is that of participation, which at the same time points to issues of local democracy. In Latin America, participation has traditionally been defined, on the one hand, as "access to public goods," and on the other, as mobilization. Today the crucial problems are defined in terms of access to and quality of the goods, and of people's representation in the public sphere. In the spheres of health care, education, work, information, and decision making, to cite but a few examples, the issue of access is accompanied by a diversified demand for quality within each sphere. This means equity is no longer measured only by access to a service but by a quality of the same level but different content for each social group, making the job of the state and public policy making more complex.

The Model of Development

The third process is the change in the development model.[5] Here the issue is twofold. On the one hand, there has been a passage from the so-called inward-oriented development to a new form of insertion in the international economy. On the other hand, there are new relations between the state—which is losing its hegemonic role as agent of development and sharing this role with the market forces—and the private sector, where business people are affected by their individual competitive insertion and their unassumed role of being among the power elites of their respective countries.

It would be a mistake to think that everything is reduced to formulas and mechanisms of accumulation. These do not by themselves define a development model and are but one of its components. Asian experiences reveal how much open-market economic development models may differ among themselves, even if they are all capitalist. What I wish to stress is that Latin America is far from having defined a new development model and is still breaking with the old one, even in the countries that seem more advanced in this regard.

Neoliberal ideas and practice have identified privatizations and, more broadly, structural adjustment, with an enduring model. Nevertheless, it turns out that these ideas and practices have been completely exhausted worldwide, and only a few fanatics who believe in them remain. This does not mean that adjustment was not necessary, in terms of economically restructuring the classic development model of twentieth-century Latin America. The structural adjustments solved some short-term problems and worsened others, paved the way for a new long-term development model, and helped autonomize the economy from politics. Yet these measures were always formulated and imposed ideologically as definitive models, and in every country they have exacerbated poverty and inequalities, which a long-term development model is supposed to alleviate. The failure of neoliberalism portrayed in the economic crisis of the mid-1990s shows that the new formulas for the relations between the state, politics, and the economy, and therefore between the state's social and political actors, are still a long way from having been defined.

The Model of Modernity

The fourth process consists of what one might designate the definition, debate, and conflict over the model of modernity. The socioeconomic changes that I referred to have brought the specifically Latin American form of modernity into crisis and have brought the new models into contention.[6] The identification of structural adjustment and market mechanisms with a model of society, which rests on the basis of identifying modernity with one historical type of modernization and reducing society to the economy, is one of the historical projects that is proposed to these countries. It is doomed to failure, except for some elites, because it does not factor in aspects of identity and collective memory, and also because it excludes most people and lacks national social actors to bring it to fruition.

An alternative vision is represented by a new kind of Catholic traditionalism. Here Western rationalist modernity is set against an essential subject of Latin American identity, founded at the moment of the Conquest and of the evangelization—the Christian *pueblo*, represented by the Catholic Church. It is understandable that this mind-set, near to that of Pope John Paul II, may have a certain social legitimacy, as it advances a progressive socioeconomic perspective concerning the disenfranchised and at times is the only one to denounce the materialism and inequalities, and even the immorality, of the capitalist or market economy. However, we have here a deeply reactionary position with respect to the sociocultural, and a certain antirationalist and antifreedom phobia.

Generally speaking, modernity—the formation of subjects capable of building their history—is usually reduced either to its rationalist-technological version, conflating it with the modernization model of certain Western countries, or to an essentialist and metasocial identity that prevents the construction of true subjects. Between these two poles there is a wide range of partial solutions, among them the media-based model of mass culture and the return to an originary identity or to a particularist community. These demonstrate that a sometimes hidden, sometimes open debate is taking place around not only the theoretical models but also the practical models of modernity.

If the phenomenon of globalization is added to the above four processes, we find ourselves even more aware of being in a new situation. The world that had been divided geopolitically—that is, by the military control of a territorial space—has changed. Today's world is defined by the hegemony of a single nation-state and the oppositions to it, and by the role of transnational market forces. But in the world of tomorrow, space and power will be defined less by territoriality, which gave a central role to the politico-military dimension, than by the communicative dimension. The models of appropriation of communicative space are models of creativity, innovation, knowledge, and subject formation. The cultural space of the twenty-first century will be dominated by those who propose models of creativity or of modernity that are capable of simultaneously combining scientific-technological rationality, expressive-communicative rationality, and historical memory and diversity of identities. Those who do not manage to combine these three elements will have no place in the world of tomorrow.[7]

The Change in the Sociopolitical Matrix

The Latin American sociopolitical matrix has been defined in various ways: I have defined it elsewhere as "classical" and "politically centered," while others have used the qualifier "state-centric." The most fitting denominations seem to be "politico-statist" and "national-popular."[8] This matrix, which prevailed from the 1930s to the 1970s, was configured through different processes of development, modernization, social integration, and national autonomy.[9] Every social action was intersected by these four dimensions, and the different conflicts reflected the fusion among these phenomena. The economic base was an "inward-oriented" development model, characterized by import-substitution industrialization, with the state playing an important role. The political model was that of a "state of compromise,"[10] represented by different types of populism, independent of the political regime. The cultural reference was a national-popular political project and a vision of radical global social change that gave political action a revolutionary stamp.

The main characteristic of these classical sociopolitical matrices, varying from country to country, was the weak autonomy of each of their components—the state, political parties, and social actors—and the tendency toward a fusion of two or three of them, with a subordination or suppression of the others. The specific combination depended on historical factors and varied from country to country. In most cases, the privileged form of collective action was politics, and the weakest part of the matrix was the institutional relations among its components—that is, the political regime, irrespective of its nature (democratic or authoritarian).

The new type of military regimes that began in the 1960s and the process of globalization, with its economic consequences, triggered the crisis of this matrix and its breakdown or disarticulation. This does not mean that a new matrix has been built in the region but rather that there exist various processes, including breakdown, the survival of new elements, and efforts to recreate the same matrix or construct new ones.

These processes point toward four different possibilities. The first is breakdown without a new model of social action. The second is the regression to the classical matrix. The third is building a new matrix characterized by the autonomy, reinforcement, and complementarity of each one of its components. The fourth, perhaps the most likely, is the juxtaposition of these different schemata. The results of these combinations will vary from country to country, and it is difficult to predict the outcome of this process. What seems relatively clear is that the institutional framework will be formally democratic, even when it is far from evident what form this democracy will take and as we will see later, to what extent it can replace the de facto powers.

Consequences for Social and Political Analysis

The above has consequences for the way in which social scientists study social movements. One must resist two temptations. One is that of becoming prophets of "the" central social movement, inventing concrete social movements that would constitute it, and overlooking the true meaning of their action. The other temptation, in the absence of a central social movement, is that of becoming the prophets of a particular identity, overlooking its significance for society as a whole. These two opposing types of certitude about social movements should give way to more modest efforts to deal with the ambiguity of social life. That means developing new theoretical visions of social change. It also entails attempting solidarity and identification along with the distancing necessary for understanding and critique.

Broadly, all social and political analysis is unsettled by the phenomena we have discussed in this chapter. The social sciences in Latin America have operated heretofore from the idea of a society defined by certain borders, by a concept of the whole of society, which had one or two parameters, two or three structures wherein one determined the other. This society's evolution was proportional to changes in these parameters, a phenomenon that clashed with the essence of Western societies throughout history. Whether under the form of dependency theory, modernization theory, or any other, there prevailed a view of society that changed according to a certain evolutionary paradigm. The actors were actors of a finished script, and thus the topics of research were usually obstacles or deviations from that trajectory, when the actors who would perform the tasks required by the script could not be found.

As we have said, what is changing is that none of the social processes we mentioned is the bearer of an overall rationality. They have different dynamics, logics, and actors. In this way, a theoretical and methodological diversity becomes indispensable in order to deal with the four sociohistorical thematic foci, processes, or problématiques laid out above, and to consider the actors and social movements that are identified with them, to which we will refer in other chapters.[11]

A new Latin American problématique simultaneously requires a reelaboration of the categories and even of the practice of the social sciences.

2

Social Change and the Reconstruction of Politics

Ambiguities of Globalization

Globalization consists of the interpenetration, in both economic (market) and communicative (media, information, real and virtual networks, computers) forms, of societies or segments of them, limiting autonomous decisions by national states.[1] It is a phenomenon of enormous importance, but it is not the only significant process, insofar as there are coexisting processes that run counter to it.[2]

I have already mentioned some of these processes, such as the explosion of ascriptive and communitarian identities based on sex, age, religion (as revealed truth and not as a choice), nonstate nationhood, ethnicity, region, and so on; the dynamics of the reconstruction of national or plurinational states and supranational blocs; and the new forms of exclusion that establish a purely passive, media-based link to globalization. So, the question that globalization and its ideologies (neoliberalism, self-regulation, technological-communicative determinism, etc.) put before us is that of who is actually globalizing—societies and the people, or only dominant sectors of them.

We should not lapse into the other extreme, which is to deny globalization and to consider it but a discourse of the ruling powers. In that case, we would incur the ideology that rejects reality as a defense against it. The truth is that we live in a complex world in which many contradictory processes, such as globalization and the countertendencies we mentioned, are found together.

Democratization and Expansion of the Political System

In Latin America today we find a contradictory situation. On the one hand, there is an expansion and strengthening of politics, as a result of the democratization processes (transitions, foundations, reforms) to which I will refer in another chapter, with all the institutionalization and consolidation of political participation this implies. This phenomenon is demonstrated by indicators of satisfaction with democracy and by voter turnout in Latin American as a whole, with the exception of some moments and some countries. So the percentage of people who vote—that is, the average voter turnout of recent years over the total of registered voters—is above 70 percent. Out of the total number of potential voters, it is 53 percent—in other words, higher than the percentage of voters in the United States. However, the levels of satisfaction with democracy, measured through polls, with the difficulty of interpretation that the direct-questioning method presents, amount to modest percentages.[3]

We can add to that the regularity of elections for selecting senior officials and, with the exceptions mentioned, greater stable political participation, the relative formalization and institutionalization of political processes, a certain potential for representation with the emergence in almost every country of party systems and coalitions that tend to assure a certain governability, and so on. On the strength of all this, it may be asserted that there is no crisis of politics as such and that an entrenchment of the polis is under way.

Structural Changes and Weakening of the Polis

On the other hand, however, there arises a phenomenon that contradicts the one just mentioned: the narrowing and weakening of politics in social life overall by processes that tend towards the destructuring of the polis. In other words, it is as if the first phenomenon we described, though quite true, were to affect an ever-smaller set of aspects of social life. Politics in and of itself works better than before, and people participate somewhat more, but its radius of action is becoming smaller and smaller, and to society on the whole it seems more irrelevant.

The phenomenon of the strengthening and broadening of politics is related to political transformations tied to democratizations and to the apparent end of the authoritarianism-democracy cycle, while this latter phenomenon of narrowing and weakening has to do with structural transformations. Let us look at some of the consequences of these transformations.

What is happening everywhere in the world, with some unique characteristics in Latin America (which we will note), is a phenomenon that we mention in another chapter and that can be stated thus: To the societal type with which we are familiar, the national-state industrial society, another societal type, which we will call globalized postindustrial, is added.[4] The referential societal type in relation to which countries could be backward or advanced, the national-state industrial society, had two basic axes: the labor and production axis, and the national-state axis, or politics. In the national-state industrial societal type or dimension, the political system is fundamental; it can be democratic, authoritarian, or any other type, but it is defining and constitutive. Thus, the social actors in this society type were predominantly tied to the world of labor or of production; that is, they had some relation to what we call social classes, as well as to the world of politics. The combination of the two results in what we called social movements.

In Latin America, which experienced this societal type fragmentarily and incompletely, this structuring through labor (or through education, in the case of students), production, and politics, had politics as its "determinant in the last instance," to borrow a phrase from the old manuals. In other words, if I had to simplify, I would say that in Latin America, actors and identities were constituted from the worlds of labor and politics, but predominantly from the latter. By politics, I do not necessarily mean partisan politics, though in the cases of Uruguay and Chile the partisan dimension did predominate in the constitution of identities. In the other cases, other types of constitutive principle might emerge, though they were always basically political. That is to say, the constitutive matrix of society—the relation between state, representation, and social actors or civil society—was, as we have said, politico-centric, national popular, and statist.

The new societal type, which we might call globalized postindustrial, does not exist anywhere in the world, or rather it only exists in principle or as a societal type combined with the previous one. Its central axes are consumption, information, and communication. In the globalized postindustrial societal type or dimension, there are no political systems; it is a societal type without a political system. Therefore, it cannot exist in any real society; it has to be mixed with a societal type that does have a political system.

That the axes of this societal model are consumption, information, and communication means that its basic social actors are of two types. On the one hand, there are the publics and various kinds of networks, which may be structured, specific, or general to varying degrees, but are characterized by not having an organization: Today, one can speak of an actor known as public opinion, which entails an overhaul of the classical theoretical definition of actor. On the other hand, we have the de facto powers and identitarian actors. De facto powers are groups, organizations, or institutions that in any society or in the international sphere exert power beyond their legitimate field of action (be it a state, the media, an economic group, the military, the IMF, etc.). When we speak of identitarian actors, one element must be kept in mind. We are speaking, against everything the great theoreticians predicted—Weber, Durkheim, Marx, Parsons, and others—about actors for whom the fundamental principle of identity building has a tendency to be ascriptive and not acquisitive. Acquisitive principles include labor, politics, what one does, or the beliefs one chooses. An ascriptive principle is that which one does not choose—place of origin, age, skin color—or things one believes because they were received, such as religion, not because they were chosen. This type of actor has a particular trait compared to those of the national-state industrial societal type: The issues of representation dealing with what one is, feels, or desires, are totally different from those dealing with what one believes, does, or plans.

As a consequence of the foregoing, the principles of collective and individual action have been transformed. The principles of reference for the actors of the classical society are the state and the polis structured as a state. The principles of reference of the actors of the globalized postindustrial society are problématiques that exceed the polis or the national state (pacifism, the environment, globalist or holistic ideologies), or in the case of the identitarian actors, the identity of the social group to which they belong (they consider themselves young people more than Chileans, women more than Brazilians, Indians, old people, people from a given region, etc.).

Denormativized Society and Abstract Politics

The structural and cultural transformation that is changing the nature of politics and social action has two other noteworthy consequences. The first is deinstitutionalization, or "denormativization," whereby ethics and morality no longer correspond, and the triad of values, norms, and behaviors is eroded. The existence of institutions of all kinds was so germane to the national-state industrial society that when there were no institutions people committed suicide, as Durkheim explained: Anomie consists of just that—the absence of norms and institutions. Today, the absence of institutions or of norms is not a pathology in the globalized postindustrial societal type; it forms part of the very nature of society. This means—as a second consequence—that we are in a situation in which economy, politics, culture, and society do not correspond to one another. To a certain level of income there does not correspond a certain educational level, form of social organization, or political line. A typical example is the young person who has a doctorate, works in an unstable service-sector job, earns very little, goes once a week to a guru who teaches yoga or to a "self-help" group, is not married or in a stable relationship but has various "encounters," is something of a leftist, but—very afraid of having his or her job taken away—votes for a rightist candidate of authoritarian stripe or for the one who offers to "solve the people's problems."

The disarticulation of the correlation between economics, politics, culture, and society, which is typical of the national-state industrial society, and the "denormativization" of society have a trait that is peculiar to Latin America. As a result of the transformation of the development model on a world scale—the transition from development models fundamentally centered on the states to development models in which transnational market forces play a major role—the state has less to offer. This makes the people's relationship with the state—politics—appear less important to them. In other words, it becomes more abstract. As politics grew more abstract and apparently less tied to the satisfaction of concrete demands because of the state's shift away from the "welfare state" role, disinterest in and incomprehension of politics were reinforced. The aforementioned paradox or tension again comes into play: In Latin America, politics works best in the political realm but matters much less in society.

Expansion and Weakening of Citizenship

Another developing tension or paradox, which we mentioned in another chapter, is between the valorizing expansion of citizenship where there are no institutions to express it and the reduction of traditional citizenship where there actually were institutions to crystallize it. In this sense, the triad of incipient civic, social, and political rights, in addition to being ill suited to our countries in that there has not been the sequential development of these rights, as indicated by Thomas Marshall, today commits the basic omission of leaving out another area of citizen rights.[5]

If citizenship is where legal subjects seek recognition of their rights and make claims before a specific power, and if that power was normally the state, today areas or spaces are being generated where people do the equivalent or something analogous for citizenship. They want to exercise rights, but the state is no longer the power before which those rights must be won, or is only partially so. We are referring to two types of rights, to two types of citizenship. First, those that have to do, for instance, with the media: the people, who devote the better part of their lives to television, do not want limits set on what they choose and would like to have some kind of citizenship (ratings or channel-surfing are attempts to hold out hope and are a poor imitation of a vote in the political arena). The environment is another sphere in which relations of power, rights, and fields of citizenship that are not referable exclusively to the state are expressed. Yet, there also is a field of citizenship—that is, power relations before which certain rights are sought to be established—that implies a revolution in the classic principle of human rights, in general, and of citizenship, in particular. I mean rights that are claimed by a particular social category and are not applicable to other citizens: those of gender, age, and ethnicity, among others. An interesting debate even has arisen recently over the rights to cities as spaces of collective life. In other words, today we have rights whose bearers are not individuals but collectivities; this is a reinvention of the concept of citizenship.

For these two new fields of citizenship, institutions do not exist, or else they exist only in embryonic and partial forms (for example, "positive discriminations" or affirmative action) that are equivalent to what the right to strike, minimum wage, job rights, or education were to economic and social rights; what the vote was to political rights; or what habeas corpus was to civil rights, to give only a few examples. Instead of institutions that regulate the duties and rights of members, there is nothing more or less than a generic claim, where the adversary and the referent are vague.

Moreover, in those classic areas of citizenship where institutions do exist, a devalorization or weakening of the ability of the institution or of the instrument that upheld citizen rights comes about. Today, habeas corpus is ineffective against crime and urban insecurity; the vote is good to elect people who, regardless of their capability, cannot guarantee the representation of the will and general plans of the citizens; the union only works for some, and for the few it serves, it does so in very limited areas, also regardless of the leaders' capabilities.

Last, let me point out that the dimensions pertaining less to rights (citizenship) and more to subjects (citizenry) is weakened also in that the integrative forms of collective action are eroded.

The New Forms of Exclusion

This issue of the transformation of the citizenship is accompanied by its flip side, which we have mentioned several times: transformations in the forms of exclusion. Exclusion was a constitutive principle of identities and social actors in the classic Latin American society, insofar as it was associated with forms of exploitation and domination. The current socioeconomic development model, based on transnational powers that operate in globalized, albeit fragmented, markets, is intrinsically disintegrative on the internal national level, though it may be selectively integrative on the supranational level. That model is redefining the forms of exclusion without doing away with the old exclusions. Today, exclusion means being on the margins, being superfluous, as is occurring on an international level, where some countries, more than being exploited, seem to be superfluous to the rest of the international community. The world of the excluded is difficult to organize or convene ideologically in the name of a relation of exploitation or oppression on a national scale. Moreover, exclusion today affects all social categories: men, women, youth, students, workers, even business people (the so-called small enterprise). All of these groups intersect in different ways along the inclusion/exclusion axis. Collective action cannot, then, be constituted around a single principle—not the social base, since that is heterogeneous; nor an ideological appeal that no longer makes historical sense for people; nor a concrete claim, since there are a wide variety of needs—that makes reference to or that gives meaning to the totality of the excluded.

Latin America at the Turn of the Century

The perspective developed here might be considered Eurocentric or North Americanist, a claim that is in a sense similar to the imputation that was made regarding the modernization and democratization processes in Latin America a few decades back. For, some would say, if the foundations for a Western national-state industrial society were never laid, and democratic institutions did not take root and become homogenizers and organizers of society, the same may be said of this new globalized postindustrial societal type. In this view, the characterization made thus far, as well as the structural, cultural and psychosocial consequences, do not recognize the "deep reality" of Latin America, instead subsuming it into a set of categories and analyses valid for other contexts.

It is true that, as we have noted, Western industrial national-state modernity was always experienced fragmentarily, and its consolidation as the organizing rationality of Latin American societies was never achieved. Yet it is also true that this modernity was a referential element of twentieth-century Latin American history and was experienced in an ambiguous, hybrid form along with other models of modernity.

This is exactly wherein lies the great drama of the future. As state-created societies that experienced national-state industrial modernity in a partially imposed, limited way, they never completely belonged to this kind of modernity. So how can they confront the impact of a new, globalized postindustrial model of modernity without breaking apart, decomposing, or disappearing, overwhelmed by those who are fully entering the world that combines these two societal types?

But this is no made-up issue or foreign invention: It is a challenge that cannot be denied and that can only be addressed by constructing a new sociopolitical matrix in each country so it can deal with these two models of modernity and their own individual identities and diversities, on the one hand, and the generation of a Latin American space, on the other, inserted with its own model of modernity into the world that is being formed.

The Reconstruction of Political Society

Political society, or the contradictory unit of the polis, shored up by political democratizations and cracked by structural and cultural changes, can be reconstructed on the basis of two great issues. One is the overcoming of the social inequalities that threaten to tear countries apart, to which we refer in another chapter. The other is a restructuring of the relationship between state and society that would give a referent to political action.

In the latter case, the main issue is the strengthening and autonomy of the state, the system of representation, and the actors of the civil society, as well as the complementarity among them on the local, regional, and national levels, and also the supranational and world levels. This criterion, beyond the classical ideological views and their technical requirements, allows an evaluation of both larger political processes and specific democratization processes as well as an assessment of specific policies which strengthen the state, the party system, the actors, and the social networks.

Instead of the classic fusion between state, parties, and society, which characterized Latin American societies through different forms and mechanisms, the reconstruction of political systems and communities calls for the shift to a matrix of autonomy, strength, and complementarity between state, parties, and the system of social actors, retaining the tensions between them.

The way to build a polis or political societies here at the turn of the century is by completing the tasks of strengthening and broadening politics resulting from political democratizations, and improving the quality of politics through a more in-depth reform of the relations between the state and society.

✻ 3

Democracy and Democratization: Concepts and Processes

Democracy and Latin American Social Thought

In this chapter, rather than simply discussing concepts and their genealogy, I examine the relationship between the concept of democracy and the phenomena involved in constructing democratic regimes in Latin America.[1]

First of all, let us try to explain, intellectually and politically, the difficulty of democratic thought, or of thinking about democracy, in Latin America.[2]

One of the intellectual reasons is the overwhelming predominance of sociological thought over political thought. In other words, there is a tendency to identify any social process as one of sociostructural origin and of a strictly societal nature. In Latin America sociology and the social sciences were mostly the sociology of development and political sociology. The weak part was political science. At a certain moment, the strongest component, apart from sociology, was economics—or rather, political economy. But as is well known, economics generally does not furnish knowledge about society itself or about processes that are not of a strictly economic nature.

This sociologizing predominance led us to think of each particular phenomenon as determined by the whole of society, which in turn was understood through all-encompassing, sweeping paradigms. Development, revolution, dependency, modernization—each of these encapsulated at some moment the whole historical problématique of society and explained all the phenomena occurring in it. That is, a dimension or element would be chosen—selected by the researcher, intellectual, or academic center—and it was assumed that the central process affecting that dimension or element was the one that directed and explained all of the transformations in every part of society.

For example, it was most common to think of democracy as a type of regime resulting from economic, cultural, or social determinants. Although many of these views did not originate in Latin America, they did have significant influence on teaching and social research in the region, as well as on the emergence of new currents of thought, sometimes in dialogue and other times in opposition. An example of determinist thought in the economic sphere is Seymour Lipset's classic *Political Man*,[3] which posits that democratic regimes correspond to a certain level of economic development. His theory is "proven" with a ranking of countries by level of development where in the list of the most developed countries are those defined as democratic. Thus, economic development leads to democracy, an assertion that supports itself not only with a theoretical principle but also with empirical "proofs." The central criticism of this theory à la Lipset or Apter[4] is made by Guillermo O'Donnell, who points out that in the most developed countries of Latin America, and perhaps in other regions, one finds military coups and authoritarian regimes, from which it may be claimed not that economic development leads to democracy but rather that a certain kind of economic development leads to or has an affinity with "bureaucratic authoritarianism." This is an absolutely correct empirical critique, but it relies on the same theoretical principle: To a certain type of economy or level of development there corresponds a certain political regime.[5] In other words, politics is the reflection of the economic.

Others maintain that democracy derives from the presence of a set of values, from the prevalence of a certain civic or democratic culture, without which there is no democracy. That culture would be found in certain national societies with a democratic tradition, basically those of English origin, and would embrace individualist and liberal values. In Latin America the cultural tradition would be centralist, communitarian, and clientelist.[6] According to this view, the region's cultural tradition does not favor democratic behavior, insofar as individualist and liberal values are subordinate or absent. Obviously, such an approach tends to be fundamentally ethnocentric, inasmuch as only certain historical kinds of culture or systems of values are called on to generate democratic societies.

Finally, we have the most sociologizing currents à la Barrington Moore or those of ECLAC (Economic Commission for Latin America and the Caribbean) on social development, as well as the Latin American Marxist currents.[7] For them, democracy depends strictly on a set class structure, whether through the breaking of the landholder or oligarchic pact with the bourgeoisie or through the formation of a middle class, or it is only an expression of the system of domination, or the adoption of formalities that respond to foreign interests.

Doubtless we are oversimplifying the arguments, nearly all of which have a grain of truth. Yet this way of thinking, however productive for efforts to shed light on processes of global social change, does not allow room for defining democracy in a secularized, precise way. Instead, democracy shows up as a dependent variable, the content and meaning of which are not specifically examined. If the central, and virtually the only, issue defining the whole of society is economic development, social structure, the system of values, or the class struggle, then a relatively detailed study of each of the various dimensions of society is unnecessary. It is thought that all of the dimensions are not only interrelated but operate by a permanent, immutable, "essential" determination—that is, under any and all historical situations—by one dimension of the others. By studying the dimension that determines the others, one gains a complete knowledge of society. On this score, everyone—rightists, leftists, centrists, modernizers, dependentists, revolutionaries, and socialists, each espousing their own theory, of course—thinks alike.

There is a difficulty in thinking about the topic of democracy in Latin America's intellectual development. Even among the analyses most focused on democracy in a nation or in the region (in the mold of Pablo González Casanova's work on Mexico, or that of Gino Germani on the region)[8] the analysis of society as a whole tends to be privileged over that of institutions or of political mechanisms. Recall the noted dilemma of "socialism or fascism," with which some authors sought to sum up the problématique in the late 1960s and early 1970s. As an alternative to a political regime like fascism, they proposed not another political regime, like democracy, but a type of society like socialism.

A second difficulty stems from political life and the ideologies present in it. In the idea of democracy there has always been an imaginary of an ideal society, in which social groups or sectors are constituted as historical subjects. In Latin America, the concept or idea of a democratic society has almost always involved the idea of an integrated, united society.[9] If for the moment we call the phenomenon of social integration *social democratization*, or simply *democratization*, one might say that what has existed in Latin America is a political and theoretical historical experience of fusing two components: political democracy (regime) and social democratization (in terms of equality, popular content, and social integration).

For instance, when René Zavaleta asked himself what democracy was in the 1960s in the Bolivian imaginary, he answered his own question: Torres's Asamblea Popular (Popular Assembly).[10] And the latter would not square with what one would call classic or formal democratic mechanisms.[11] Or if one asks oneself what democracy is for the Argentine working class, obviously the answer will be Peronism. And Peronism has little to do with what we would call formal political democracy; it may have to do with the democratic ideal, with the protagonism of the popular sectors, or with the people as subject, but not with what we call democratic institutions. What about for Mexicans and Cubans? Unquestionably, democracy was the experience of the revolution and its institutionalization, however little the latter may have had to do with the liberal republican principle. Elsewhere, we have the cases of Chile and Uruguay, where the processes of social democratization were accomplished through channels of political democracy. What is democracy in these cases? It is the experience that everyone, individually or collectively, has had of social democratization, brought about through voting, democratic-republican institutions, and political parties.

So, in Latin America the idea of democracy has been identified with particular historical experiences of social democratization or integration, of being a part of the nation, of being involved in processes of creating equal opportunities and the assertion of subjects. This means that what was taking place was the fusing and overlapping of various classic democratic ethoses. One is the liberal ethos, in which democracy is represented as freedom; another is the socialist ethos, according to which democracy is equality; and a third is the communitarian ethos, in which democracy means belonging to a collectivity, participating in a subject that is an "us."

In its political constitutions, Latin America has always put forth the liberal ethos, which, save a few exceptions, it has hardly ever respected in its history. Until the 1970s, social and political processes in the region were always directed toward the egalitarian, participative, or communitarian ethos, much more than toward the liberal ethos.

Thus we have a practice, a political life totally pervaded, saturated, or soaked by the social, which is reflected in thought and in theory. That explains, in part—and this is a deficiency that we are paying for today— how, strictly speaking, there has been no Latin American political theory of democracy, as there was for dependency and development, to counter theories imported from other contexts. There was a theory of the structuring of social action in politics called the theory of populism, or the theory of the State of Compromise, in addition to others in which the thought was very rich, independent of the level of agreement there may have been between all these theories. Nevertheless, the theory of democracy, if there was one, was the repetition of the abstract concept of democracy taken from other contexts and was basically a theory of social democratization and its effects on political life. In other words, it was much more a theory of social conflicts, struggles, and processes than a theory of institutional frameworks or mechanisms of citizenship, decision making, or partisan and electoral representation.

This dearth of inquiry and theoretical reflection on institutional matters is partly explained by the fact that the weak link of Latin American social and political life, with exceptions beyond the scope of our present study, was always the institutional component. Institutions were essentially instruments or mechanisms by which groups defended or gained what was in their interest—to be accepted or skipped over as each saw fit, especially among the privileged and powerful sectors—rather than legitimized principles and frameworks for social life and individual and collective action. In this respect, one may think of two kinds of legitimacy of social and political institutions, particularly for the democratic ones: intrinsic legitimacy, in which democracy or a specific institution is valued in its own right and not as a means to an end, and instrumental legitimacy, in which the democracy or institutions are valued insofar as they serve some purpose or the meeting of a demand.[12] Without rendering a judgment on the ethical quality of one or the other, we should acknowledge that intrinsic legitimacy is what makes politics an irreplaceable component of a good or desirable society, worth becoming involved in for more than whatever material gain can be derived from it. In this sense, it is a more solid basis for guaranteeing that democracy prevails. What is certain is that in Latin

America, if democratic legitimacy did exist, it was basically an instrumental legitimacy. To illustrate my point: We weren't the English who went off to vote in the middle of a bombing raid; we would have done so had we thought the results would benefit us rather than to bolster an institution for itself. One need not see Manichaeism in this, with intrinsic legitimacy representing the good guys and the instrumental the bad guys or the calculating ones. The ethical erosion that many democratic institutions suffered at the hands of the dictators and oligarchies (let us not forget the frequency of elections and the existence of parties under Somoza and Stroessner, or the U.S. military interventions following election outcomes that were not to their liking) largely explains the exclusively instrumental valorization of democracy that may have developed.

The Redefinition and Revalorization of Democracy

In this overview of democratic practice and thought—in which we are stressing this contamination between political democracy and social democratization—the military dictatorships of the Southern Cone, and the authoritarian components of regimes that elsewhere would not, strictly speaking, be defined as military regimes, are a watershed that are bringing about a shift in political life and in theoretical reflection. Why? Because under these circumstances the fundamental idea of ending the dictatorships cropped up—though that might not solve other problems or change other ills in society—since the dictatorships were viewed as denying human life and as an evil in themselves. In other words, what mattered at that moment was ending a particular kind of domination, even though that did not do away with capitalism or exploitation. What mattered was that the people be able to live, salvage the basic principle of life, and declare it to be good. That is called human rights. In asserting human rights, a regime is proposed in which those rights prevail, and anyone with power cannot just take them away or violate them with impunity. Democracy appeared to be the historical exemplar of such a regime, allowing the intellectual space to consider it in and of itself for the first time, even though perhaps there were no economic or cultural conditions or social structure for it. What mattered was the political factor: all the key actors of society wanted an alternative political regime, which they called democracy, to the dictatorship. Democracy was secularized, starting from certain ethical principles, with respect to other dimensions. It became the referential value in relation to a crucial issue for the ideal society: the relationship between the state and the people—in other words, the political regime. Democracy became the ideal political model worth thinking about and fighting for, irrespective of whether or not other ends were served or other benefits were won, however important they might be.

As the ethical, intellectual, and political space opened up for conceiving of democracy as a regime and not as a kind of society, the concept was narrowed, of course, but not the power of its ethical principle, which would even be extended metaphorically to other realms of social life, such as the family, school, and gender relations. Yet this is clearly only a metaphor, a use of the democratic ethical principle to consider other realms without referring to the use of institutions and mechanisms that are a defining part of political democracy.

What we wish to underscore is that the concept, strictly speaking, was limited to naming only one kind of political regime. Now, what is a political regime? As I have already stated, a political regime is a very particular sphere of society, though it may have a more encompassing role involving the general running of society. It is distinct from both the state and politics, though it may refer to the relations of the former with society and though it may be part of politics. As I have noted, by political regime I am referring to the system of institutional mediations between state and society that serve to resolve certain matters of social life, such as the nature of government, citizenship, the institutional regulation of conflicts, and demarcating the space for collective action. Thus, there are corporative, fascist, military, authoritarian, totalitarian, and democratic regimes, depending on the principles and mechanisms with which they define and solve these three issues. The democratic regime is the regime that resolves the issues we mentioned with principles like popular sovereignty, the rule of law, public liberties and human rights, political pluralism, and the rotation of power, and with mechanisms like voting, the existence of parties, political constitutions that set the jurisdictions of each authority, the separation of powers, and so forth.

What I am speaking of is a dimension of society that is not *the* society and that can change, progress, retreat, regress, independent of—that is, related to but not determined by—the mode of production, the system of values, and the social structure. This dimension, which I call democracy, is a concept and not a theory, though various theories have been formulated regarding the conditions that allow its constitution, development, fall, and recovery, the types of democracy, and the relationship between democracy and other spheres of society. In the concept of democracy there is always a normative-value component and an institutional-practical component. The various democratic visions and struggles emerge from the tension between these two components.

Thus, just as at one time it was common to study the transition from feudalism to capitalism, from capitalism to socialism, from socialism to the market economy—or however one wishes to call it—from traditional to modern societies, from rural to urban societies, from extended family to nuclear family models, from interpersonal communication to mass media, and so on, one can now study how the passage from one political regime to another takes place, whether from a nondemocratic to a democratic regime, or from the latter to some other kind of regime. To state that an intellectual and scientific space has opened up for such an enterprise is not tantamount to endorsing any particular theory—or all of them, for they could all be misguided. Rather, it means merely acknowledging the validity of the object of study: in this case, democratizations or transitions to democracy, which we would rather call "political democratizations" here, for reasons to be discussed.

For the moment, let us say that this validation of the change in political regime as an object of study requires at least three conditions, which are equally applicable to the other examples of changes, shifts, or transitions I mentioned. The first is to define adequately and rigorously the points of reference, the starting and ending points. The second is to refrain from all manner of teleological analysis of processes under way or explanations that predetermine the outcome; in other words, to refrain from evolutionist-style thought in which the scripts are written in advance and all actions are explained based on that script, which leads to a prearranged objective from which any departure would constitute a "deviation." The third is to avoid making the political democratization process out to be the only fundamental process affecting society and having all the others depend on it without duly attributing to them their autonomy, as the autonomy of processes or changes of regime was ignored previously.

Actually, one of the main risks in embarking on the study of political democratizations is that of conceiving of them with the same mind-set by which previous processes were considered in the Latin American social sciences. In other words, saddling processes of democratization with the idea of the utopia, the society worth living and dying for. Naturally democracy may be worth living and dying for, provided we are aware that it does not bring happiness, nor can it, since societies and the human condition are never exhausted by a single dimension. Democracy, like politics, cannot solve the sum of society's problems, but in that unsubstitutable realm of society that is specific to it, democracy solves problems better than any other regime, and thus is a value in itself.[13]

Therefore, the worst mistake would be to make transition theory or, rather, the theory of political democratizations into the new single paradigm for looking at social phenomena and not into a thematic focus that, while central at certain times, is only partial. In other words, to think that the regime defines the entire society and that just as before there was the passage from a traditional society to a modern society, or from a capitalist society to a socialist society, today the passage is from authoritarian society to democratic society. That was one of the main problems that needed facing at the outset of these studies. Granted the reality of general oppression by the dictatorships that seemed to lay waste to everything, and given the crisis of the categories with which the process of development and frustrated revolutions were conceived and experienced, one might think that this was *the* new problématique, replacing that of development, socialism, or the revolution, and *the* new theoretical-analytical paradigm, replacing that of modernization, dependency, or the world capitalist system. In continuing to conceive of the new realities with the old mind-set, one ran the risk, once again, of passing from theoretical analysis into ideological discourse.

Today, it may be said that economic development or growth solves only part of the problem. In fact, it produces and exacerbates environmental problems, and, left to its own devices and without the intervention of redistributive policies, it generally tends to increase inequalities. In the same way, we cannot consider the topic of political democratization as the general solution or the new global paradigm. Actually, *the* theoretical-analytical paradigm no longer exists, since each of the different processes Latin American countries are confronting would require at least one paradigm of its own. The building of democratic political regimes, social democratization (understood as social integration and cohesion and the overcoming of inequalities and exclusions), the reinsertion of Latin American economies into the world economy with national and regional development models, and the definition of a model of modernity different from the classic Western one we know, are not univocal or unilinear processes. One cannot be subsumed into another through a theory or a single analytical paradigm, nor can they be carried out by a single predominant social actor. Within each one of these processes there are tensions, contradictions, autonomies, and unique dynamics. There are different actors for each, since a democratic actor can be antidevelopment, an egalitarian actor can be antiliberal or antidemocratic, and an actor who asserts subjects and their modernity can be "loaded" with identity in such a way that they scorn universal institutions. So, there is not *a* subject, *a* basic or single process, or *a* single theory of global change, since today the very concept of social change refers not to a guideline, as it did once, but to several—at least four, as we mentioned above and in other chapters.

Political Democratizations

Studies of processes of political democratization, improperly and inadequately called "transition theories" or "transitology,"[14] contributed to the understanding and participation in actual processes of political democratization in three simple ways. First, they studied how democratic institutions—democratic political regimes—were generated and established where there were nondemocratic regimes or where authoritarian institutions prevailed over democratic ones. Second, they moved away from all-embracing paradigms, comprehensive theories of social change, and determinist theories in which one structure is the consequence or reflection of another. Third, they differentiated between processes of political democratization.

This last point seems extremely important, since views like those of Fukuyama, Huntington, and others have considered political democratizations, or transitions, in terms of a third or fourth wave, depending on the author. In other words, they stuck all the Latin American democratizations of recent decades into the same bag as all those initiated from the time of the Portuguese and Spanish transition, including those of Eastern Europe and even some African and Asian cases, as if they were of a single kind. There is no question that this is another of many media and journalistic improprieties, because viewing democratizations as "events" or "occurrences" that are somehow all related obscures the existence of very different phenomena. In this sense, one contribution made by studies of political democratization is that they allow us to understand very different processes.

In Latin America there are at least three kinds of political democratization. First, democratic foundations, the kind analyzed classically by Barrington Moore's historical sociology and Dankwart Rustow's political science.[15] These are societies or countries that have not had experience as democratic regimes, that are installing democracies for the first time, and that tend to approach the global society model of change, as with the original establishment of democracy in European countries or in the United States. In recent decades in Latin America the process of democratic foundation has appeared mostly in Central America. It involves building a basic nucleus of democratic institutions after the collapse of the oligarchy and the patrimonial dictatorships, drawn-out civil wars, guerrilla movements, and revolutions.

This type of political democratization features three major characteristics related to this aspect of civil war, revolution, or global change. First, there is the complicated conversion of those who were armed combatants into political actors. Actors who sought to wipe out their enemies become actors who have to enter into conflict, represent, and negotiate in order to govern and reconstruct a country within a shared institutional framework. Second, and as a consequence, the building of democratic institutions is joined with a process of pacification, national reconciliation, and even national reconstruction. Finally, the other characteristic that foundations have is that, depending on how confrontational the situation is, the influence of external actors (single or multiple) can be fundamental, as illustrated by the Central American case, in which U.S. policy, European social democracy, and Latin American mediator countries have played an essential role in the development and especially in the outcome of these processes.

The second kind of political democratization, which at one time was thought to be the only one, is that which we call transition.[16] Semantic debates aside, here we mean the passage from a formal military or authoritarian regime to a basically democratic regime, however incomplete or imperfect the latter may be. This is the case with countries such as Spain, from which the analytical guidelines for our region were adopted at first, and in South America, especially the Southern Cone, broadly defined.

Unlike foundations, transitions are not, and do not trigger, sweeping changes. Insofar as the power holders are the military, transitions do not occur by the overthrowing of the latter but through mobilizations, political negotiations, and institutional mediations, which may take the form of plebiscites, elections, or the mediation of a higher institution between the conflicting factions. So there is no ouster or military standoff with the power holders, as occurs in foundations. But transitions involve removing and replacing power holders in order to generate democratic institutions; that distinguishes them from the third kind of political democratization, democratic reform.

Democratic reforms seek to create, extend, and broaden institutions in order to turn them into real democracies; in the long run they may prove to be deeper or more radical than foundations or transitions, but they are not the same. They consist of an extremely complex process of progressive, gradual installation and creation of democratic institutions starting from within the regime and, generally, starting from the previous power holders. The removal or replacement of power holders is not strictly necessary, as it is with the other two kinds of political democratization we mentioned. Obviously, this democratization "from above" is always set in motion by pressure and mobilizations from below.

We are not referring to just any kind of political or democratic reform, or to the extension or broadening of an existing democratic regime, such as the extension of elections to certain spheres that used to work by appointment or nomination, or of suffrage to certain social groups heretofore excluded from the political arena (for example, elections of local or regional governments, or extending the vote to the illiterate and to women). Doubtless these extensions can be part of the reforms we are discussing. Yet when we discuss reform here as a kind of political democratization, we are talking about an intentional, comprehensive process of transforming political institutions to make them democratic. While we know when transitions begin and end, with reforms we know roughly when they begin but are not clear about when they end. They are very long processes, full of progress and setbacks, where there are spaces that open by degrees and where it is not possible to pinpoint and celebrate *the* moment when democracy is inaugurated, as happens with foundations and transitions.

The paradigmatic case of processes of reform in the 1990s is Mexico. In the early 1990s Colombia seemed to be headed in this direction, though later it was mired in an involution and the decomposition of the state and the political system. These are situations in which there is not a transition from a formal authoritarian regime or from a military dictatorship to a political democracy; these are processes, rather, in which lead actors, obviously not the only ones, are the government or the government party or parties.

We should note here that these three processes, different in nature but all oriented toward political democratization, do not exist in a historically and totally pure state. Rather, each one contains components that are characteristic of the others, so that they face shared problématiques at certain moments. For example, in the case of Argentina, in which for the first time one administration has succeeded another on democratic terms, there is a foundational component within a typical transition process. In the case of Chile, the transition, strictly speaking, ended some time ago, yet the democratic regime there is incomplete, and there is an unfinished process of reforms to democratize the institutions that are legacies of the military regime.[17] Clearly, that case is not the same as the Mexican case, since in the Chilean case the power holders who were replaced were the military, but both cases have aspects in common, such as the transformation of the political constitution so as to do away with authoritarian legacies.

Now that these three kinds of political democratization are defined and studied, the pertinent question for some years now has been how to size up these different types. Our first comment is that, independently of the outcome, these are completed processes in almost all cases, though there are exceptions. To say, for example, that in Chile we are still in transition, or to speak of a second transition, either means that the process is so long-term and aims at such a complete or perfect objective, or that later we will need to refer to a third or a fourth transition, thereby rendering the concept useless. It is more fitting to assert that the bulk of the foundations and transitions have been accomplished. In the case of reforms, as the Mexican case demonstrates, there are fundamental components that enable us to say there is no turning back.

Of course, still-unresolved situations persist, in which a political system breaks down or partial authoritarian regressions occur. In general, with these exceptions, the main unresolved problem is no longer the regression to a new authoritarian or military regime, to a situation of civil war, or to an autocratic system with a democratic facade, situations that had been points of departure. Rather, the problem is the quality of the democratic regime that is installed. To illustrate this point, consider the major political crises that have been unleashed in Argentina during the Alfonsín-Menen succession, Collor de Mello's Brazil, Fujimori's Peru, Bucarán's Ecuador, Chávez's Venezuela. They were not solved as before with a coup and military regimes as was once the norm, but (except in the Peruvian case) with something of a democratic consolidation, though it be of low quality.

Are these authentic and complete democracies? Unquestionably, they are not, but in every case they are closer to democracy than they were a decade or two ago. Broadly speaking, we could say there are five types of situations, some of them highly variable: cases of breakdown, democratic regression, or uncertain forms of recomposition, such as that of Venezuela, Ecuador, and Peru; cases of breakdown of the political system without democratic regression, such as in Colombia and Peru; incomplete democratic regimes that have not achieved consolidation, such as Paraguay and Ecuador; stalled democratizations, such as the Chilean case and some Central American cases; the most successful cases of finishing and consolidating democratization processes, such as Uruguay and, above all, Brazil, Bolivia, and Argentina, with varying degrees in the quality of their regimes.[18]

The Ethical Problem with Democratizations: Reconciliation

In many cases, the military dictatorships and civil wars left the formation of a unified, viable society as an unsolved and pending issue. That has given rise to the debate over reconciliation and national reconstruction. The topic of reconciliation in societies in general, and in Latin America in particular, in secularized terms and having shed its religious robes, arose after times of great national upheaval.[19] In history, reconciliations are accomplished implicitly with the passage of time or with an act or specific moment in which people decide that it is better not to kill one another and to coexist, not lovingly, but recognizing one another as members of the same community. In this sense, reconciliation is a matter only of acknowledging oneself as a part of the same space as another, accepting the existence and development of the other—that is, recognizing rivals rather than enemies who must be destroyed. Reconciliation is, then, a process of recognition of the legitimate field of coexistence, understanding, conflict, and struggle. Process means something never finished. A legitimate scope of coexistence, cooperation, and conflict means that for there to be reconciliation, there must be institutions and rules of the game that apply to all, without which the demands implied by subjective intentions and expressions do not go beyond the level of discourse.

On the level of the nation-state, after major upheavals, reconciliation aims for a process of reconstituting the basic unity of society without eliminating strife and conflict. This national unity (which can perfectly well be plurinational) entails overcoming three great divisions.

One is that of historical unity and continuity, which means reconciling oneself with the country's past, its history, and its ways of life. This coming to terms with history means accepting the value of each stage in which there has been a collective effort to build and of all the social groups that embodied it. It also means recognizing the negative moments of history, purging them through truth, justice, and reparation so as not to set the stage for them to be repeated. Without this, there is neither country nor shared history.

The second dimension of basic national unity or of reconciliation is the social one. It involves overcoming the problem of having several countries in one, where some live in a kind of social apartheid or ghetto. We are referring, of course, to the problem of extreme socioeconomic and cultural inequality. In this dimension it is clear that reconciliation is a long process and not a specific moment.

The third division to overcome is political. This fragmenting of society tends to be deeper than others, since here the division tends to be total rather than a matter of degree: the other is eradicated (exile, imprisonment, torture, disappearance, etc.) or rejected. This divisiveness is born of a process in which there were conquerors and conquered.

The idea of reconciliation, then, aims to overcome these three divisions: historical, social, and politico-ideological. But in the recent case of political democratizations, the topic has pertained mainly to the historical-political dimension.

There are four models of historical-political reconciliation on the level of overall society. The first is forgetting and the simple passage of time, with no explicit stances taken toward the past, as was the case with Franco-ism in Spain. The second is the "clean slate" or "end of story," in which an explicit act of memory loss and "royal pardoning" takes place, leaving society plunged into a hidden trauma that rears up from time to time in the form of settling scores or new amnesties. The third is that of arrangements and accommodations through some truth about what happened, and with partial justice and reparations, depending on the correlation of forces. Last is the moral model, which consists of acknowledgement of truth, justice, and reparation. This is simultaneously a process that unfolds in time and one that requires concrete acts or gestures that trigger said process (for instance, the role that the truth commissions play in the Argentine, Chilean, and Guatemalan cases, to name the most well known, or the trials of those responsible for human rights violations, or the laws of reparation). In the cases of Latin American democratizations, there was a combination of these models, with the first three predominating and the moral model being somewhat weaker.

The central issue at stake in talking of reconciliation is the creation of institutions in which various people, sectors, and actors recognize one another as part of a single society, though without this entailing any precondition apart from this recognition.

The Current Problems of Democracy

If the bulk of political democratization has already been achieved in some cases, and at least the basic breakthrough to initiate democratization in others—with some exceptions—already was achieved, then what is the main problem with democracy in these countries? If the looming problem in most Latin American democracies is not a regression to the democracy-authoritarianism cycle, what is the challenge they face?

We can indicate two kinds of problems. The first has to do with the very nature of the political democratization processes, in any of their three formulations, which left incomplete democracies, basically because of the persistence of authoritarian enclaves. When referring to authoritarian enclaves we are not talking about economic slowdowns, poverty, and inequality, all of which can be very troubling to and a formidable task for democratic governments. Rather, we are calling authoritarian enclaves those elements of the previous regime that persist in the democratic regime.[20]

These enclaves can be institutional, like constitutional provisions and laws limiting the popular sovereignty and the rule of law. They can also be of the ethical-symbolic type, like violations of human rights under the authoritarian regime, which force the new regime to solve inherited problems in matters of information, justice, pacification, and reconciliation. They can also be actor enclaves, involving paramilitary, civilian, military, or foreign groups; put otherwise, actors that work like agents of the previous regime and do not accept the democratic game but adapt to it because they are forced to while waiting to derive any opportunity from it. There may also be cultural enclaves, which are of greater importance in the Central American countries, of relative importance in Mexico and Colombia, and a very minor presence in the Southern Cone countries. These are perceptions and habits that prevent the development of democratic mechanisms. Examples are corruption, the fraudulent use by dictatorships or single parties (*partidos únicos*) of electoral mechanisms, and noncompetitive elections, which devalue the meaning of voting in the eyes of the people.

One can draw the conclusion that, once the bulk of the transitions and foundations and a large part of the reforms were finished, the upshot has been not so much authoritarian regression as the consolidation of generally incomplete or weak democratic regimes, with a deficiency of democracy, due especially to the presence of authoritarian enclaves. Thus, the first kind of problem the Latin American democracies are facing in large part involves the effects of democratization processes and can only be overcome through democratic deepening.

The second type of challenges these democracies face is tied less to these outcomes than to a complex, worldwide phenomenon that affects Latin America in a particular way. Here the theory of democracy fails us, since this theory was conceived for one kind of society, that of the polis. We have already stated that a polis society is a space where there correspond, however contradictorily, an economic system, a political organization, a model of cultural identity and diversity, and a social structure. In other words, the economy, politics, culture, and society are shared historically by a people. That means it is also the space in which a political community is defined and a center of decisions for those who are inside it, which is called the national state. The others, those on the outside, also have their own decision-making centers, their own national states. This is what we call a country or society. Today, the referential polis society of Latin American countries, the "modern," "industrial," or "nation-state" today has come apart because of the phenomena of globalization and internal fragmentation. This affects issues of citizenship, as we have noted, which in turn are impacted by the new kinds of social exclusion.

All this leaves a state relatively cut off from society, and actors—split between their universal membership in a sociocultural category and their membership in a local, regional, and above all national space of which they still feel a part—identify with a country, though that identification may be visible only at important moments or during events of a symbolic nature.

The institutions that work well for us for the national industrial component do not work for the globalized postindustrial component. We need to rethink, then, a theory of democracy for a society that brings these two components together, since the processes and theory of democracy with which we are familiar were conceived for a kind of society that is no longer the only referent.

In summary, just when Latin America sees the possibility for political democracy as an autonomous, legitimate struggle for the first time, which doubtless constitutes a historical leap in polis building, there are also trends that undo or erode the polis. Formulas and the theory of democracy do not exist for the new societal forms as they did for a kind of society emerging at the end of the eighteenth century, and consolidated and furthered through the nineteenth and twentieth centuries, but that is no longer the only kind of society in which we live.

Both the legacies of authoritarianism and the problems issuing from the structural and cultural transformations we have mentioned suggest that the main problem democracies face in Latin America is not so much the threat of authoritarianism or militarism, nor does the problem mainly lie in consolidating the postauthoritarian regime, in the sense of preventing regressions. Rather, the difficulty is in overcoming authoritarian enclaves and in the quality and relevance of the democratic regime. The latter means that the great risk is that, with a democratic regime in place rather than an authoritarian or military one, the regime may be irrelevant or ineffective. In other words, it risks seeing its legitimacy vanish not because another regime project, such as a form of authoritarianism, opposes it, but because it has neither the capacity nor the quality to fulfill the tasks that all regimes have to accomplish.

Relevant democracy means that those aspects that a political regime has to solve (government, citizenship, the institutional framework for social conflict, and the representation of civil society) are defined by the political regime and not by the de facto powers. As we have said, these de facto powers are organizations—the media, national and international actors, and economic, military, paramilitary, or civilian groups—that themselves take on the topics proper to the regime at the edges of institutionality. But they can also be de jure or institutional powers that overstep the duties that are entrusted to them and the actions allowed them. Hyperpresidentialisms, majority or minority coups in parliament, political decisions made by constitutional courts or other deliberative institutions, and the legal proceedings of the judiciary when it assumes powers greater than those it has through judges or the police, are all examples of de facto institutional powers.

The Future of Democracy in Latin America

On what will the future of democratic regimes depend? This question cannot determine the factors that make democracy possible, since at times there may be democratic regimes simply because the people want them, because the main actors in society prefer democracy, even if the "objective" preconditions for it are not present, to killings or oppression by a dictatorship or domination by de facto powers at work in the marketplace, civil society, the state, armed powers, or transnational forces. If we had to advance a hypothesis that did not turn democracy into a purely dependent variable but rather made it a factor active in the building of a society, and that did not incur ideological or structural determinisms, we would assert that the future of democracy in Latin America will depend largely on the capacity for building political legitimacy that allows, in turn, for strong states, parties, and social actors that are autonomous, yet complementary to one another.

It might seem historically incongruent to speak of strong, and probably large, states. Yet if we look closely at the serious problems of public security or scientific and technological development—the media, the reinsertion of nations or blocs into the globalized economy, the environment, education, and health care, to name some of those that are cited as the most pressing and overdue for a solution—there is no way to intervene in them without a considerable investment by the state. That requires, over and above improving efficiency, an increase in human and economic resources, for which the state will have to cut back in some areas, such as military spending, but overall the state should grow and become strengthened. We refer to this in the following chapter.

Nevertheless, a strong state—and the countries that have experienced it are proof—has to be socially controlled, which can only be accomplished through the party system, if we wish to maintain a democratic regime, and with the knowledge that the parties are not going to represent every interest. In some countries this begins with the basics—having parties; in others, there is a need to build party systems, since there exist one or two individual parties that absorb the state and society. In most countries it is necessary to build stable majority coalitions that assure social change and democratic governability; in others, the relationship between the parties and society must be rebuilt. In sum, there are countries that will have to take care of one or all of these tasks. Each country has a different problem, but all are in some way involved in a complex process of attempting to strengthen a party system that could control a strong state.

For their part, both a strong state and a strong party system have to be controlled by the citizenry, which requires strong social actors and networks that are autonomous from the state and the party system. This poses a very difficult issue in societies that are experiencing the collapse of their classical actors, the erosion of the state referents of collective action, new forms of mass exclusion, and a weak structuring of the social base for new public issues and matters.

This view provides a yardstick with which to measure political action. Nowadays, concrete political projects, politics, and policies, within a democratic framework, make sense not so much if they tend toward a society based on some ideology or if they aim for the building of heaven on earth, as we used to think of them, or if they solve only one problem or situational demand, as is often thought today, but if they can give a meaning to personal and social life in a given society and improve its quality. And that, in today's climate, depends less on the content, which can vary widely for the different actors and viewpoints, than on the capacity of individual and collective action to take part in individual and national fate, which entails asking ourselves in each case whether projects or policies strengthen the state, the system of representation, and the social actors. This goes for broad projects, the platforms of parties or party coalitions, and public policies. Any public policy—including public security, control of crime, health care, education, housing, decentralization, and combating poverty, to cite but a few examples—over and above technical and economic criteria, should be evaluated for its contribution to this triple strengthening.

At the heart of this view is the central issue of the reconstruction of a polis society where democracy might have roots and be sustained because reconstruction of a polis society means the building of a solid system of relations between the state, the system of representation, and strong actors on very different levels: on the local and regional level of each country, on the national level, and also on the supranational, regional, and global levels.

To return to the central argument made throughout this book, instead of a fusion between state, parties, and society, which was the typical scenario in Latin America, this is a shift to a matrix of tension, autonomy, strength, and complementarity without absorption among state, parties, and social actors.

At a moment in which the transition from authoritarian or semiauthoritarian regimes to regimes of a democratic tendency seems guaranteed, this triple strengthening seems to be the only way to address the main problem that political democracy in Latin America faces now and henceforth: to make of it a relevant regime that is not at the mercy of de facto powers past or future.

✹ 4

The Transformation of the State and Social Policies

Ideologies Surrounding State Reform

The antistate perspectives in vogue these days, which are both ahistorical and empirically false, come from two contradictory angles.[1] One proclaims the market as a cure-all, and the other, the protagonism of civil society confronting the state. These views clash, in the first case, with the observed trends in public opinion, in which a kind of bureaucratic and inefficient state is rejected, but the state is expected to play an active role as an agent of redistribution and as a principle of national unity. In the second case, it is contradicted by the current weakness of social actors, to which we will refer in other chapters.

In Latin America and internationally, debates around state reform have been fueled by different ideological visions, which at first included the idea of the state's virtual disappearance but later evolved to take on notions such as the shrinking of the state apparatus, or its administrative decentralization; the reduction of its functions, replacing it with mechanisms of self-regulation that always match the regulations established by economic powers; the reduction of resources for the sake of fiscal austerity; and the need for automation and technological development, which are defined as the modernization of the state. All these views only partially address the issue and do not consider state reform from a comprehensive perspective. In practice, actual policies of state modernization, including necessary reforms oriented toward improving service provided by the state to beneficiaries, have been regarded from different angles with a pronounced anti-state bias and with a short-term perspective. Thus, it may be said that a process of dismantling, or of administrative reform that transfers the criteria of efficiency and productivity from the private sector to the public sphere, has prevailed over the idea of the substantive transformation of the state.

The shift from *asistencialista* policies (comprehensive social welfare benefits distributed on a national scale) to "targeted policies" (policies assisting those sectors deemed most vulnerable to the negative effects of adjustment policies), as we will see later, eclipsed the need for a thoroughgoing state reform that would allow for a better combination of emerging needs with a long-term view in which the structural redistributive effects of social policies are assured. This shift is largely due to antistate critiques and the resistance that the business sectors and the political right express on the topic of state reform, as well as the danger of increasing public spending and imposing greater tax burdens. Thus there is the paradox of demanding social responsibilities of a state that lacks adequate funding, which rebounds in a critique of its bloatedness and inefficiency.

Let us recall that many of the economic reforms made in the name of and under the ideology of structural adjustments may have had some success in resolving short-term problems and in reinserting the economy in the transnationalized world system. They also, in part, were able to change the traditional subordination of economics to politics. Nevertheless, the reforms also enormously increased inequalities, dismantled mechanisms for the protection of the most vulnerable sectors, impeded the workers' movement, increased poverty, and failed to establish a new, socially regulated relation between economics, politics, and society.[2]

A New Prospect for the Transformation of the State

Starting from the need to palliate the negative social and political effects of structural adjustments, correct an economic model in which growth was dissociated from social integration, and reconstruct national sociopolitical systems, a new view of state reform that seeks to move away from the purely instrumentalist vision has gradually been advanced.[3] This involves recovering and rearticulating a state that intervenes in the orientation of development and has the capacity to allocate resources and fulfill regulation duties, all in connection with new relations with society, particularly the system of representation and the constitutive base of the social actors, or civil society.

The starting point for a new relationship between the state and society should be the recognition of the historical fact that no contemporary national development has been able to dispense with a predominant role for the state. But it is true that an age characterized mainly by "inward-oriented" national development in which the mobilizing state was the indisputable and unopposed agent may be ending. We are witnessing the emergence of development integrated into transnationalized market forces. Yet that does not mean the loss of the importance of state action but rather the modification of its forms of organizations and intervention, and the redefinition of its relation to the other actors of society.

In other words, if the state's integration into a new sociopolitical matrix is examined, far from eliminating the principle of "stateness," the issue is to create it in some cases and to strengthen it in others.[4] What is called for, then, is not the reduction of the state's role but its transformation: its modernization, decentralization, and participative reorganization, so it fulfills its role as one of the agents of development.

But this double strengthening—value-normative, with regard to the principle of autonomous stateness, and institutional-organizational, in terms of the state's role as agent of national unity and development—requires both eliminating its more bureaucratic tendencies, associated with past forms, and strengthening the levels of representation and participation of society.

In this latter idea there are at least three aspects. The first has to do with the phenomena of decentralization and the strengthening of the local and regional powers, matters tied to problems of administration, management, and participation of actors in the social base. The second involves the topic of parties and the political class. We will address the latter in another chapter. Here the idea is to make the transition from weak, vulnerable party systems—a result, depending on the case, of the irrelevance or excessive meddling of parties in society, their tendency to cannibalize or absorb each other, or their overideologization or total lack of differentiation—to strong party systems. Such a system should be characterized by its tendency toward inclusion, the internal democracy of its parties, the capacity for negotiation and agreement in order to form broad coalitions, and the establishment of channels that guarantee the expression of the new social themes and conflicts of society. In sum, what is involved is the issue of representation. The possibility of forming majoritarian coalitions, in turn, goes through institutional changes in its form of government. This, in turn, implies a reexamination of extreme presidentialism not only from the perspective of efficiency or accountability, as some have done, but also from the perspective of the constitution of majorities and the strengthening of political parties.[5]

Simultaneously strengthening the principles of "stateness" and representation entails a third aspect: that politics be transformed and that civil society, or the social actors autonomous from the state and political party system, increase in strength and density. The new waves of liberal economics have been concerned here only with the strengthening of the entrepreneurial actors vis-à-vis the state. However necessary in some cases, such a narrow focus is wholly insufficient and, to some degree, distorting. It is necessary to consider all of the actors in society in terms of increasing their levels of participation, which, taking on a symbolic dimension, should include the actual resolution of problems. Here again we touch on the issue of decentralization of state power.

The issue of state reform cannot be approached with disregard for the general principles we mentioned—stateness, representativity, and the autonomy of social actors, which define the new relations between state and society and constitute the context for any reform.

The Practical Principles of State Transformation

The reform of the state, or rather, its transformation, should take these relations into account and steer clear of the purely instrumental or administrative illusion under which efficiency problems are posed without taking into account the complexity of the state's insertion into the historical context of the society.[6] Moreover, it is not a matter of eliminating the instrumental or administrative dimension, the "internal" aspect of the state, but of contextualizing it. For if we talk about reform or transformation, in the final analysis we are talking about concrete strategies directed at an apparatus of institutions and organizations that, in turn, must contend with the wider issues of social transformation to which we have referred.

All this means that state reform cannot be limited to a dogmatic question of size and scope: The principles and function that make the size of the state into a dependent variable should be considered. It is necessary to move away from the tradition of solving problems by adding new departments and agencies to the state without changing them, and also away from the neoliberal argument that claims that the magic solution to all problems lies in reducing the state apparatus. This could mean that in certain areas, such as justice or redistribution, over and above the necessary reforms of existing structures, there would be an increase in human, institutional, administrative, and bureaucratic resources—that is, an increase in the size of the state apparatus should be considered. At the same time, the reduction of this state apparatus in certain responsibilities, especially some of its military duties, should be considered. Generally speaking, with regard to the matter of size, roles related to the redistribution of wealth and to social integration should follow a pattern that is the opposite of that of coercive roles.

Strengthening the principle of state or "stateness" without falling into statism means a clear distinction should be drawn between what constitutes state policy and what constitutes the policy of a particular administration. The former is found chiefly in consensus, while the latter follows the principle of the majority. New issues, like those related to human rights, the environment, and especially overcoming poverty, should be included in state policy.

The transformation of the state also entails the application of various principles, depending on the areas of state intervention involved. In some of these areas, such as the law, a deep transformation that affects norms and personnel is in order. In others, reform efforts are primarily geared toward modernization, lightening the bureaucracy, decentralization, and retraining state civil servants. Finally, there are some new matters that the state will have to address at times with executive authority and at other times only in a regulatory capacity. This will require new structures (environment, innovation) or new norms (communication, information technology) or even a restructuring of existing agencies with new responsibilities (culture, education), perhaps more related to regulation, orientation, and assessment than to administration.

The terms in which the access both of individuals and of society to the state were posed have changed. As far as state services are concerned, it is not a simple matter of access to services or their range of coverage, even for the most marginal sectors: What is at issue today is the quality of the service or good. This means that quality has become a precondition for equity and that we can no longer separate these two aspects. This observation goes not only for housing and health care but also, especially, for education and justice.

With regard to decisions of state, without abandoning the principles of state autonomy and "stateness," institutional participation by individuals and society at central and decentralized levels has made it necessary to introduce principles of direct democracy for certain matters and, in other cases, to reform the state structure so as to allow the presence of noncorporative representation on national committees or advisory boards in various spheres of national action.

In sum, the reassertion and strengthening of the principle of statehood entails the transformation of the state and not only its modernization, reduction, or expansion. The state has a variety of roles, to which there apply various principles of transformation, depending on which particular role is called for. The reform or transformation of the state should likewise be placed in our general perspective—that of building a new sociopolitical matrix characterized by the strengthening, autonomy, and complementarity of its components.

✵ 5

Social Policies and Equality

The Meaning of Social Policies

Despite the importance they have taken on, social policies continue to show up on the conceptual plane as a residual category, especially with respect to economic policy.[1] Thus, when one speaks of the latter, it seems clear that it is geared toward economic development, which entails, among other things, growth, the maintenance of macroeconomic equilibrium, and self-sustainability. Investment, monetary, and other policies typically are defined around these objectives. When one speaks of social policy, by contrast, the exact aim is not clear; rather, we have a grab bag of policies—a kind of shopping list that gathers very different, not always interrelated items.

If the purpose of economic policy is to steer the economy toward the satisfaction of the material needs of individuals, in my view, social policy has the purpose of producing the conditions that guarantee the existence of society itself. That means a certain degree of equality between its members, a quality of life defined in accordance with the cultural diversity of those who make it up, and the existence and development of social actors and networks that provide support for the citizenry. I reflect on this definition of social policy below.[2]

Social policies are developed and take on meaning in the specific sociohistorical contexts of their objective, which is to produce society. We have already referred to the new Latin American sociohistorical context. With that framework, for the purposes of this chapter, I will highlight the topics of political and social democratization.

As we have said before, beyond being a political regime and a set of institutions in the realm of sociopolitical life, political democracy is the search for a solution to a sociohistorical problem: how to organize society from the political dimension. It is therefore the expression of an ethos, or a set of ethical principles and values, which is never fully realized in institutions and mechanisms. Democratic institutions and mechanisms seek to reify the democratic ethos, which leads the latter to go beyond the institutional system.

Thus, democracy is also a movement and an act of political creation by society, and consequently cannot be explained by any external determining condition (economic factors, social structure, the international situation) in the absence of the will of the significant actors involved. I have also noted that in Latin America the democratic ethos has been much closer to the egalitarian, communitarian, integrative ideal than to the libertarian, individualistic one. Democratization has been understood in the collective historical memory more as a process of incorporating and constituting a collectivity—that is, more as social democratization or "fundamental democratization"—than as the building of government institutions or political democratization. The idea of democracy is associated more with the constitution of collective identities, the reduction of inequalities, and social integration and cohesion, than with the liberal ethos and electoral returns.

The presence of authoritarian regimes and policies that sought to dismantle and reverse processes of social democratization led to an incorporation of the liberal ethos and a revalorization of political democracy and of the building of institutions belonging to it. Political democratization has been experienced in Latin America as a process that unites the ethical principles of freedom and equality. In recent years it has tended to split into two autonomous processes, in which both ethical principles seem to be absolutely necessary, and one cannot be privileged over or sacrificed in pursuance of the other.

Thus, on the normative-value level, a balance has been struck and a mutual strengthening between the two principles has taken place, without their being mistaken for one another. In practice, however, political democratization seems to have come much further than social democratization, which, again, does not mean that the former has resolved all of the problems of democratic establishment and consolidation, to say nothing of those of quality and deepening. It must be recognized that the rise of liberal and individualist principles, while indispensable for the legitimation of political democracy, is not necessarily conducive to a climate that favors the principles and mechanisms of equality. The challenge today, beyond consolidating the political democracies, is to succeed in making these into true, quality democracies in order to neutralize the de facto power structures that could easily replace the formal political regimes.

The process of social democratization, which involves reducing inequalities and building autonomous social actors able to mobilize and have their demands represented, faces the problem of the multidimensionality of inequality to which we will refer, and the absence of solid, organized social actors. The structural adjustments, which meant the difficult transition to a new development model and a greater autonomy from politics, invariably caused a rise in poverty and inequality, as well as a dismantling of established relationships between the state and social actors, weakening the organizing and ideological capacity of the latter. A recomposition of these relations has still not taken place, nor has there been a formulation of a development model that, aside from guaranteeing growth, would allow the reduction of inequalities and a greater social integration.

Equality and Equity: What Is behind the Words?

The discourse today on equity and equality is necessarily fragmentary. One reason for this is that there are no longer societal references for the issue of equality as there were in the past, when the utopia of a socialist society, or of one without private property, was put forward as a model of an equal society. Another reason is that the topic of equity tends to become an ideological substitute for that of equality; as we will see, the former only refers to one of the dimensions of the latter.[3] A conceptual debate is in order, then, that would allow us to restore complexity and legitimacy to the concept of equality, unfastened from the historical models and ideologies with which it has been identified.

There are two basic theses on this topic. The first is that the space of equality, unlike the dimension of equity, is the polis society, or rather, the nation-state (which includes the idea of multinational states), the centrality of which is now challenged by the processes of globalization. The second is that one of the conditions for the nation-state and for the very idea of society to be viable is socioeconomic equality.

In the theory and social practice of progressive and leftist tendencies, the distinguishing principle was the second item in the *liberté-égalité-fraternité* triad proclaimed by the French Revolution. In fact, the three great Western utopias were organized around these principles, which branched off at some point in history: Liberty gave rise to the liberal-democratic utopia, whose subject is the individual/citizen; equality gave rise to the democratic-socialist utopia, whose subject is the citizen/people; fraternity constituted the essence of the Judeo-Christian utopia, with its subject being the community/people of God. The Christian utopia, above all in its Catholic version, was always closer to the theme of equality than to that of liberty. The modern locus of these utopias basically has been the nation-state, though in certain cases, such as the Judeo-Christian, they were proclaimed on the level of humanity. In contemporary society, all historical projects must move along these three axes, which in the case of colonized, dependent, or subject nations, are organized around the principle of national independence.

Equality and equity appear as two faces or dimensions of the old concept of "social justice." They are two distinct ethical principles that cannot be assimilated with one another or used interchangeably. Whereas equity refers to the equality of individual opportunities for the satisfaction of a set of basic needs or socially defined aspirations, equality refers to the distance between social groups in terms of power and wealth, or if you will, in terms of access to instruments that determine power over the personal and over one's surroundings. A society can be at once equitable and unequal. It is possible for equity to increase without inequalities decreasing. The size of socioeconomic gaps is irrelevant from the perspective of equity, provided that individuals can meet their basic needs. From the perspective of equality, the socioeconomic gap between social groups is not good, but sociocultural difference or diversity is. The latter is another ethical principle that has as its subjects not only the individual or social groups in general but also identity, generally though not exclusively of the ascriptive type. Equality and diversity both have a certain community or society as referents; that is, they assume the legitimacy of society as something different from the sum of legitimacies of individuals (human rights) and target a cross section of it.

Degree zero of equality is equality before the law but refers only to individuals and assumes no gap between social groups, which is not the reality. Equity places a lower limit; equality a lower and an upper limit. Equity is an absolute principle; equality is limited by freedom and socio-cultural diversity.

This conceptualization raises the question of why the issue of equity currently prevails over that of equality. In the first place, there is the decline of universalizing utopias or blueprints of society, required by equality but not by equity. Freedom, for its part, only requires mechanisms, and not a type of society as equality does. In the second place, the image of the individual predominates over that of social groups and collective behaviors. That dominance is explained in part by the questioning of the idea of society and of the political community or polis, which was the locus where the problem of equality was considered, due to phenomena of globalization. In society as a whole and in the market, there are individuals and there are corrective policies. Theoretically, the market, with corrections, can resolve problems of equity, which is not the case with the issue of equality. In a world in which social actors are weakened, one can still make progress in equity, but these actors are indispensable for struggles for equality.

The Multidimensionality of Social Inequality

Various phenomena, which I have mentioned in another chapter, have worsened and redefined the outlook for inequalities in Latin America, redefining the meaning and scope of social policies. The first is the new nature of exclusion, which hinders any kind of concerted collective action: atomized structural bases, divided and fragmented social groups, and the lack of an adversary or interlocutor to oppose or make claims before, other than the whole of society. Can one speak of a nation as a sociopolitical community? There is no possibility for revolutionary action or for taking refuge in fundamentalisms, on account of the presence of the mass media culture and the (purely symbolic) penetration of the market.

Second, one must remember that poverty and abject poverty of a structural nature increased significantly during the 1980s. The progress in reducing poverty in the early 1990s—later counteracted by crises and recessions—can be explained not by redistributive phenomena but rather by an increase in employment and wages (wage earners and women improved their lot) due to economic growth (the so-called trickle-down effect). The rise in social spending did not lead to redistribution, since social security was regressive, save in certain cases. All that meant that inequalities did not drop off (if there are fewer poor people, it is not because the rich are less rich, but because they are even richer) and that the economic growth has already borne its greatest fruit and showed its limits in terms of effects.[4] In other words, today the model of economic growth on a national and global level is inherently contradictory with societal integration, which compels its regulation—intervention "from without," in other words, from society and politics.[5]

Another dimension of social inequality should be added to the above-mentioned phenomena of exclusion and poverty, namely, the one issuing from diversity in terms of ascriptive criteria (gender, age, religion, ethnicity).[6] The paradox here lies in that ascription is an increasingly valued source of diversity and social differentiation. It is what is involved, beyond demands for equality before the law, in struggles for identity and for making one's own processes of modernization and transformation. Yet this same principle of ascription is a source of discrimination, and certain ascriptive groups (women, youth, the elderly, groups defined by ethnicity or region) are more vulnerable and suffer greater inequalities.

Unless they undergo a very thorough and radical conversion, the doctrine of human rights and democratic-liberal principles, which made hard-won progress in recent years, at least in theory, and which assert the universality of rights and equality before the law for all, can scarcely take account of this situation and help overcome this kind of inequality. This is because the struggle for equality in these respects cannot be accomplished except through the assertion of rights that stem from difference and are not universalizable. In other words, the struggle against inequalities based on ascriptive categories requires that institutions utilize "positive discriminations," favoring disadvantaged groups or parity in issues of gender. That clearly means subordinating individual, universal rights and the principle of equality before the law.

Finally, let me reiterate that the expansion of the normative horizon of citizenship beyond civil, socioeconomic, and political rights to encompass different fields such as the environment, communication, gender relations, local and regional life, and globalized world space, has not been accompanied by institutions that would allow these rights to be exercised by all.[7] That is compounded by the above-mentioned disputes arising not only over access to long-established rights but also over the content and quality of that access. Hence first-, second-, and third-class citizenships are produced, which in turn widens the field of inequalities.

Social Policies and the Fight against Inequality

The first aspect to analyze here is the exhaustion of revolutionary models for resolving issues of inequality, insofar as they have demonstrated historically a certain incapacity to resolve questions of freedom. Actually, the longer these models have postponed a democratic-liberal solution, the more the gains they certainly made in equality were likely to erode. The universalized aspiration for democratic political systems and the international geopolitical situation itself mean that egalitarian utopias have to abandon the revolutionary method of seizing power if they are to be achieved.

The populist formula that entailed the mass availability of public services is no longer valid today either, though at first it made a basic democratization possible.[8] Without going into an analysis of the economic issues involved in the populist formula, one must realize that the latter defined the process of basic social democratization as access to a given good or service. Hence the universalist and expansive nature of the social policies. Today, access is being redefined, in terms of the quality and specific content of the good or service one obtains. Moreover, mere access to certain institutions or fields, which was a precondition for equality some time ago, also serves to reproduce inequalities today. That holds for education, health care, information, and any other field of social life. Quality, defined according to diversified needs and objectives that general policies do not recognize, is becoming a precondition for equity.[9]

Yet if the revolutionary and populist models seem not to offer solutions today, neither can the gradualism of the trickle-down effect and of growth alone achieve the incorporation, in terms of equity, of the large numbers of the excluded. It would seem that the development models in vogue cannot achieve the massive structural incorporation of the excluded within the ethically allowable time frame of one generation. Rather, such models tend to cause new segmentations and reproduce inequalities.

In this connection, after more than a decade of structural adjustments and neoliberal formulas, and the corrections made to them, assessments of the social situation show the inability of such policies to address poverty and generally serve the populations most vulnerable to market mechanisms.

The idea of the subsidiary state, which was dominant during the first phase of the structural adjustment, had assistentialist policies as its corollary. At their most severe moments, the latter were social control mechanisms (for example, minimal employment programs, to alleviate the high unemployment rates, in the Chilean case) for dealing with the most marginalized sectors. These policies were accompanied by institutional changes that, instead of transforming the state from within, rather tended to create new agencies, shelving a more radical change in state structure. Various studies show that the privatization of social services (education, health care, social security) along with the assistentialist mentality, has generated stable, lasting conditions for the dualization of society: on one side are those able to gain access to market mechanisms; on the other, those who necessarily will be forced to be "assisted" forever by the state.

The vision of the subsidiary state also produced a cultural change in the way the poor are viewed. The latter were transformed from subjects of social policies (with mechanisms for processing their demands and, in some cases, participation mechanisms) into "beneficiaries" of targeted policies. The ideologues of the neoliberal formula made assurances that economic growth would automatically generate the necessary resources to raise the citizenry's standard of living. The reality showed that coming to grips with the social situation would require specific policies, adequate institutions, and, above all, resources that could be distributed through public social expenditure. Studies show that public social expenditures in Latin America fell during the so-called structural adjustment. Its recovery in the following years, as we have indicated, scarcely had a redistributive effect.[10]

A critique of the inefficiency of the welfare state was followed by targeting of the so-called vulnerable groups. Throughout the region, governments steadily implemented compensatory policies as the policies of choice. This has prevented an integrated restructuring of social policy, as the tendency in the region was to ascribe to targeted policies the character of stable policies that gradually replace state institutionalism in traditionally social matters. The emergency funds undoubtedly had immediate and generally positive results, including visibility for the targeted groups, greater flexibility in procedures, better collaboration with nongovernmental intermediary bodies, and the potential to generate new participation mechanisms among the so-called beneficiaries. On the other hand, the emergency fund policy runs the risk of creating new clientelistic relations, generating long-term dependency in the recipients, duplicating government efforts, or simply, given that they are subject to less monitoring, being conducive to cases of overt or concealed corruption.[11]

The targeted policies should therefore not eclipse the need for a sweeping reform of the state in this area, basically aimed at regaining the legitimacy of redistributive state policies of a structural nature. The traditional institutionalism of social spending should be modernized and decentralized and, at the same time, should be able to integrate the new institutionalism of the targeted policies. What is needed is a better combination of meeting emerging needs (vulnerable groups and buffers against poverty) and a long-term perspective in which the "firm" goals of social policies are guaranteed: equality and quality of life in keeping with sociocultural diversity and in dimensions such as better distribution of income, health care, education, social security, and housing. Targeted policies and emergency funds did not resolve these issues.

In sum, we are facing the exhaustion of models capable of addressing the issue of equality. To state it in extreme terms, no model or policy will be effective on this score if, in addition to positive discriminations, welfare measures, and targeted policies, there is not structural redistribution.

However, a redistribution of this sort faces two problems. The first is a political "squaring of the circle." No redistribution can be accomplished today outside of democratic mechanisms—that is, through a revolution or the imposition of ethical principles by physically coercive means. If the active agreement of those who will be affected by a redistribution cannot be counted upon (consider the simple example of taxes), at the least their resistance must be prevented. That assumes such measures will be democratically legitimated, which requires political power. There is no democratic political power without forming broad majorities to reach national political agreements that are policies of the state rather than of a particular administration. These agreements are very difficult to reach since they contend with powerful interests, but they are unavoidable if the democratic framework is to be preserved.

The second problem is determining what needs to be redistributed, both on the level of individuals and of social actors. For the era has passed when everything was reduced to an issue of economic power, equated with wealth, capital, or property. It is not that there is nothing to redistribute in this area. But in addition to fulfilling the above-mentioned democratic requirement, this does not encompass all of the issue of power, which today is multidimensional and highly diversified. On the level of individuals, it is necessary to redistribute the capacity to "prosper in life." That, in part, is known as education in the widest sense of the term, but it also includes the expressive and affective dimensions—social and cultural capital. On the level of social actors, what is needed is a redistribution of the capacity for collective action through organization, institutions, and a strengthening of the new dimensions of citizenship—in other words, social capital and political power.

Conclusion

I have stated that the objective of social policies or what is proper to them—in comparison to their equivalent, economic policies—is to produce society. In operative terms that means socioeconomic equality, a quality of life with respect for sociocultural diversity, and strong, autonomous citizenries and social actors able to negotiate representation in the political and state arenas.

Nevertheless, these issues presuppose an affirmation of the legitimacy and the value of society or the political community as an irreplaceable space in which individuals can realize their aspirations. The worldwide failure of neoliberal formulas has allowed the need for political communities and the state itself to regain legitimacy. But the same has not occurred for the ideas of equality or redistribution, much less for the mechanisms to achieve them democratically.

In the absence of a proposal for a type of society that guarantees equality, we return to our basic hypothesis: the threefold strengthening, autonomy, and complementarity of the three components of the sociopolitical matrix —the state, the system of representation, and the social actors, all of them mediated by the democratic political regime. That does not guarantee equality but the conditions for the struggle for it; without that struggle no society is viable.

✳ 6

Political Parties and the Crisis of Representation

In this chapter[1] we revisit a few ideas on epochal change advanced elsewhere in this book, then apply them to the problématique of representation and the role of political parties.[2]

The Current Historical Context of Political Representation

Today there is talk about a change of era, sometimes in terms that are too vague. We will touch upon two dimensions of this change, to which we have made extensive reference in this book.

First, what we could call the type of modernity—or model of modernity or the societal type—is changing. The national-state industrial society is on the wane as the only real or referential societal type. This type, in diverse variants, was organized around production, labor, and politics, and its principal social actors fought for basic definitions at the state leadership level; to that end, they generated systems of representation. This whole process was predicated on the idea that an economy and a type of social organization corresponded to a certain political system—democratic or authoritarian, depending on the case or historical moment—and to a certain cultural model. These four dimensions could be at odds or in contradiction, but there was a basic correlation between them.

It is precisely the idea of society in its polis-society dimension that now seems to be exploding. That is, the fundamental unit by which collective life was considered and the interaction between human beings was understood, the polis society, is called into question today. It has not disappeared, but it is threatened by two processes. The first is what is commonly termed globalization, in which the polis society is intersected by highways of every kind and transnational markets that rob it of its "center" of decision. The second is the explosion of particularisms and identities whose basic reference is shifting from the state or society to subjective experience around categories of ascription. Today identities are constituted around labor, income, and beliefs or ideologies (doing or accomplishing), and around gender, color, age, and nation or place of birth (being or ascription).[3] We are witnessing, then, an explosion of society. Currently, the political systems do not coincide with the whole of what is called society but only with a part of it.

Second, not only are different models of modernity being constituted, but also a profound transformation in the model of change, modernization, or development is under way. In other words, the shift to modern society is changing in character. It ceases to have the resource-accumulating and -distributing national state, around which social actors based on production or politics used to mobilize, as its only agent. This mobilization around a state that led development—which characterized welfare states and capitalist systems of various kinds, social democracy and different types of socialism, and populisms and national liberation movements—seems also to be yielding to a development model in which transnational market forces are key elements. It is not the case of the end of history or of the only model of the future, but only of a historical cycle that began with the crisis of the 1970s and the so-called structural adjustments, which acted more as elements of rupture than as defining elements of a stable development model. In this scenario, the main problem is how a political system and a state are reconstituted—quite the opposite of the prevailing ideology, which claims that building markets is what is at issue. That may have been the problem with the previous model, in which the state and politics seemed to be the exclusive agents of development, subordinating and subjecting the economy. But today the task before us is rather to control and regulate the blind transnational market forces emerging as the exclusive engine of growth, in other words, to reconstitute political communities, nation-states, and polis societies.

This scenario leads to the separation between what we could call "the political" (the problématique of the common good or the general functioning of society) and "politics" (activity tied to the administration of the foregoing). When economy, politics, culture, and social structure correspond in a society—that is, when there is a society polis—the political and politics are somehow the same. It must be remembered that, as I have said, there was always tension among all of these dimensions, which implies that they never corresponded perfectly to one another. But what I want to suggest here is that we are in societal situations in which the traditional forms of correspondence are disappearing. As this dissociation occurs, the political dissociates from politics as well. This means that the basic institutions that expressed this relationship between politics and the political are called into question. Along with the state, political parties are one of the main institutions of this type.

New Problems of Party Representation

Let us turn to the issues of representation and political parties in Latin America today. One should bear in mind that political parties are not only institutions of representation—the latter is only one of their responsibilities. Parties have the roles of representation, leadership, management, convoking, developing projects or proposals, government administration or opposition, unifying demands and channeling conflicts, and recruiting from the political class for state or public service positions. None of these responsibilities is met exclusively by political parties, but the parties are the only institution in contemporary Western society that meets *all* of these responsibilities. Political parties accomplish all these things by definition, while many other actors perform only some of these duties.

One could say on this point that the role of leadership is as deeply in crisis as the role of representation, if not more so. However, we should avoid thinking in relations of simple causality: Since they do not represent anything, therefore they do not have leadership. Political parties can perform leadership functions without fulfilling any representational role at a given moment. For instance, authoritarian or revolutionary parties can be quite unrepresentative and yet have great success at convoking and mobilizing. Mobilizing and representing are not the same thing.

When it is said that parties represent and that representation is in crisis, the question of what the parties represent should be asked. What dimensions are hidden under the concept of representation? First, and this was one of the basic dimensions to which contemporary political analysts referred—parties represent the principal conflicts, cleavages, or divisions in society. For example, a society in formation essentially debates whether it will be organized along centralized or federal lines, or how regions will be represented. In that context, in some cases, parties were generated on the basis of federalist associations or centralist parties. For its part, the conflict between church and state introduced the division between liberals and conservatives or between laicism and confessionalism. In the twentieth century, in the Latin American case, the main cleavage was in terms of social justice, the divide between rich and poor, capital and labor. Hence the right/center/left division or cleavage emerges. Political organization, in terms of democratic, authoritarian, or other types of regimes, is another conflict that divides society; on that basis political parties were formed as well. The political party systems we are familiar with, then, are built sometimes only as an expression of one of these cleavages, and sometimes as the aggregation of geological strata of these different rifts, representing one pole of these dualities. In any event, the party classically organizes the whole of its proposal starting from one of the cleavages or divisions, whether representing ideological or cultural groups that share a single vision, or a homogeneous or classist social base with common needs, interests, and aspirations. When capitalism or socialism was spoken of, for example, that choice arrayed the party spectrum from right to left, and the socioeconomic proposal of each was necessarily associated with its proposal for all the other dimensions of social life.

What, then, constitutes the crisis of representation in this dimension? In my view it arises from the existence today of manifold divisions and cleavages, none of which is reducible to another. Thus, those who occupy a given position in one of the divisions hold conflicting positions on another of the axes of division or conflict. For example, there is a moment in which the capitalist business actor is fundamental for gaining political democratization or the end of dictatorships—but that same actor is not the best ally if one subsequently wishes to resolve the issue of poverty. Certain actors can be closely joined on the growth-economic stagnation axis, or that of social justice, yet be adversaries on the environmental axis. In other words, the conflicts are not overlapping axes in which everyone is at the same end, but rather a multidimensional expression of cleavages, in which the repairing of one division cannot transfer over to another. One might say that this has always been the case, but, in fact, cleavages and conflicts used to be viewed and acted upon as a single totality reducible to a central conflict, the settlement of which would settle all the others.

Thus, on the one hand, it is becoming more difficult for the classic cleavages and conflicts that gave rise to the party system to be represented in their entirety by a single political actor. On the other hand, other kinds of essential, key issues are emerging that have not yet found expression in terms of conflict or cleavages. It is not known of what a partisan positioning would consist with respect to one or another new kind of cleavage. Just as in the birth of the industrial, capitalist conflict the positionings and projects had not been determined, insofar as it was not known what they were about or what was at stake, many of the characteristics of globalized postindustrial society, which overlap with the national-state industrial society, are perceived as problems or negatives but without yet giving rise to defined positions around which rivalries and projects might be constituted. There are tensions and cleavages in society, many of which cannot be defined in confrontational terms, that have yet not given rise either to stable actors or to proposals that would allow the delineation of a party spectrum or a continuum of representation with respect to proposed solutions.

Second, the parties represent and have represented interests gathered around general societal issues, as well as the more specific interests of a given social group or social organization—what we call corporative interests. This representation occurs before a general interlocutor, the state, which cannot be reduced to the administration but includes the executive and legislative branches; the economic, cultural, and military entities of the state; and the centralized and decentralized levels. With the weakening of the role of the state as an agent of development and distributor of resources, even on the symbolic level, those who represent interests before it lose power, importance, and ability to convoke. Those with specific interests seek basically corporative forms of representation that compete directly in the marketplace or become de facto powers.

Third, along with representing antagonisms, interests, and social projects, political parties represent social actors: middle classes, popular sectors, shanty-dwellers, laborers, campesinos, regional elites or local actors, business people, and professional associations. In this area, the classical actors (classes and movements formed around production and distribution, and around politics) now tend either to become corporativized, basically as industrial interest groups, or to become atomized or segmented, as is happening with the so-called sectors of extreme poverty or the excluded. For their part, the new actors tied mainly to cultural issues or to matters of the environment, human rights, gender, and defense of cultural identity are certainly able to bring topics into the public forum and agenda, and even make them hegemonic in society, but can only guarantee their stable political representation in actual parties, as happened with environmental and women's movements, with great difficulty. Instead, alongside organized social actors there is emerging the phenomenon of public opinion, which can be general or segmented, and which in many cases plays the role of social actor.[4] It would seem that polls and the media recognize or represent this new "actor" better than the parties do.

Fourth, political parties have historically represented the demands of citizenship. What was stated elsewhere in this book on this score should be borne in mind, namely, that the phenomena of citizenship are now affected by two contradictory processes: expansion in scope and broadened exclusion.

On the one hand, we are becoming aware today of the existence of diversified fields of power, including gender relations, communication, the environment, local and regional authority, and supranational issues (such as those involving migrations, global communications, and economic treaties or pacts). These all constitute potential fields in which to claim rights—that is, fields of citizenship. Yet unlike civil, political, and socioeconomic rights, there do not exist institutions or organizations here analogous to those of the aforementioned, where citizenship can be exercised. How will political parties represent these new demands of citizenship?

On the other hand, in Latin America exclusion was always synonymous with domination and exploitation, and the parties on the left, and also at times the populist and centrist ones, sought the integration of these social sectors. This took place through situations that made the excluded a single group. Proposals and ideologies of integration were able to convoke large conglomerations, insofar as they took aim at well-defined adversaries and the overcoming of situations of exploitation and oppression common to all the excluded. We have noted several times that today exclusion does not so much resemble exploitation—though this does survive on a broad scale for vast sectors—as total marginalization from society and the loss of common ties and opportunities for the excluded. This kind of exclusion permeates all social groups, creating tremendous obstacles to any kind of political representation.

Fifth, in addition to conflicts and divisions, vested interests, social actors, and citizen demands, political parties represented and expressed ideas and projects, visions of the desirable society, and from there, critiques of the existing society, and policies or programs to improve it wholly or in part. Political parties were sites of and actors in public debate.

Everyone knows that there is no one single type of desirable society nowadays. No one has an image of such a society as the socialist or the capitalist, the Christian, the liberal, the Marxist, the democrat, the authoritarian, the progressive, or the conservative did. We have no blueprints of societies. We realize that there is not a feasible utopian project around which to present projects or positions. Projects or positions will have to define and apply broad ethical and utopian principles only partially to one sphere of society or another, without there being a coherent plan that at once encompasses the economy, politics, culture, and society, as the familiar utopias did. In that context, political parties have enormous problems in representing ideas and proposals; for that reason other actors come onto the scene looking—unsuccessfully—to replace them.

Finally, political parties represented what could be called the political class. From the moment in which, as we noted, politics loses its exclusive identification with the political, and the two dimensions split, the political class that is represented through political parties inevitably begins to revolve around itself in a kind of void. That is, the parties continue to represent the political class, but it is more difficult for the latter to represent society and easier for it to represent its own views and mainly electoral and bureaucratic interests, which are certainly legitimate but are not necessarily identified with any view of the common good. This is surely the hardest problem to solve, since in relation to the other aspects we have noted, there could be institutions and organizations that try to represent interests, actors, conflicts, and projects, although always partially and without entirely replacing the political parties. But with respect to the representation of the political class—the class that concerns itself with the political activity of the state and of society—there is no institution other than political parties, and their replacement in this role can only lead to generalized corruption or radicalized corporativism.

Political Parties and Historical Projects

In sum, independent of their actual quality and performance, or their historical success or failure, political parties in Latin America sought to represent great historical alternatives. Whether in the populist, vanguardist, clientelist, electoral, or personalistic forms, they took one stand or another on the issues of development, social integration, the building of and independence of the national state, revolution, and democracy.

I have noted that today one can no longer speak of these problems as if they encompassed the whole life of a society. In other words, if one wishes to speak of development, it is necessary to reformulate its meaning for each sphere of society, since there is no longer "development" in the singular but rather economic, political, cultural, and social development, the structures and processes of which do not match up one to one, and which prove the undoing of the concept. Development is not unidimensional but multidimensional.[5] It is very difficult to speak of a model of development, since the terms of each of these dimensions do not correlate. Political democracy does not guarantee social democratization, and both can inhibit the expansion and growth of markets. Sustainable development certainly affects economic growth, which in turn greatly affects social equality. Insertion into globalization can mean economic progress, but it threatens national, regional, and local cultures and identities. Social equality is difficult to achieve in democracy and may, in turn, limit the expansion of gender- and age-related subjectivities, and those of civil associations or simply individuals.

This absence of an automatic or structural correspondence among economy, politics, culture, and social organization calls to mind again the four different tasks that lie ahead, discussed at the outset of this book: political democracy, social democratization, reinsertion into the world economy, and the generation of modernity itself. Unlike the old concepts of development or revolution, these are neither the prerequisites for nor the effects of one another. In each of these areas there are different ethical considerations, each one unavoidable, each requiring policies, proposals, and actors among which contradictions and antagonisms may exist.

Political parties are the only entities that can coherently articulate the contradictions present among these four dimensions. What, then, will the political parties represent? They will represent not a single historical option but forms of articulation of different dimensions in tension, for which they do not have a monopoly on representation and which are not found assembled in an already configured, comprehensive project.

If the political parties do not do this, the markets will, or the enlightened technocracy, the force of money or the media, or authoritarian individualism camouflaged as direct democracy, or the movementism that eliminates pluralism and difference. Forced to choose between partyocracy (*partidocracia*) or the market, technocracy, movementism, or fundamentalism, the parties are a safe bet. But these are not the options that come into play; rather, the simultaneous strengthening of the state, the regime, political parties, and autonomous social actors is at stake, as we have reiterated throughout the book.

There will be neither society nor polis without a strong state. There will be no strong states if there are no strong political parties and partisan systems. There will not be political parties if there are no autonomous social actors. Some might say that things are going in the other direction today and not toward strengthening the state, parties, and social actors. If that is the case, there will be a need for the voluntarist act of affirming a basic ethical-political principle: the irreplaceable site of representation of society that the political parties represent.

Apart from that, the most deep-seated trend at the beginning of the 1990s, along with criticizing politics and the parties themselves, was toward reconstructing the parties and their systems where they lapsed into crisis, fell from view, or never existed in practice. In some cases, the sectors that took part in uprisings or civil wars have been incorporated into the party system; in others there was an effort to constitute solid, individual parties; in others the single-party or bipartisan monopoly of the system was broken up, making the system more representative; in others party alliances that express broad social consensuses were constituted; and in others the relationship between parties and social actors was redefined, leading to greater autonomy and complementarity between them. But at the end of the decade and the beginning of the 2000s a new wave of skepticism vis-à-vis politics, and a loss of prestige of political actors, especially in the Andean countries, seemed to break up or pulverize the party system, and new expressions of antiparty movements appeared. This reality and the very low prestige of parties do not mean that these societies can dispense with them or replace them with a messianic civil society or with grass-roots movements.

On the contrary, all this reinforces that the major issue today is the construction of a system of parties and representation that would allow the rebuilding of a political community in the face of the brutal subjugation of the market and the emergence of identities that often take on a fundamentalist guise.

✳ 7

Civil Society, Social Movements, and Democratization

Two preliminary observations on the concept of civil society are in order.[1] First, we use this concept in a purely descriptive sense—and not a normative one, as the prevailing view has been in recent years—to refer to the set of actors, organizations, and networks that do not form part of the state or the formal political system. Second, and in apparent contradiction with the foregoing, civil society has always had a very precarious autonomy in Latin America, and there has been a very ambiguous line dividing the state, politics, and civil society, since these societies were constituted mainly from the state and from politics.[2]

Civil Society and Democratization

It is possible to distinguish at least four major phases of civil society's presence in processes of change from authoritarian regimes and of political democratization. Before the onset of democratization, when military and authoritarian regimes are still strong, civil society is virtually dissolved and is absent from the public space. This is due, above all, to the repressive nature of the regime and to the retreat—and traumatization, in some cases—of the middle classes, among whom many have viewed the authoritarian coup as a return to tranquility, and stability as the defense of gains they had achieved during the national-popular period. It is a moment of withdrawal, depoliticization, and the forsaking of all public life.

The second phase, which, strictly speaking, marks that of the beginning of what I have elsewhere called "the invisible transition," appears when that political withdrawal is disrupted.[3] This is more of a social phase than a political one. It involves the emergence of protest and criticism from various sectors against repression or against the most brutal forms of economic transformation undertaken by authoritarian regimes. It is not a protest against the dictatorship per se, but against some of the measures and reforms that have affected certain gains made by these sectors. Such protest is basically led by classical actors such as the unions. It should be recalled that, in general, these authoritarian regimes coincide with processes of economic change that seek to move from an import-substitution industrialization development model to neoliberal-style models dominated by transnational market forces. It is precisely in such moments when the authoritarian regimes attempt to dismantle and hinder politics.

At this point, the different sectors that had been in leading roles during the regime (democratic or populist, depending on which kind preceded the authoritarian one) gradually begin to develop forms of social mobilization. At the same time, a cultural phase appears as well, in which intellectuals and artists begin to gear their works toward human rights and other themes with content that is in some way political, with a view to delegitimizing the dictatorship. In Brazil, for example, movements of artists, shanty-dwellers (*favelados*), blacks, and homosexuals arose, as well as urban and other movements. In Chile, gender, human rights, and ecological movements, singers, recitals and even novels cropped up at that time. In other words, a variety of social and cultural expressions appear, creating a climate that little by little unifies the different oppositions, the various ways that civil society rejects the regime's reforms and measures, and shepherds them toward a vast democratic movement for human, social and cultural rights. The different protests become tinged with a component of democratic demands, and the rallying cry calling for an ouster—*Y va a caer* (It will fall)—goes up in the streets.

This phase is marked by the problematic relation between the social and the political. On the one hand, the question is how to bring together the different demands from very heterogeneous sectors in such a way that, without effacing their individual claims, they might be geared toward ending the dictatorship or toward the search for any other formula (free elections, plebiscite, referendum, etc.) with the same aim. Thus, with an activated civil society carrying out protests and mobilizations, there is also a political actor, which was very repressed in some countries, or dissolved and turned to dust in others, such as Peru. The matter can be summed up thus: how to ensure that the public outcry, which is starting to be heard in street protests, is unified around the political, and how to reconstitute a political apparatus, a party system able to politicize civil society's demands and guide them toward the goal of ending the dictatorship.

Here one enters complex territory, since throughout this phase civil society generally has shown distrust toward political parties, among other reasons because it is thought that they were the ones who triggered the crisis that led to authoritarianism. The disrepute of the political parties exists and conspires against their ability to convene. At the same time, in this phase the parties are normally weakened and scattered, and cannot muster a unified action that would let them recoup their numbers and the civil society's trust. Moreover, it is the time when political leadership becomes indispensable, since in its absence there can be a civil society virtually having a democratic experience itself, but submitted by an authoritarian political regime. In other words, there is a total split between the social and the political.

Thus, in this second phase the revalorization of the political and, particularly, the reorganization of a party system, enters into the balance. The parties, in turn, have to be less concerned with what they stand to gain after the dictatorship and more concerned with how to bring down the dictatorship and rebuild a government of the majority. That is the whole point: how to build a government of the majority upon the departure of an authoritarian government. That cannot be accomplished by civil society; it is the job of the political parties.

That brings us to the third phase, which is that of mutual subordination: that of political parties to the dynamics of the civil society, that is, understanding what the demands and claims are in order to unify them; and the subordination of civil society to political parties because, otherwise, with whom will the dictatorship be negotiated, since we are not talking about an overthrow? Except for traditional, one-man, patrimonial dictatorships, á la Somoza or Trujillo, in general there are no formulas for overthrowing or mounting insurrections against those dictatorships or authoritarian regimes constituted by institutionalized parties or the armed forces. That obviously makes it very difficult to confront them in the military sphere; in the last decades there have been no overthrows of military dictatorships or "new authoritarian" regimes in Latin America.

Therefore the relationship between political parties and civil society is fundamental. Civil societies alone do not remove institutionalized dictatorships; neither do political leaders alone. This type of authoritarian regime or dictatorship is not removed, is not toppled, so to speak. They leave power through mobilizations by the civil society, negotiations between the dictatorship and the political class representative of that civil society, and often mediations by other institutions: at times the Catholic Church; the monarchy, as in Spain; a foreign presence, such as the Contadora Group in Central America; and even U.S. intervention.[4] There can also be cases of internal collapse due to criminal ineptitude, such as that of Galtieri in the Malvinas Islands, or due to a number of acts of fraud and corruption, as was the case with Fujimori.

The third phase is therefore that of the predominance of political solutions around which the civil society, which at times has lost faith in political society, must be mobilized. For instance, in Chile, when the opposition decided to go to the plebiscite after having stated for ten years that any plebiscite by Pinochet would be a sham, the Catholic Church itself took a stance to the left, and the social organizations felt that everything invested thus far in the mobilization process was going to be staked on a throw of the dice in a fraudulent plebiscite. The task before the Chilean political opposition was, first, to come to an agreement to go to the plebiscite without insisting that an agreement be reached first on a platform of postauthoritarian and democratic transformations; without excessively debating the issue of who was to blame for the crisis that led to the authoritarian regime, for that would cause divisions once again; and without making the issue of who would gain what from the alliance into the main issue.

There was, then, a double process of transformation of the civil society: moderating its social extremism in terms of its sectoral demands, knowing that they would not be able to achieve many of the items that were proposed, and steering all that toward political extremism or radicalism—out with the dictator. But that requires political direction or leadership, which up to now has come only from political parties.

What should be taken into account is that all the examples of political democratization show that at the outset, the political party system was in disarray and disarticulated. In the Chilean case, for example, even though the parties were fewer and were somewhat better structured, they were dismantled by the brutal repression of the dictatorship. In the Argentine case, the first expression of the last military regime, that of López Rega, is a Peronist sector that, from the government, fought the other Peronist sector, which was armed; the Peronists and radicals, in turn, were lifelong enemies and so never could constitute a first government together following the dictatorship, even though they had been able to create an opposition together. In Chile, Christian Democrats and socialists were at each other's throats in 1973, and the vast majority of Christian Democrats, with the important exception of a few leaders and militants, explicitly or implicitly supported the coup. The simultaneous experience of dispersal, distance, and fusion between civil society and politics affects practically every case of political democratization.

Each country rebuilt its partisan system and rebuilt the civil society's relations with the parties in accordance with its own tradition and following the changes wrought within the civil society itself. In the Chilean case, the parties that now govern are those that were eliminated by the dictatorship. In Spain it was the Socialist Party, totally transformed, that governed to assure the transition. In Brazil the parties that had been rooted to some degree were restructured, and those created under the dictatorship were consolidated—though precariously, like all of the Brazilian partisan system. In the Peruvian case, a reestablishment of a partisan system seems inevitable, and reestablishments of partisan systems take time.

Social Movements and Actors

Associated with the classical sociopolitical matrix was a type of social action that might be characterized as a central social movement (see Chapter 1). It defined a central conflict and was geared toward overall change: the national popular movement (NPM).[5] Historically, particular social movements formed part of this central movement, despite their identities. Each particular, concrete social movement was at once modernizing, developmentalist, and nationalist, was geared toward overall change, and made reference to the "people" (*pueblo*) as the single subject of history.[6]

Generally speaking, the emblematic social movement was the labor movement, more for its symbolic significance than for its structural power. Nevertheless, at various moments this leadership was called into question by the impression that the urban workers, forced to make commitments, had lost their revolutionary drive. Consequently, other movements, such as those of campesinos, students, or even the revolutionary parties, were called on to step into these leadership roles.

This central social movement was made up of various concrete actors and movements. Its main characteristics—and here we are referring mainly to the urban sectors—were the joining of a very strong symbolic dimension that sought a comprehensive social change with a dimension of very specific, particularist demands, and the turning to the state as interlocutor for demands, as well as the site for taking power in order to change society. Consequently, the structural weakness of classes as a foundation for social movements was made up for by their force of attraction on the level of ideological and political mobilization that was at once integrative and revolutionary.

The military authoritarianisms, the structural adjustments, and the above-mentioned transformations mentioned in other chapters—namely, the breakdown of the classical sociopolitical matrix—had profound consequences for the social movements and actors.

Under the military dictatorships, social action was threaded with interwoven meanings. The first was the reconstruction of the social "fabric" ripped apart by authoritarianism and economic reforms. The second was the politicization of all demands, insofar as each action was directed toward the end of the authoritarian regimes. Thus, the relation to the state and to politics changed dramatically for the social movements: They became more autonomous, more symbolic, and more geared toward a search for their own identities than toward instrumentality or concrete demands. Self-defense and survival, at first, opposition to authoritarian social transformations later, and, finally, an orientation toward politico-institutional formulas for transition, marked the evolution of collective action during these regimes.

The attempt by authoritarian regimes to change the role of the state, and the economic and societal changes to which we referred, transformed the spaces for the constitution of social movements, even in the countries that did not experience this new wave of authoritarianism. Their structural and institutional standing was significantly weakened by the repression, marginality, and informalization of the economy. More than organized movements, the main collective action during the military regimes was social mobilization of a symbolic nature.

One could say that it is the democratic movement that takes over—that is, a central social movement that for the first time is geared not toward comprehensive and radical social change but rather exclusively toward a change in political regime. The ending of the authoritarian regimes and the establishment of democracy became the main objectives of collective action. With this change the central social movement won in instrumental terms, but the price paid was that particular demands began to be subordinated to political objectives. At the same time, this gave political actors the leading role, as we said above.

Negotiations and agreements on the level of elites replaced social mobilizations during the democratic transition and the processes of consolidation. In this sense, the process of political democratization tends to split each collective action into two logics with which all social movements are imbued. One is the political logic aimed at the establishment of a consolidated democracy as a condition for any other type of demands. The second is the particular logic of each social movement directed toward securing concrete claims in the social democratization process as a condition for actively supporting the new democratic regime.

The existence of authoritarian enclaves (to which we have referred in another chapter) after the inauguration of democratic regimes maintained the importance of human rights movements in the dawn of the new democracies. Nevertheless, the risks of an authoritarian regression and the negotiations over other legacies (institutional, military) of authoritarianism gave the governments and opposition political actors the central role in social action; the principles of action of other actors were subordinated to the logics of these central actors. At the same time, the demand for economic stability, tied in certain cases to the processes of democratic consolidation, privileged the exigencies of the economic adjustment, discouraging collective action that was thought to potentially put these processes at risk. The outcome was a certain deactivation of the social movements; the fact that the only major objective had been that of establishing democratic regimes, or on several occasions, of adapting to and defending oneself from the structural adjustment, left the social movements without a central principle for the future. Thus we may ask whether the national-popular movement, and later the democratic movement that replaced it, will be followed in Latin America by a new central social movement that gives direction to the sum total of particular social movements.

At least three issues make the emergence of a new central social movement somewhat difficult. We have already mentioned the increase in poverty and the new type of exclusion. This means that the great contradiction in these countries is between those who are "inside" the socioeconomic and political system, irrespective of their position relative to its interior, and those who are "outside" that system. As we pointed out earlier, this segmentation affects different groups, actors, or social actions to varying degrees, making organized collective action more difficult. On the other hand, this also means that the predominant model of modernity is challenged not only by the marginalized, whose interests over and above inclusion are highly contradictory, but also by those who play a subordinate part in the system. The rural indigenous world, the informal sector, and the unemployed or precariously employed are examples of "outsiders," even if in cultural terms they are integrated by the media. Women, youth, and especially workers are examples of groups imbued with the "inside-outside" contradictions. In sociological terms, there is real conflict around the model of development, not between those who are in the system and those who are not, but rather between those who are inside it. Those who are outside the system are seen as unnecessary and seem to be superfluous. Currently, there is no conceivable revolutionary ideological model that takes them into account, as there was in the 1960s, with the possible exception of those attracted to desperate fundamentalism. But the latter are weak in Latin America.

The breakdown and reconstruction of a sociopolitical matrix, after the disarticulation of the politico-statist and national popular matrix, creates a new obstacle to the emergence of a central social movement. Actually, the old matrix had the advantage of fusing the different problems and dimensions of society. The new emerging matrix, if it can be consolidated, will have its components differentiated, with greater autonomy, tension, and interaction among them. This means that the role of politics will be changed and that it is still unknown what will replace the state, the party system, and the populist movement in the constitution of social actors and movements. It seems likely that each sphere of society will separate and, with its own contradictions, give rise to heterogeneous collective action with few shared principles. Therefore, at the same time that diversity and social identities are enriched, the symbolic and organic links capable of unifying this diversity in a new central social movement are weakened.

Beyond the political democratizations, there are cultural changes that will influence the characteristics of a potential central social movement and of the particular social movements. In the classical sociopolitical matrix, struggles and conflicts were oriented mainly, as we have indicated, by egalitarian, libertarian, and nationalist principles and objectives. These principles were taken up by various anticapitalist, antioligarchical, democratic, antiimperialist, or nationalist tendencies and movements. The national popular movement included these three dimensions or principles, and politics was the main sphere of social action. These principles and struggles are as yet unresolved and still incite numerous collective actions. But each of the above-mentioned principles has become more technical, autonomous, and complex. Thus the old forms of organization such as unions, parties, and corporatism are becoming insufficient and are unable to find a single formula for all these dimensions in classical politics. At times, the achievement of some progress in one of these dimensions has actually been accompanied by rather severe regressions in the others.

Meanwhile, changes in civil society have brought new kinds of demands and principles of action that could not be expressed through the traditional struggles for equality, liberty, and national independence. The new topics of daily life—interpersonal relationships, personal and group accomplishments, aspirations to social recognition, a sense of belonging or social identities, all of which refer to the model of modernity at stake— belong rather to the dimension of the pursuit of happiness or of subject formation, and cannot be replaced or represented by the old principles and mechanisms of collective action (unions, political parties, etc.). They are not private affairs either but rather are expressed as demands in the public sphere. Naturally, this new dimension does not take the place of the previous ones but adds even greater diversity and complexity to social action, insofar as it is not directed at a specific adversary, as was the case of the classical social struggles, and rests not solely on confrontation but also on agreement and solidarity.

What can be expected in the foreseeable future is a variety of forms of struggle and mobilization, which will be more autonomous, shorter, and less directed by political actors. They probably will occur in an institutional framework and will be oriented more toward sectoral demands, partial modernizations, and gradual social democratization and integration than toward radical systemic changes. Their content will be split between the demands of inclusion and, at the same time, the quest for meaning and an identity of one's own in the face of the universalization of modernity that the forces of the market and its agents propose. If these demands go unmet, likely abrupt and isolated outbursts will develop, or there will be withdrawal into apathy or seeking of refuge in community, or a combination of these formulas, rather than the creation of coherent and stable revolutionary movements.

8

Changes in Latin American Political Culture

Classical Latin American Political Culture

Political culture may be defined as the set of values, opinions, attitudes, behaviors, and, more broadly, the cultural orientations and styles, both informal and institutionalized, that are present in the power relations related to the overall functioning of society—that is, what I am calling politics.[1] In a given society there are predominant traits of political culture, but it is difficult to ensure that there is "a political culture." Rather, one should speak of the coexistence of diverse and sometimes contradictory political cultures.

Classical Politics

At one time, politics was basically two things: On the one hand, it was an important path to access certain goods and standards of living through the state; on the other hand, it was where individual experience met and joined with integration into a collective project, where a person was identified with society, with an idea of nation. Politics allowed the attainment of benefits through the state (housing, education, health care, and sometimes employment) and gave meaning to people's lives, individually and collectively. Political culture was, then, at one and the same time pragmatic or instrumental and transcendental: one belonged out of self-interest but also out of a quest for meaning. There was, then, an ethical and religious component to Latin American politics, insofar as one became a part of something larger than oneself. Other societies, by contrast, ascribe a religious meaning to the economy or to other realms of social life.

Politics was thus a meeting place for individual experience and the epic. In order to "be happy," one needed to be integrated into some political project. Take, for example, slogans such as "Make love and the revolution," coming from abroad, or, more typically Latin American, "In the streets we're much more than two," or *The Captain's Verses* by Neruda (for example: "Bésame de nuevo, querida. / Limpia ese fusil, camarada.") [Kiss me again, my dear / Clean that gun, comrade].

Political culture was much more a culture of democratization than of democracy, more one of mobilization than of representation. That is, democracy was not prized mainly for its political aspects, as a form of government, or as a set of rules and institutions, but as integration into a society, as a way of being a subject in it.

This double dimension, instrumental and transcendental, explains the coexistence of the logic of negotiation with the logic of friend-vs.-foe and revolutionary logic. The list of terms of a social movement called at once, especially in the 1960s, for concrete benefits and ideological demands, that is, "food, clothing and shelter" and a "socialist society."

In general, this was a noninstitutionalist political culture, in that more than being distrusted, institutions were ignored; one was above or below them, and the same was true with classical juridical and political procedures. This political culture will crystallize in different kinds of styles and behaviors, depending on the characteristics of each society. Thus, one can differentiate the Argentine society, for example, from the Chilean and Uruguayan societies, in that in the two latter cases this crystallization of habits happened on the basis of voting and the party system. The vote was the equivalent, in a sense, of what revolutionary action was, especially in the Chilean case. In other words, the vote was not valued in itself as an expression of citizenship but was appreciated as a mechanism to change everything if one wished to, since it enabled one both to reap material and symbolic benefits and to seize power of the state.

Democratization and Political Culture

The advent of the military dictatorships and the processes of political democratization, which may, as I have stated, take on the forms of foundations (Central America), transitions (Southern Cone), or political reform (Mexico), brought about changes in the political culture. These changes moved in the direction of valuing institutionality. There has been a passage, then, from a purely mobilizing, content-based politics to a politics that understands that forms and procedures are also content and are also substantive. The institutions tend to be valued and distrusted at the same time but no longer go unacknowledged. Thus, in the answers to questions asked in public opinion polls about institutions, one sees that distrust runs very high. Nevertheless, everyone ultimately defers to institutionality. Let us take an extreme example—the plebiscites to change the constitution and carry out a presidential reelection. Certainly, this is an attempt to manipulate the citizenry, but this is very different from remaining in power or calling out the military for support. The plebiscite will perhaps be of a Caesarist, nondemocratic character, but it is an institution legitimated by those who participate in it and by the acceptance of its results. Through a plebiscite, even though attempts may be made to rig it, one can win or lose, which means that institutional norms, however ambiguous their democratic meaning may be, are present. To this effect, forms of recognition of institutions are emerging today—that is, rules of the game that obtain for all, though they may not benefit one individually. This is the great achievement Latin American political culture has made.

With regard to institutions, including elections, the judiciary, and so on, there is, then, a dual movement of acceptance or recognition along with distrust. This ambivalence is seen in public opinion polls that ask whether political parties "are indispensable to democracy" and whether "the current political parties only serve their own interests, instead of serving the people." In both cases, the percentages that agree with these statements are extremely high. Moreover, we mentioned in another chapter that the last elections held in Latin America reveal that approximately 70 percent of the total of registered voters actually vote, and 53 percent of the total of all those of voting age do so. The first figure demonstrates the similarity to European statistics, and the second percentage is higher than that of voter turnout in the United States.[2]

Thus, there seems to be a shift from a political culture that is contemptuous, dismissive, or negative with regard to institutions, and that is centered only around mobilization, the affirmation of subjects, and instrumentalist negotiation to satisfy the interests and projects of those subjects.

The shift is toward a political culture that understands that institutions are necessary and accepts them, and that consequently accepts their sanctions and negative effects, such as defeat at the polls.

Reality and Myth of the "New Politics"

Alongside triumphalist visions of the "new economy" that confuse myths with reality, the vision of a "new politics" is arising from the right. It was in evidence in several presidential campaigns in late 1999 and 2000, such as those in Chile and Mexico. In both cases, the banner of change was flown, in the sense of a change in traditional politics. This slogan's communicational impact has been so huge that, for one thing, it is tending to give a new identity to the right in various places, detaching it from conservative or authoritarian ideological discourse. But that is not all: It is also influencing the other camps of the political spectrum, including those of the left, which are tending to combine some parts of this new discourse with old and rather timid elements taken from traditional politics.

This new politics basically consists of the assertion that, more than creating projects or large society-building ventures, it is necessary to face the problems that concern people, and this is measured by polls and focus groups. In theory, to do that, one need only listen, and without proposing anything, so that acts of government or representation are made into a series of technical answers to these problems. Something to be said in favor of this discourse is that it emphasizes nonconfrontational dimensions and that it calls, albeit usually demagogically, for addressing the problems that are said to concern the inhabitants of a country. The downside is that it ignores the history of societies and denies what is specific to politics.

It is true that for many people today politics seems to be less crucial for solving a number of issues involving access to goods and services. It is also true that it is less of a source of meaning in the lives of large sectors that it once brought together. But for that very reason, politics can be more political today and less of an interference in everything. The ultimate goal of politics is to build a good society, which presumes different views of what a good society is and how to go about creating it. This process of building a good society, which is never finished, is not exhausted by solving individual people's problems, not only because that is never achieved but also because there are matters that, while they may not be among the concerns of "the people," are still enormously important for the life of society. Insofar as people are diverse and their problems are all different, insofar as many of those problems are not resolved by the state, and insofar as people are gaining ever more autonomy to resolve those problems, it is incumbent upon politics precisely to resolve those questions of the organization of society that many people cannot see directly but that are indispensable for the very reason that they enable people to act and resolve their problems. These issues entail conceptions, ideas, projects, and proposals that will never be the sum of partial solutions; there is a specificity to politics that does not end in the resolution of everyone's specific problems.

Moreover, "the people" (*la gente*) is something very heterogeneous, and the term masks the tremendous diversity of those who live in a country. Politics needs to account for this diversity but also to be guided by a view of the whole, without which society vanishes, atomized into markets, subjugated by media, or controlled by de facto powers. Also, one must not make the mistake of thinking that "the people" only have specific concerns related to their individual needs, privations, and aspirations. People also exist as a citizenry that is concerned about the future of their country. Therefore, many people whose individual problems have been solved by a certain administration or party nevertheless vote against them when they feel the latter's views have been wrong or the administration has been poorly run overall.

While it is true that some dimensions that often are overlooked by traditional politics are addressed by the discourse of the new politics, the latter is nothing more than that: an ideological discourse that empties politics of its society-transforming content, turning it into an electoral game or a way of playing with the hopes of individuals.

A New Political Culture?

Yet, there exist real problems that are eroding the revaluation of representative political democracy and of institutional politics that I mentioned earlier. Certain structural and cultural transformations in Latin America, which I have discussed elsewhere in this book, are weakening the very reality that today we are more institutionalist, more trusting in representation than in mere mobilization. That is because these changes have transformed politics itself.

As I have already noted, until the time of the dictatorships, politics was the place where people accessed the benefits of society much more than through other spheres or activities. It was also the place where projects were constituted in which personal experience and collective events merged.

In the present day, politics offers much less than when it was characterized by those two elements. Among other reasons, this is because structural transformations and the change in the development model have meant that the state has lost its monopoly on the supply of material and symbolic goods, health care, housing, social security, and communications, which today have been privatized. The state, and through it, politics, are no longer the only large suppliers, and what they supply is less apparent and more abstract: social life in a political community, in the polis. Therefore, politics is no longer the necessary vehicle to generate those goods, while subjectivity is expressed in many forms besides ideological-political ideas or projects.

This multidimensional expression of individual and collective subjectivity outside of politics is particularly visible among youth: in music, interpersonal relations, a certain ecological consciousness, and in a complex youth culture that somehow says, "I don't need to be either leftist, centrist, or rightist to be happy."

The two basic roles of politics in Latin America have changed, then, but have not vanished. In changing, politics is losing its centrality just when we are learning and taking into account that institutions are important. As I noted in a preceding chapter, there is a movement of separation of "politics" from "the political," where "the political" continues to matter as a concern for the "good society" and for the general orientation of society but is distant and disconnected from "politics," which is seen as a specific activity, professional and remote. It is not that the political does not matter to people but simply that they feel politics is not the best way to express themselves in that dimension. Politics begins to revolve around itself to some extent, and, consequently, it becomes much more abstract from the people's lives, which continue to have an ideological dimension, but of a more concrete nature. People ask, Why should I bother with politics if it is so far removed from my search for personal fulfillment? And the latter means not only satisfying material needs, not only everyday consumption, but also being a social subject.

This is not well understood by a guilt-ridden, perplexed political class that is used to a different historical situation and a different task. According to some sectors of that class, individuals demand that politicians concern themselves with and resolve the people's problems. Politicians thus attempt to become priests, psychologists, doctors, builders, managers, providers of goods and services, and door-to-door salesmen of sorts, devoted to solving "the people's problems." In actuality, people want to resolve problems on their own and are in need of spaces, organizations, and resources. From politics, people demand ideas, meaning, and direction, though no longer totalizing, with respect to the life of the society and to the political community, for that is what the people do not find in their own everyday activities.

At the same time, we are told that the media are transforming the individual from "homo sapiens" into "homo videns"; that is, into someone who consumes and produces images more than thoughts.[3] This means that the capacity to understand abstract thought in today's society has been diminished. This is precisely what complicates the matter: It turns out that politics is becoming more abstract, but our surrounding environment is reducing our capability to understand the abstract. On the one hand, there is a need for representation, political parties, and appreciation of institutions; on the other hand, a certain tension is evident with respect to the abstract character, detached from individual experience, that politics is acquiring. The relationship that existed before is thus broken.

In this new political situation, the phenomena of citizenship and government exceed the classical institutions in which people just recently began to believe. There is a lack of institutional creativity and a general incapacity, with some exceptions, to create new institutions. Rather, the classical ones are reformed in accordance with particular, immediate interests (for example, the constitutional reforms to make presidential reelections possible). It is becoming necessary to create flexible institutions in social and political life, where the people and collective subjects can generate different types of ties between the political and politics, such as the popular participation law in Bolivia or the creative de facto interactions in some countries between elements of parliamentarianism and presidential regimes, to give just two examples from Latin America. In a different context, the South African constitution demonstrates such institutional creativity.

After decades, the importance of classical institutions has come to be recognized in Latin America, just when those institutions are everywhere undergoing a profound redefinition in order to adapt to the world of the twenty-first century. There has not been an effort at institutional creativity that would make the phenomenon of appreciation and building of democratic institutionality compatible with another contemporary phenomenon, that of institutional erosion due to the emergence of a political culture in which the meaning of politics itself has changed.

Let me make a final observation on the varying ways in which different generations see this change in politics and political culture, a difference that further complicates treatment of the subject. In effect, adults—and therefore most of the political class—live in a world that has changed, yet they are doing the same things they know how to, even though they seem not to work. Adults and the political class live in a city destroyed by an earthquake or have entered a forest of some species that they think is familiar but that in fact is something else.

By contrast, the youth are entering a new world in which they do not try to do what they already know, since they never learned it. For them, the world, social life, and politics are a forest in which what is to be found is a mystery: If they stay on the margins, it is because of their fear of the unknown.

In both instances there is a structural distance between politics and society. Adults experience this change as loss and as nostalgia, while youth experience it as an uncertainty from which they must protect themselves.

PART II

Crisis and Democratic Recovery in Chile

✳ 9

Democratic Crisis and Military Coup: Thirty Years Later

Chilean Democracy and Its Crisis: An Overview

With the exception of the decade of the twenties and the period of military rule from September 1973 to March 1990, Chile has had a very long democratic civilian rule under constitutions embodying separation of powers, regular elections, and the orderly transfer of power.[1] The first governing junta independent from Spain was formed in 1810. Unlike its neighbors, Chile succeeded soon after its independence in establishing a stable political system, embodied in its constitution of 1833. In this early period, the government was shaped largely by the conservative aristocracy as a republican system with a strong president. Toward the end of the nineteenth century, several liberal reforms were introduced, inducing a parliamentary-like government that lasted until 1925. Politics throughout the period were dominated by ideological conflicts, first between the conservative and liberal parties and later joined by the radical and democratic parties that were created to represent the emerging middle class.

Growing industrialization and urbanization in the early twentieth century generated new social cleavages in the country and led to the emergence of a new middle class and working classes (mainly miners) that began to exert political pressure and to demand social legislation to protect their interests. To give political voice to these rapidly growing groups, new political parties emerged, from the Communist Party in 1922 to the Socialist Party in 1933 and the National Falange in 1935 (a faction separated from the conservative party that would become Christian Democracy in the 1950s). The period from 1920 to 1932 was one of instability and military interventions. A new constitution was promulgated in 1925, embodying the reality of the new social order, but it was implemented only in 1932, when the first of a series of elected governments came to power and initiated four decades of democratic stability. From the 1930s to 1973, Chileans elected governments from all the colors of the political spectrum. In 1973 a military junta took control, and democracy in Chile broke down.

The Chilean democracy that broke down in 1973 had been a restricted democracy until the sixties. Women did not get the right to vote until the 1950s, and peasants and the urban poor were excluded from socioeconomic participation until the 1960s. Often they were excluded from voting because of illiteracy, or their participation was manipulated by the electoral system prevailing until 1958. Despite these limits to real political participation, however, multiple parties, from the extreme right to the extreme left, provided for a broad and complete ideological spectrum. Negotiation among parties was a necessity since no single one could win a majority on its own. Both these features were crucial for integrating the population into modern social life and for reaching agreements on institutional rules of behavior that kept the military from interfering directly in political affairs until 1973.

The relative weakness of civil society compared with political forces allowed considerable autonomy for the political class. Its ideological polarization was tempered until the 1960s by the pragmatism of the Radical Party, which routinely forged alliances with other parties across the political spectrum. Although every political group that aspired to the presidency played by democratic rules and built up political alliances in order to win elections and push through its legislative agenda, there were no incentives for broad and majority-based governing alliances because so much power was in the hands of the president. The outcome was a series of governments that pushed their radical agendas of social change without majoritarian legislative support for their programs. Thus the legitimacy of democratically elected regimes was weakened at a time of crisis because this legitimacy was based more on instrumental calculus than on shared democratic values.

During the 1960s political participation was extended to peasants and the urban poor. The party system became more rigid and polarized among three poles: a more authoritarian right unified around the National Party, an ideological center led by the Christian Democracy, and a radicalized left mainly formed by the Socialist and Communist Parties. The dominant belief was that compatibility between capitalist development and social democratization had reached an impasse. The last attempt to make the two compatible was the so-called revolution in liberty led by President Eduardo Frei, whose Christian Democratic Party governed from 1964 to 1970. It was caught between a right-wing opposition that was deeply affected by agrarian reform and a left-wing opposition that criticized these same reforms as merely an attempt to prolong capitalism.

At the end of the 1960s, the political class was sharply split between those favoring greater democratization and social integration by reversing the course of the capitalist development and those favoring a deepening of capitalism by reversing the process of social democratization and income redistribution. These two options were represented by the candidates for president in 1970. On one side, the candidate put forward by the right presented a more authoritarian program. On the other side, the Christian Democratic candidate favored deepening the social reforms initiated under the Frei government, and the candidate nominated by the leftist coalition (the Popular Unity) of Socialist, Communist, and other center and leftist groups stressed anticapitalist measures, social reform, and popular participation, along with continued democratic rule. Because none of the candidates won an absolute majority of the popular vote, the Congress had to decide among the two highest relative majorities. The candidate with the highest one was elected—Salvador Allende, a Socialist senator and the Popular Unity coalition candidate. Allende was sworn in as president in November 1970.

The escalating political conflict from 1970 to 1973 revealed the polarization of Chilean democracy and led to a legitimacy crisis. The rightist opposition, with the support of the U.S. government, resorted to both legal and extralegal means to overthrow Allende. The Popular Unity government was unable to create a consensus for its program and kept on implementing it. The Christian Democrats ultimately became trapped in the insurrectional strategy of the right. By the end of 1973, the deepening economic crisis and polarized antagonism between all political forces and the institutional crisis of legitimacy opened a space for a successful military insurrection.

The military coup of 11 September 1973 began seventeen years of hard repressive rule by a rightist military regime led by General Augusto Pinochet at the head of the military junta formed by the commanders in chief of the army, the navy, the air force, and the police. Pinochet attempted to establish a new social order through neoliberal economics and authoritarian institutional reform. He imposed a new constitution in 1980 that institutionalized military rule until 1988, giving him authoritarian power. The constitution provided for a plebiscite to elect Pinochet for eight more years in 1988. However, Pinochet's social and political opposition won this plebiscite by a large margin and unleashed the return to democracy. This coalition, organized as the Concertation of Parties for Democracy (Concertación) and composed of centrist (mainly the Christian Democratic Party) and leftist forces (mainly the Socialist Party and a newly formed Party for Democracy) then won the presidential election in 1989. The elected president, Patricio Aylwin, leader of the Christian Democratic Party, took office in March 1990. His successor in the elections of December 1993, who was also the candidate of the Concertación, was Eduardo Frei Ruiz Tagle (son of the former president), who took office in March 1994. In December 1999 and January 2000, new elections took place. In the second round the candidate of the Concertación, this time a representative of the axis formed by the Socialist Party, the Party for Democracy, and the Radical Party, Ricardo Lagos, won. He was inaugurated in March 2000.

The Triple Significance of the 1973 Military Coup

The military coup of 11 September 1973 involved three different aspects: (a) the culmination of a crisis of democracy, and thus of the political system; (b) a coup d'etat, that is, an insurrection; and (c) the beginning of a counterrevolutionary process or capitalist revolution headed by the military.

There is no necessary relationship between the first aspect and the other two. There were other possible solutions to the existing crisis. The military coup was neither absolutely inevitable nor necessary. Nevertheless, between the second and third point, there *is* a necessary relationship. The military coup could not be carried off, there could be no coup d'etat, without a subsequent military regime—an "etat du coup," as some have called it, though no one had foreseen the specifics of it. And it was clear that this military coup was in it for the long haul, that they were not inclined to go right back to how things were. There is a necessary relationship between the coup and what would come later, which still was not entirely mapped out, but there is no necessary relationship between the crisis of democracy on the one hand, and the coup and subsequent counterrevolutionary project on the other.

September 11, 1973, brought down a political system, the Chilean democratic regime. Here we are referring basically to that, not to other aspects of the crisis, such as the economic dimension.

Fortresses of Chilean Democracy

Around the beginning of the 1970s, Chilean political democracy had been successful in resolving certain problems and had left others up in the air, which gave rise to a latent crisis. Among the problems that in some ways it had resolved—especially if we use the other Latin American countries as a point of comparison—we find, first, that of stability: From the 1930s on, there were not recurrent cycles of democracy and authoritarianism in Chile, as there were in other countries.

Second, the problem of representativity was partially solved. In Chile there was a political party system in which virtually the entire spectrum of political ideologies was in some way represented, and sometimes by more than one organizational alternative. This point is noteworthy, since a big problem in some countries, such as Argentina, is that there was never a major party on the right, while in others, particularly Central American countries, there was an institutional exclusion of the left. In the Chilean case, there was a political system with a full spectrum. In this sense, the problem of pluralism and of political ideological representation was in large part resolved. Of course, this came at a price. Toward the end of the 1950s, only a fraction of the population voted, since not everyone was incorporated, and women's suffrage came fairly belatedly. Still, one could make the argument that at least there was a democracy that resolved the problems of stability and representation.

Moreover, the political regime in place also had solved the problem of effectiveness. In other words, the government governed—for better or worse, but they did it. There are governments that do not govern, that do not accomplish what they set out to do. In the case of Chile, governments governed, even though they had some problems, such as the instability of public policies and the inability to generate majoritarian governments. But the country had a relatively stable, representative, and effective democratic regime. Also, it proved able to solve conflicts institutionally and to be the privileged site for channeling social demands—those that reached it, naturally.

To the extent that this is true, it helps explain why the armed forces did not step in: The ruling elite were able to bargain, to bring themselves into agreement, and to have an institutional system that enabled them to resolve their problems without having to resort to calling out the military, as with almost all political regimes in Latin America. Nevertheless, there were major problems pending, which is why the situation was a latent crisis.

Weaknesses and Latent Crisis

What were the main unresolved problems burdening Chilean political democracy? The first of them stemmed from the structuring of society, the result not of good or bad original intentions but of the complex development of different factors, in which the political party system absorbed the whole of civil society. It was a country with a strong political system but a weak civil society. This had at least two aspects. On the one hand, political conflicts were transferred swiftly to society at large (for example, the political-ideological filter for positions in self-governing institutions such as universities). All the conflicts were in some way a reflection of political conflicts. Society was not really autonomous but reflected the conflicts that originated in the political world. Moreover, the principal actors in this were the political parties. When the political parties, which we could call the political-intellectual class, are very strong, they tend to become autonomous from society. This tendency—which is relative, in that in the end it is controlled by a system of periodic elections—in practice simply means that the ruling political class tends to ideologically invent the country. That is, the representative system tends to become a closed cultural world. In Chile, a political party was much more than a political party: It was a way of life, a way of dressing, a way of singing and speaking; each had its own language and world view. The problem is that there is a very strong tendency to devise different worlds when one is locked into closed universalizing concepts. Thus, the tendency toward polarization is also very strong.

The most important result that comes of this structuring of society is that, though it was a politically "viable" or "governable" society because the political party system was representative, a latent crisis lingered, for if at any moment the negotiation consensus was undone, the entire society would be rendered defenseless.

The second problem is that no institutionalism existed to guarantee stable majoritarian democratic governments. The battle between the president and Congress was firmly entrenched. This was a presidentialist system in which the grand revolutionary or counterrevolutionary projects could be launched from the executive branch. By revolutionary projects, I am referring not only to the left but also to all political movements, since in the last presidential election before the crisis, in 1970, three revolutionary projects were presented: that of Radomiro Tomic with the Christian Democrats, who promised an "antineocapitalist revolution," that of the "new republic" and deepening capitalism of the rightist candidate Jorge Alessandri, and that of the "Chilean road to socialism" of Popular Unity candidate Salvador Allende.

But the institutional political system did not guarantee majoritarian governments for such far-reaching projects. Therefore, there was a great likelihood of political instability within the regime itself. There was no institutionality that would force majoritarian government coalitions in a polarized multiparty system. There could be coalitions, but they were merely in response to short-term electoral goals. Therefore, one of Chile's main political problems was that minoritarian governments ruled for thirty or forty years. And the Popular Unity was no exception to this rule.

A third problem lies in that the political culture had contradictory features. On the one hand, parliamentary negotiation and procedure were favored. One of the critiques that foreign hard-liners made on this score was the "scandal" of friendly relations between members of Parliament from rival political factions. In point of fact, one of the tendencies of the political culture was negotiation and for a very simple reason: Since no one made up a majority, there had to be continuous negotiation, making alliances and forming agreements.

On the other hand, the political culture showed a clear tendency toward grand, exclusionary projects, that is, extreme ideologization. For example, there was a union social movement and a partisan political movement, which mixed, to remarkable effect, the most intensified instrumentalism with total ideologism. The particular demand and the quest for socialism were the union movement's two revindications. And both demands went hand in hand.

When I say there are exclusionary projects and ideologies, what I mean is that all the actors are potential revolutionaries. All have the latent or explicit idea for a grand project, which includes taking over the state and using that platform to carry out sweeping transformations of society. This is found on the right, the center, and the left. This revolutionary view is potentially antidemocratic, since in the end, between bargaining and "my" truth, one can choose the latter and hold onto it at all costs. This ideologism greatly strengthened the tendency toward polarization and checked the tendency toward bargaining, since in a climate of grand ideological projects, no bargaining occurs. For this reason one can argue that we had a contradictory political culture.

Another contradictory element lay in that the democratic political regime was a legitimate regime; rather, the people believed in it and did not demand a different one. And those who did were a minority, who through a vote were forced to bend to this massive legitimacy. But in the Chilean case, legitimacy was much more instrumental than value-oriented; rather, it was based in large part on the various actors' reckoning of the competition's ability to satisfy their interests. At all events, even a legitimacy of this kind is better than none. Nevertheless, a purely instrumental legitimacy, which is not based on valuing democracy as an end and not simply as a means to satisfy other interests, has a weakness: At certain times, in moments of crisis, different sectors could succumb to the temptation to adopt other means to achieve their ends. These, then, were the positives and negatives of Chilean democracy. The latter were factors with potential to contribute to a deeper political crisis.

Democracy in 1970 and 1973

The big question was how these elements would play out in 1970. Actually, in 1970 the democratic regime suffered no legitimacy crisis. There were, nonetheless, many aspects in crisis or at least that were perceived to be in crisis by the most significant actors.

Thus, there was a crisis between the development model and social democratization. Some maintained that the development model was preventing accumulation, and others held that the development model was holding back social democratization. The model of the capitalist road, the import-substitution road with state participation, was also in a legitimacy crisis; everyone wanted to change it, in one way or another, as the 1970 presidential campaign attests. Also the political leadership of the parties that theretofore had been in the government was somewhat in crisis. In this sense, the left, with full legitimacy, emerged to take advantage of an opportunity that all the other political sectors had already had.

But what was not in crisis was the democratic regime itself. Though the need for changes was declared, despite disagreement over their direction, in the end everyone participated in the elections, since the people believed the political system to be the place where conflicts and projects for society are resolved, even when the discourse of some sectors on the left had radicalized momentarily on this score, as happened with the Socialist Party in their 1966 Congress.

This changed dramatically, however, in 1973. But how does one go from a partial social crisis—the democratic regime itself was not in a legitimacy crisis—to a total crisis? In other words, how do we explain the legitimacy crisis *of* the system, namely, that people—including all the most significant actors in the political process—came to lose faith in the democratic regime?

In our view, what happened from 1970 to 1973 is that all the actors behaved in such a way that they tended to erode institutionalism and, therefore, the legitimacy of the democratic system.

On the one hand, the Popular Unity's strategy for carrying out the transformations it had promised was strictly legal. Yet it broke the principles of legitimacy based on bargaining. This is especially apparent in the formula used to expropriate private capitalist firms that would become part of the "social property area," the programmatic core of the "Chilean road to socialism." Thus, Decree Law 520, which allows state intervention in companies under certain conditions, and the overruling decrees signed by all the ministers to intervene or expropriate when the office of the comptroller rejected this action, were legal, but obviously its enforcement broke the tradition of parliamentary bargaining over an act of expropriation or any other important incident.

Therefore, the strategy chosen by the Popular Unity had the effect of eroding the legitimacy of the system, which was based on the idea of bargaining and negotiating. In this sense, the Popular Unity continued what had been done by all the important political projects that had existed in Chile: proposing and promising social changes without having a strategy for building majorities to accomplish those changes, which is indispensable in any revolutionary change that excludes violent overthrow. However, in this case, in addition, there was an attempt to actually bring about those changes.

It also would have been impossible for the right to carry out the platform of the "New Republic" in a democratic regime, and so it had to wait for the ascendancy of the military regime to set it in motion under the guidance of its very authors. Recall, moreover, that Tomic's platform, which won 28 percent of the popular vote in September 1970, was, in his own words, to launch the impending revolution and do away with "capitalism and neo-capitalism." All the actors, without exception, put forward revolutionary projects without having a viable strategy for building majorities.

In the particular case of the Popular Unity, this coalition sets out an extremely ambitious platform with the same lack of a viable strategy. In this case, such a strategy would have meant an agreement with the Christian Democracy. One might say that this was impossible, that the Christian Democracy did not want to do it; in any event, many reasons could be given. In any case, whatever the reasons, there was no strategy for building a majority. For this reason, the Popular Unity's platform would impair institutionalism and the legitimation of the previous system.

On the right, there were at least two key early attempts—one taking the insurrectional path and the other, the legal "loophole" road—to break with the country's political tradition. The former is the conspiracy that ended with the assassination of General René Schneider. The other was to elect Jorge Alessandri, who finished as first runner-up in the presidential race, only to be elected through the Plenary Congress, step down immediately, and call for new elections, in which past president Frei Montalva would be elected. Even if they failed or were not carried out fully, there is no question that these attempts were made. They took aim at a very early alternative, which in time would develop into a strategy: the end or overthrow of the Allende government.

The idea of overthrowing President Allende was present in U.S. governmental sectors even before the September 1970 elections, and in sectors on the right, at least since Allende's election in September 1970. But it was not majoritarian in the opposition bloc. And it was not majoritarian in the ranks of the opposition, above all, because of the strength of the democratic regime's legitimacy. Nevertheless, a strategy for his ouster arose from the very first from the right, which would subsequently make use of all sorts of tactics to see it through. There were legal or constitutional tactics, such as the bid to gain a majority in order to overthrow the president constitutionally, though this certainly was a departure from Chilean political tradition and therefore fed the institutional legitimacy crisis, paving the way for its outflanking and ruin. But there were also other actions that were patently illegal, such as the economic boycott strategies or the terrorist attacks, which struck especially in 1973. Other tactics included denouncing electoral fraud in the March 1973 parliamentary elections, which everyone knows was a false accusation intended to undermine the legitimacy of the electoral system as a mechanism to resolve conflicts. If methods were used by the government to see its program executed at all costs, the opposition made use of every recourse to erode and put an end to the Popular Unity's regime.

The Christian Democrats nevertheless bore a great responsibility for the legitimacy crisis in the democratic system. They brought into play a strategy that sought to neutralize both camps, based only on electoral calculus, a strategy that could be defined as initially ensuring the continuity of the regime in order to use the erosion of the government in such a way as to ensure its replacement after the six-year period. Later on, in the climate of polarization, the Christian Democracy had no alternative but the overthrow strategy and was swept up in it. In fact, the insurrection strategy on the right was not followed in the name of the real interests and projects they defended, but rather they turned to the idea provided by the Christian Democracy: to defend "democracy and freedom."

There was not a single actor, with the exception, at certain times, of the Church, which backed the system; the country; or the support of the regime itself. The strategies were corporativist or classist; groups identified their own projects with national interests. If on the left there was a democratic revolutionary ideology and an obsessive drive to carry out its platform with nondemocratic potential, on the right there was nondemocratic, insurrectional, counterrevolutionary behavior from the beginning of the Popular Unity government, and an objective subsuming of the Christian Democracy into the rightist agenda. All bet on their own project, and this is what started to greatly undermine the legitimacy of the regime.

This crisis, in which everyone acted on behalf of their own project and not the country, had institutional expressions. There came a point when no one believed in the rules of the game. Nor did anyone believe that they were fighting to defend democracy when the chamber of deputies made a pronouncement on the government's legitimacy crisis in August 1973. This agreement is a call for a military coup, though not all those who ratified it intended that and though others among them explicitly were opposed to a violent resolution. But a call for a coup at that time was not exactly defending democracy.

Another institutional expression of this crisis, to refer to only two, were the events surrounding the main ideological-political conflict of the era. In the end, this was a problem of ownership of large, monopolistic, capitalist firms, that is, the development of the area of social property, through different forms of nationalization. The approval for the project from Confederación Democrática (Democratic Confederation; CODE) senators Juan Hamilton and Renán Fuentealba, which entailed a constitutional reform, consisted of forcing the Popular Unity to make expropriations through a law. The debate over presidential vetoes led to a very complex problem of interpretation on the president's ability to enact part or all of the bill. Normally, this kind of conflict should be solved by the constitutional tribunal, which on this occasion declared itself as having no jurisdiction. Thus the basic institutional conflict of the era remains without a legitimate or consensual solution.

All this makes up what could be called a systemic crisis of the democratic regime, which had not existed in 1970. The economic crisis was, in this case, secondary. The situation was the exact opposite of what happened in the years 1929–31, in which there was a typical case of political crisis triggered by an economic crisis, ending with the dictatorship of Carlos Ibáñez del Campo. In this case, by contrast, the economic crisis was strictly a side effect of the political crisis, which, naturally, then would impact the political crisis, worsening it and polarizing it even more. But the economic crisis was the result of all the actors' behavior, not only the government's. Otherwise, there is no explanation for why on 12 September 1973 the supermarkets were fully stocked. This means that an economic boycott and hoarding were going on.

To this point we have noted that there was a crisis in the political system, the result of the behavior of all the actors and not of a conspiracy, or if you will, the result of many conspiracies. The fact is that this does not explain the coup, since there can be different kinds of solutions to a crisis such as that one. One very poor solution was shown on 11 September 1973, and the task remains, then, to explain why that response was chosen and not another.

From the Crisis to the Military Coup

We have stressed that there is a legitimacy crisis, and if there is one, no one believes in one another, much less in the rules of play. And in an all-encompassing legitimacy crisis, in which no one has a monopoly on legitimacy nor is anyone legitimated by anyone else, the one who has the strength or physical power will define the conflict. This is not the case because he has legitimacy or because he has been asked to intervene, or because the people believe in him, but because he has the strength, that is, the weapons.

Neither did people believe, as some hold, that the armed forces were the moral repository or bastion of nationality. This is simply ideological. No institution or sector is unto itself the only moral repository or last bastion of nationality. But the military as an organization are the only ones who have the physical and instrumental strength to intervene at that moment. By definition, the one who has concentrated strength and power when a legitimacy crisis arises, intervenes. Of course, this intervention is neither legal, nor constitutional, nor legitimate, since there is no consensual legitimacy at that moment. Let us make no mistake on this score. In a situation like this one, the armed forces intervene because they have the strength to do so.

Then the question comes up of what is the character and nature of the armed forces that can carry out this intervention. To answer this question, we have to look into why and how the armed forces were inserted into society and into national politics. And we find that the kind of insertion decided on by the ruling elite through political-institutional agreements was a very particular kind of civil-military relation that did not exist in other Latin American countries: the *cloistering model*.

The cloistering model means that the armed forces are confined to the tasks that are defined as germane to them, since society has its own legitimate mechanisms for conflict resolution, without need to resort to armed force. To that end they have to develop, like all human groups, an ideology, that is, a way of representing what they are doing. And if a given group or sector is simply devoted to upholding an institution because there is no war on, it cannot justify an ideology based sheerly on the defense of territory and sovereignty. Consequently, the ideology that develops in the armed forces—and ideologies are always a mix of truth and self-justification—is the professionalizing, constitutionalist ideology because this is the one that best depicts their reality and not because the military police are "essentially" democratic, nondemocratic, or whatever. But here there is something very important to realize. These cloistered armed forces, isolated by the political class, are armed forces characterized by a constant: their affiliation, through their officers' enrollment in courses and institutes, sanctioned by bilateral or multilateral treaties, with the hemispheric defense system hegemonized by the United States. Thus the ideology of national security, characteristic of the Cold War, of the division of the world into blocs, and of the incorporation of Latin America into the U.S.-led bloc, was progressively developed.

This system was based on one crucial idea, which in turn solved the identity crisis the armed forces suffered in the latter half of the twentieth century, which arose because the national state was already constituted and there was no risk of boundary wars. The idea was that the armed forces were guarantors of the free Western world against potential Communist attacks, which would not come directly or militarily from the Soviet Union but through subversive forces that cropped up inside each country, as the Cuban revolution illustrated. Therefore the armed forces internalized the idea that they were the moral repository of the nation and the greatest guarantee of national unity.

In countries divided and torn apart by infighting without a consensual institutional context, the military could see in this doctrine an unmediated reflection of reality. But in a country such as Chile, in which the political class resolved its conflicts fairly well, and, moreover, where right, center, and left confronted and negotiated, as we noted, the armed forces could not hold themselves up over other sectors or institutions as any kind of special moral repository. This idea remained a latent one in Chile, to be put into practice in moments of crisis. It stood as an ideological reserve for when the need to intervene should present itself. Yet intervention would hinge on what happened in society.

In 1970, when some "impatient" voices—as they were called at the time—made overtures to the armed forces for them to potentially take action in the political problem in order to block Allende's rise to power, the military responded that they had no choice but to accept the institutional political order. There was a constitution, a legitimate election was held, and so the situation was in the hands of the political class.

Another situation came up in 1972, when, apropos of the lockout organized by big business bosses, the armed forces were asked to participate in the Allende government. Then a rough draft of a project proper appeared, with the concept of guarantors of constitutionality, which at that moment meant defending the legitimate government. For all that, at the time there was no systemic legitimacy crisis either of the government or of the different branches of the state.

Conversely, in 1973 the armed forces were facing two alternative projects. The first, coming from the Allende government, was to fulfill their constitutional duty, that is, to repress the insurrection unleashed by the most hard-line opposition sectors, backing the government and subordinate to it. The second project, coming from the right, encouraged them to take power to resolve the crisis autonomously. These were the two alternatives on the table.

Obviously, something happened inside the armed forces between October 1972 and September 1973. The institutional project supporting the constitution and a troubled constitutional government were left aside in order to adopt the second project, which allowed them to seize power and take over the nation.

To single out the doctrine of national security as the cause of this change is to point only to ideological underpinnings. What really triggered and set the subversive project in motion can only be defined as a plot from within the ranks of the armed forces.

Some could say in all honesty that they agree there had been a conspiracy and that it was necessary, and others could even justify it, saying it was the only remaining solution to the conflict. What cannot be said is that there was no conspiracy. The dictionary defines conspiracy as "the act of a group conspiring, uniting against their superior or sovereign, or against an individual, for the sake of doing him or her harm."

The problem gets complicated for the armed forces, since either the leader of the military coup agreed in the eleventh hour to take part in it, which means that what is told in Pinochet's memoirs *The Decisive Day* would be untrue, or the leader of the coup took part in the conspiracy, which means he would have had to lie for an extended period to the legitimate constitutional power, the president. At all events, at some point he would have had to lie to the president to hide either the planning or the execution of the coup. This is the real dilemma, which can only be solved by accepting that those who led the coup had to commit treason. So what happened in Chile in 1973 was the result of a *betrayal*.

By "betrayal" we mean the use that someone makes of the trust placed in him by another in order to destroy that person. Betrayal is not a simple act of disloyalty. There were many opponents of Allende's government and many who were for the military coup who never betrayed anyone because President Allende never conferred any duty on them, nor did he place his trust in them. As is revealed in the great literary works on drama and the human condition, such as Greek theater or Shakespeare, for example, and as the poet Raúl Zurita accurately recalls, a betrayal lies at the root of all tragedies.

The military coup has a betrayal at its root. This fact explains the distance between the crisis of democracy and the military coup.

From the Coup to the Counterrevolutionary Project

A final observation is in order on the transition from the "military coup" to the "etat du coup," that is, to the military regime proper. Whatever the ideology of the authors of the coup, there were two pressing tasks that needed to be accomplished.

First, they had to stabilize the economy. Obviously, they were not going to do so with socialist practice, since for that they would have supported Allende's government. Obviously, the path they chose would be the recomposition of the capitalist system.

The second task consisted of containing, repressing, and detaining the people who had supported the Popular Unity government. In other words, systematic repression, and thus, the DINA (National Intelligence Directorate)[2] or whoever fulfills its obligations, are intrinsic, essential, to the coup and to the military regime, and are not accidental, superfluous, or mistakes. For its part, a centralized organization for intelligence and repression were requirements for a personalized power within the armed forces, especially if we consider that, in a conspiratorial coup, there are different views and projects with respect to what is to be accomplished. If the coup needed the commander in chief of the army in order to be carried out, when the latter becomes head of state, his "political" legitimacy could be called into question by some officials who may have differing political ideas. In other words, the repressive and intelligence-gathering organizations in these cases are used not only against society and the opponents or "enemies," but inside the new regime's very institutions, to keep its "friends" in line.

These tasks bring to mind the main features of a regime that would last seventeen years: the regime will have to have an authoritarian and capitalist refoundation in order to sever the kind of ties between economics and politics that existed until then.

A second conspiracy emerges now, this one from inside the group that took power. Once power is gained, plots must be hatched in order to make a given project prevail over the others. And in this second conspiracy not only will the military sectors have a hand, but also civil sectors will be involved, and each of them with a different project. For it is obvious that what some who led the economy at the outset of the military regime wanted was not exactly the same as what would be imposed when a specific group took total control of economic politics as of April 1975, for instance. Moreover, in the absence of a democratic regime, conflicts between different views necessarily become conspiracies to impose one project or another, deals struck by some behind the backs of others.

This is when a second betrayal comes about, which is the betrayal by the civilian and military group that was to direct the regime's political and economic project of the rest of the people who supported the coup but who did not necessarily want a long-standing regime, to say nothing of the project that now was being thrust upon them.

Conclusion

To sum up, the coup on 11 September 1973 cannot be analyzed without making complex references to these three aspects: (a) a crisis of democracy with shared responsibilities, even when this does not explain the coup; (b) a military coup that involves a conspiracy within the ranks of the armed forces and an act of treason to the Allende government and to the constitution; and (c) a counterrevolutionary or revolutionary project—however one wishes to call it—that implies a conspiracy and an act of treason within the group that has taken power.

In our view, the reason certain sectors have such a hard time refraining from trotting out thirty-year-old justifications time and again, and trying to analyze and understand what happened in that era, is that it is tremendously difficult to grasp that we live in an age brought forth by betrayal.

✻ 10

Political Opposition and the Struggle
for Democracy under the Military Regime

This chapter analyzes the development of the Chilean opposition to Pinochet's military regime that began 11 September 1973 and ended 11 March 1990, and its role in the democratic transition and consolidation. We understand this development as a learning process with regard to the type of struggle needed to end the Chilean dictatorship. First, we will refer to some of the particular traits that characterized the Chilean democratic opposition. Subsequently, we will describe the different phases through which the opposition passed, ending with the 1988 plebiscite and its implications for the transition to democracy.

The political transition we discuss in this chapter consists of the transition from authoritarian, dictatorial, or military regimes to democratic ones. Their conceptual aspects have been developed in another chapter of this book. Let us recall that transitions are different from the revolutionary or insurrectional model in that the power holders are neither militarily defeated nor overthrown, but rather are pressured to step down. This implies that, along with the processes of internal breakdown or of opposition mobilizations against the regime, transitions involve implicit or explicit negotiations between the power holders (in this case, the armed forces) and the opposition, and a regulated area of confrontation between regime and opposition that solves the conflict between both (plebiscites, elections).

From this point of view, the opposition's task is to generate the best space for institutional confrontation with the regime. If they do not achieve it, this space will be imposed by the regime, whether to prevent a transition or to stake the space's boundaries in the best terms for the future circumstances of the current power holders when the regime changes over. Thus, for the assemblage of political actors facing processes of transition unprecedented in their historical memory, one might speak of a learning process. In it, both successes and failures inevitably come into play, and the opposition starts redefining its role in the transition as it begins learning what the transition entails.

The Original Characteristics of the Chilean Opposition

The September 1973 military coup ended President Allende's government and the democratic regime, and ushered in a military regime or dictatorship characterized mainly by three basic traits.[1] First, the legal political power combined the increasingly personalized political-military leadership of General Pinochet with the authority of the armed forces. The different branches of government were subordinated to the army, which was placed under Pinochet's command.

Second, the regime, together with the dismantling of the previous society, attempted a rearticulation between state and society that entailed a new model of capitalist organization and reinsertion in the world economy that was characterized by the drastic reduction of the role of the state and by the transposition of market principles to the most varied arenas of social life. This implied a model of social organization. Thus, the military regime developed a plan to found a new order, which was manifested politically in the constitution imposed by the 1980 plebiscite. This constitution institutionalized a military regime of fifteen years' duration (1973–88) and an authoritarian regime, as of 1989, of indefinite duration. The latter was to be largely civilian but would grant tutelary power to the armed forces, restrict a political arena that excluded certain social and political sectors, and ensure inviolability of certain institutions that determine the nature of the state's model of economic and social relations. The transition from one regime to another was guaranteed in 1988 by a plebiscite that would allow General Pinochet to stay on as president for another eight years.

Third, the repressive nature of the dictatorship did not succeed in preventing opposition sector spaces of social, cultural and political expression. In other words, the state did not absorb society; it repressed, excluded, and controlled it. The expressions of civil society and its organizations were not quelled, though they were restricted, and above all, systems of representation before the state were eliminated.

The opposition to the Chilean military dictatorship was made up of an assembly of political and social actors who generally were heirs to the previous democratic regime. The opposition had an inherited character even when new actors arose and inevitable generational changes were brought about. This inherited nature meant that certain traits that typified the relation between politics and society under the previous democratic regime were reproduced.

We have referred to these traits already; at least two are worth recalling. First, the preponderant role of the state and the party system in constituting social actors assured representation of the actors but gave them scant autonomy with respect to the political system. Second, the resultant influence of a political class prone to be relatively autonomous from its bases of representation exacerbated the problem of partisan identities in an openly competitive system. The political parties emerged as subcultures, which led to a high degree of ideologism, and in certain circumstances, to sharp polarizations of the political system and to obstacles in forming alliances.

But the military regime profoundly dislocated this relation between politics and society when it suppressed the representational sphere of sociopolitical actors, though it could not do away with them outright. This dislocation happened due to the institutional nature of the regime, as well as the type of structural transformations that their capitalist recomposition project brought into society.

The main consequences of this dislocation were the following. First, the Catholic Church emerged over a long period as an actor fulfilling surrogate opposition duties and as a substitute for the political arena, without ever being able to replace it. Second, the party structure remained relatively unchanged, though its relations with the social base became more troubled, and its purpose became the search for spaces for political expression. Third, relations were maintained with the social organizations' leadership and political parties, but the former's role went further than the search for space for political expression; they wanted to express and satisfy demands from their social bases. Fourth, the two dimensions of political action during the democratic period—the instrumental dimension and the expressive-symbolic or ideological dimension—which came to be identified with different social and political actors, were dismantled. Lastly, a state referent as a basis for the organization and representation of demands was lacking.

We should add to the traditional features of political actors the extreme political polarization and divisiveness as the democratic regime was being toppled, as well as the structural and institutional transformations under the military dictatorship, and the novel experience of living under a dictatorship and fighting against it.

Thus the political opposition was facing a triple challenge, which constituted its problématique in this period. The first challenge was to reestablish relations between partisan political actors, the organizations, and the rank and file of civil society, while at the same time reconstituting party actors themselves. The second one was to reach an agreement between partisan actors to bring unity to the political opposition. The third challenge was to confront the dictatorship, both by opposing government policies and by seeking to end the regime.

Since this was a type of regime totally unknown in the historical memory of the Chilean political actors, as we have said, as well as a process of transition that was totally unique in South America, the opposition contended with this triple challenge in different ways, whether applying the experience of the democratic period to the antidictatorial struggle, or resorting ideologically to models that had arisen in other historical contexts and that had no feasible correlation here.

All this bolsters our basic hypothesis that the action and development of the Chilean political opposition should be understood as the learning process of a political class whose formation, practice, and historical memory qualified it to rule or to oppose democratic governments successfully, but not to confront dictatorships.

The Early Phases

For the purposes of this chapter, by "resistance" we mean the level of individual and organizational subsistence of those who oppose the military regime; by "dissidence," the oppositional struggle that does not seek to transform or eliminate the regime, but rather expresses its rejection of it. By the "opposition," we mean the actors and struggles that seek to transform or change the regime.

One cannot technically speak of an opposition in the early years of the military regime but rather of resistance from the sector defeated by the coup—the political parties and social sectors that supported the Popular Unity government. These groups sought to ensure the survival of their members and leaders, many of whom were murdered, imprisoned, or exiled, and to maintain what they could of their organizational apparatus.

Moreover, the Catholic Church occupied a semioppositional space, headed by Cardinal Silva Henríquez.[2] The Church's official duty was to defend victims of repression and to accumulate and disseminate information to that effect. But it also performed the role of material and cultural meeting space for remaining political and social actors seeking to reconstitute themselves. In this period, the Church was the only actor to confront the state-military power. Yet the very nature of this actor held it back from fully assuming the opposition role. Third, the Christian Democratic Party (PDC), which with certain exceptions had tacitly or explicitly supported the military coup, grew critical of the military regime, a typical process of dissidence. Fourth, minor groups such as the Revolutionary Left Movement (MIR) made armed attempts on the regime.[3] The attempt, due to its precariousness, took the form of armed resistance, which was violently repressed and never amounted to much in the opposition camp overall, nor did it appreciably affect the stability of the regime.

During this time, in the country as well as in exile, opposition forces debated the events and nature of the 1970–73 process and the causes of the Popular Unity downfall, and also the type of dictatorship that was installed. This twofold debate still has a conspicuously self-justifying nature, with elements of self-criticism issuing from intellectual quarters. The opposition identified this type of military regime as fascism or neofascism, and the costly result of this misreading was that people believed it had to be an "antifascist democratic front," which lacks any basis in reality.

Two major circumstances brought about some changes in the opposition forces. First, the Christian Democratic Party's clear move to the opposition, and second, the outlining of the foundational nature of the military regime, which, starting in 1976–77, began a process of in-depth structural and institutional transformations in the country that were designed to recompose national capitalism and reinsert it into the world economy. This latter development led to a new political institutionality, which we will refer to shortly. The changes in the opposition camp are as follows.[4]

First, the PDC, though officially declared "in recess" by the military regime,[5] emerged as the most important public expression of the political actors opposing the regime. For their part, the parties on the left acted underground and still were subjected to a harsh repressive process that has all but eliminated several tiers of leaders. Some of these parties engaged in significant opposition activity in exile, focusing on Chile the attention of international public opinion and organizations. Party debate tended to be self-critical over past actions and followed a different course inside the country than it did in exile. The parties, though disparately, began to discover the military regime's true nature, a discovery manifested mainly in the concern, beyond mere organizational survival, for reengaging with the social movement. There was no strategic debate proper, and those summoned to the "large fronts," especially by the Communist Party, met with the rejection of the Christian Democratic Party and the distrust of the Socialist Party. The latter suffered a deep cleavage in 1979, where part of this political debate combined with infighting over old leadership.[6]

Second, most opposition activity, complementing and largely linked to the Church's efforts alluded to earlier, concentrated on the social and cultural more than the political. This is seen primarily in the emergence and expansion of a fringe of militant and activist organizations (political, cultural, social, intellectual or paraacademic, political parties, churches, popular education, human rights, etc.), which maintained a certain autonomy toward their political affiliations and provided opposition activities in different social arenas with continuity. Moreover, new forms of organization emerged in the union and student arenas, some related to the new institutionalism generated by the regime, others at the margins. In the student sector, they acquired the forms of institutional demands and, especially, cultural activities. Union activists tried to rebuild grass-roots unionism up from the new labor laws. They also tried to reestablish some kind of general coordination of the large labor organizations, which bore the stamp of partisan political identities and the structural divisions developing in the working class.[7]

Finally, the purpose behind all these struggles and activities—though they called for "the struggle against the dictatorship," which they wanted to end and to bring about the "rapid reestablishment of democracy"—is mainly to put up resistance to the transformations imposed by the regime, to defend old gains, and to maintain and recreate threatened collective identities.

The Regime's Institutionalization

The constitution imposed by the regime in a 1980 plebiscite meant the end of the regime's institutionalization process.[8] The constitution consecrated maintaining a military regime until 1989 and subsequently its transformation into an authoritarian regime, civilian in nature, with restricted political involvement and tutelary power for the armed forces. The regime attempted to have this transition from military dictatorship to permanent authoritarian regime confirmed by keeping Pinochet in power through the 1988 plebiscite. In it, the commanders in chief of the armed forces would propose a candidate for an eight-year presidential term, during which the definitive constitution would go into effect. The basic power scheme installed with the 1973 military coup would be kept until 1989: personal dictatorship and military regime, with Pinochet as head of state, and the junta of commanders in chief of the armed forces as "legislative power."

Something of a repoliticization in the upper echelons of the political parties took place in the 1980 political institutionalization. Nevertheless, it was happening at a time that was extremely favorable to the regime in light of its apparent economic successes, which later dried up in the recession of 1982–83. The Christian Democrats assumed public leadership of the opposition in the constitutional plebiscite called by Pinochet, though there was no cohesive, concerted strategy with the parties on the left for how to deal with the plebiscite. The government won by means of widespread fraud, which was denounced by the opposition, and led the Church to invalidate the plebiscite without the political actors reaping the consequences of it. The perception that the regime would last indefinitely yielded several consequences in the opposition.

In the Christian Democratic Party a period of disarray began, fueled by the death of their leader, Eduardo Frei Montalva, and the exile of their president, Andrés Zaldívar. After two years, they managed to solve their internal leadership problem by supporting the alternative that proposed greater flexibility in alliances with leftist sectors. In these sectors various processes were under way, with contradictory results for converting an opposition space into an opposition subject. The Communist Party, for example, came to a turning point in its strategic-political line as well as in its growth process. It shifted from a gradualist, reformist conception that normally placed the party "to the right" of the Socialist Party to a concept of mass uprising, which brought it more in line with revolutionary ways. This included accepting the possibility of armed struggle and the growth of a Communist Party branch tied to a military organization. Without forsaking its workers party essence, this led it to considerable growth in youth, student sectors, and especially underclass sectors (*sectores poblacionales*).[9]

The Socialist Party, which until then had been very divided, began a twin process. On the one hand, it underwent an ideological renovation that distanced one group from the more orthodox conceptions associated with 1960s Marxism-Leninism and led it to be grouped with or tied to the groups that emerged from the split between the Christian Democratic Party and the political center in the Popular Unity era (such as MAPU and independents).[10] On the other hand, a partial reunification occurred that would later mean the coexistence of two large socialist parties on the scene—one with the spirit of renovation, the other of a more classical persuasion—though both would strategically converge about 1988. Smaller groups would gravitate around these two parties, such as the MAPU, which grew ever closer to the socialist parties, and the Christian Left, which would see party infighting over whether they should incorporate into the socialist camp or remain a party with their own identity and mission.

At all events, these processes are characterized by certain traits that set them apart from the subsequent period. Thus, politics still did not fill a recognized public space and inhabited a partially open and partially clandestine realm. This branded the party processes as mainly elitist and weakened party relations with the social actors. The latter were facing transformations orchestrated by the regime and its perception of a new social order that stood in the way of, and redefined their fight for, certain demands. Moreover, an incipient strategic debate was under way, but one burdened with the perception that the regime was immutable, lacking in theoretical referents and practical experience for this kind of struggle, and weighted too heavily with abstract matters of legitimation or delegitimation of the regime through opposition activity. An example of this was the debate on the legitimacy or illegitimacy of the constitution (though illegitimate, it nonetheless was imposed and took effect), which demanded another way of perceiving it and challenging it if progress was to be made in a process of democratization.

The Opposition in the Public Space

In 1981–82 the foundational effort of the military regime entered a stage of crisis, mainly as a result of the failure of its economic model. The failure was manifested partly in the collapse of the financial system, the replacement of the economic administration team, a heavy foreign debt, and the generalized indebtedness of vast middle-class sectors.[11] The most important sociopolitical expression of the crisis inside the regime, which many opposition sectors mistook for a terminal crisis, was the sparking of protest movements starting in May 1983. This represented a rebirth of the mass movements and forced the regime to an incipient opening (*apertura*).[12] This *apertura* sought to restore the support of civilian sectors that were distancing themselves and to bring the opposition into the institutional fold of the 1980 constitution. About halfway through 1986, with the discovery of weapons arsenals and the assassination attempt on General Pinochet, for which the Frente Patriótico Manuel Rodriguez (Manuel Rodriguez Patriotic Front, the armed branch of the Communist Party) claimed responsibility, the cycle of protests and mass mobilizations seemed to come to an end. For its part, the regime succeeded in recomposing part of its economic plan and concentrated all its efforts on following the itinerary stipulated in the constitution, to which we have already alluded. The period from the onset of the protests in May 1983 with the irruption of politics into the public space, to the moment in February 1988 when a majoritarian opposition pact was struck to confront the regime in the 1988 plebiscite by rejecting the armed forces' candidate, brings to an end the chapter of what we have designated the opposition's learning process. This process cannot be understood without referring to other transition experiments, such as those of Uruguay, Argentina, Brazil, Spain, the Philippines, and Korea, and without the insights into these experiences provided by various intellectual groups with ties to the political opposition at home in Chile and abroad, in addition to some political leaders' firsthand experience with the other transitions.

The cycle of mobilizations begun in 1983 is directly related to the regime's internal crisis, that is, to the collapse of its economic model and to the way this affected middle-class and popular sectors, the latter of whom were already impoverished and oppressed during the years of the dictatorship. Yet this crisis would not have had the political outcome it did without the level of organization that certain union groups had recovered, the survival of the political parties and their underground activity, and the presence in many arenas of social life of the sociopolitical fringe of militants or activists. The crisis in the foundational dimension of the regime met vast potential for social discontent as well as organizations that could channel it into forms of collective expression.

This accounts for the process of mobilization lasting three years, during which there were activities that nearly brought the country to a standstill, such as huge rallies, street demonstrations involving various sectors, especially students. To this list should be added the opposition electoral wins in all social organizations, which isolated the regime's supporters. Popular protests, including the raising of barricades and clashes with police, were violently repressed by police and military reinforcements. The favored form was the monthly demonstration in which the various social and political sectors expressed their opposition to the regime under the unifying idea of "Democracy Now" (*Democracia Ahora*).[13] Those calling for these protests would vary from unions to political organizations, though normally they switched off—not without tensions, as we will see.

The surprising enormity of the early protests led to three perceptions in the opposition as they debuted in public space. First, they felt that the end of the regime was imminent if the momentum of unrelenting pressure and mobilizations was kept up. Second, they thought that the unity of the political organizations was needed in order to take control if the regime was being overthrown. Finally, they perceived that the traditional connection between politics and the social movement was remaining relatively intact. We refer to these three aspects in the pages ahead.

The Debate over the End of the Regime

Over time, the perception that the fall of the regime was imminent gave way for the first time to a strategic debate, albeit a relatively incomplete and unrealistic one. The basic idea, which replaces that of a workable strategy or formula for transition, was that the process of mobilizations could by itself create an "ungovernable" or destabilized situation in the regime. This, in turn, would lead to the armed forces disposing of Pinochet at some point in order to negotiate their withdrawal from power with the civilians. In the opinion of some observers, a collapse would occur, prompting an automatic withdrawal of the armed forces, and the civilian forces would fill the power vacuum that had been created. The idea of "Democracy Now" reflected this perception of an imminent fall, and of the lack of an adequate formula or strategy to end the regime. Some sectors with closer ties to the political center, called in by Cardinal Fresno to "negotiate" with the regime in August and September 1983, put the departure of Pinochet on the table as a condition for any negotiation, which made it inviable. The sectors on the left refused to negotiate on any terms.

The whole opposition took the threefold idea of "Pinochet's departure, provisional government, and constituent assembly" as their watchword, claiming that the 1980 constitution and any provision written into it was illegitimate. Thus the classical insurrectional model clearly prevailed, even when using peaceful formulas, by which no transition from a military regime to a democracy has been accomplished in recent history. For its part, the Communist Party realized that its change of direction toward insurrectional forms closer to armed struggle led to the PDC's refusal to form any alliance with them. By contrast, the shift found acceptance in a significant contingent of young radical shanty-dwellers (*pobladores*), who distrusted the institutions and formulas of concerted political action. All of this bolstered the PC party line of embracing "all forms of struggle" and favoring those with the most violent and heroic substance. This explains the consolidation of the militarized forms of the Manuel Rodríguez Front and of the Rodríguez militias with the Communist Party, though the party later would distance itself from both.

In every case (negotiation geared toward unconditional surrender, mobilization that seeks the collapse of the regime, or revolt of the masses aimed at the regime's military defeat), there was no strategic plan. A proper plan would have taken into account the nature of the regime, its level of institutionalization, and the dual nature of a personalized dictatorship with a resistance to negotiation, and a military regime that adheres constitutionally and hierarchically to that personalized dictatorship. The cost of all these deficiencies was that the mobilizations, lacking a transition strategy and institutional formulas that would make the armed forces' withdrawal viable in moments of weakness, reinforced the "bunker" mentality of the regime and were weakened. Thus vast middle-class sectors retreated, fearful of the more radical forms of mobilization. This led to the isolation of the most militant groups and those most inclined to more hard-line methods that would cause unrest and pave the way for a regime collapse.

Undoubtedly, the regime was transformed throughout this period of mobilizations, hitherto-unknown spaces of collective action were opened up, and civil society was strengthened. But it is likewise true that all this was not enough for the political opposition to accomplish its purpose: ending the dictatorship and reestablishing democracy.[14]

The Issue of Opposition Unity

The opposition unity paid the price for the inherited character and the influence of ideological organizational identities of the Chilean political class. Thus, when it first burst into the public space, and in view of the fact that a wide variety of political parties had survived and established a political presence, the agreement was made neither on a formula of transition nor on the necessary actions to pursue it jointly, that is, on the procedure for becoming a multiparty coalition. What came of it was a grouping into ideological blocs more concerned with the identity of those included in or excluded from each bloc than with drawing up a concrete proposal for confronting the regime.

It is true that the makeup of these blocs represented a clear break-through from two standpoints. First, an effort was made to overcome fragmentation against an apparently monolithic adversary. Second, major changes appeared in the PDC. They broke with their customary inclination to act alone and entered into alliances, mainly with sectors on the left, though always excluding the communists. Change appeared also in some socialist sectors, which no longer made unity of the left (with the Communists) a binding condition of their partnership in alliances. But as the first ideological-political opposition blocs were formed in 1983, some of which sought a partial solution to the opposition split, and others, to solve unity problems within the ranks of certain fragmented camps (socialists), a way of dealing with the matter of opposition unity crystallized, despite that everyone proclaimed unity as the necessary condition for the regime to fall.

This way of solving the problem of unity favored ideological identity and affinity—hence the exclusion of dissenting ideological views—over agendas to end the regime and make the transition to democracy.

All subsequent efforts until 1988 were of the same order, and the many different blocs (known as *referentes*) that were created throughout these years tried to overcome the problem of exclusions, though never wholly, by favoring historicoideological affinities and without referring to specific problems of strategy in order to end the regime and recover democracy.

Some of these opposition unification attempts that were built around ideological-political blocs first emerged between August and December 1983, and served as a blueprint for the ones to follow. At that time, the Democratic Alliance was formed (small groups of the right, the PDC, and some smaller centrist parties, and some socialist parties and groups), as were the Democratic Popular Movement (other socialist parties and groups, the PC and the MIR) and the Socialist Bloc (of a different nature, since they were seeking to unify the socialist camp by grouping together socialist sectors that were in the Alliance, plus the Christian Left and the MAPU). All these blocs agreed on the abstract platform of "departure of Pinochet, provisional government and constituent assembly" and on what they called "social mobilization strategy." But beneath it lurked different perceptions on the nature of transition, which became apparent in the difficulty they had in setting a common course. Partial attempts at unification, such as the Democratic Intransigence (a group of public figures) or the Civilian Front (inspired by the Socialist Party, which was in the Alliance) either could not overcome their marginal status or simply disbanded quickly.

After a few years that had raised the political class's profile through these blocs, the Democratic Alliance lost its leftist contingent, the Socialist Bloc dissolved under the constant pressure of centrifugal tendencies that wanted above all to safeguard the partisan identity of certain groups, and the Democratic Popular Movement gave way to the United Left in June 1987, incorporating the MAPU and the Christian Left. But the latter endeavor, which recalled the old theme of the "unity of the left" and was an attempt to break out of the Community Party's isolation, ran up against the fact that at that time those very parties disagreed over how to confront the regime in the 1988 plebiscite. Various United Left parties agreed to the rest of the opposition's terms of the confrontation, and thus the United Left was held over as a possible long-term project, though it lacked a platform or strategy in the short or medium term.

In August 1985, the opposition would attempt to regroup again, this time on the Catholic Church's initiative, under the auspices of Cardinal Fresno, in what was called the "National Accord for a Transition to Full Democracy" (*Acuerdo Nacional para una transición a la democracia plena*). The importance of this agreement, which incorporated major parties on the right that supported the regime and the opposition front but upheld the exclusion of the Communists, was the wide political spectrum it represented. The reference, albeit incomplete, to certain transitional procedures —such as that of a plebiscite to reform the constitution—that brought the opposition deeper insight into the nature of these transitions, was also important. But the exclusion of the communists and the precariousness of the right-wing's support, as well as disagreement over the type of operation needed to set off a transition, left the Accord more as a symbolic reference than an effective political pact. In fact, attempts to deepen or refine it led the sectors most closed to the dictatorship to regroup and opt out of the Accord, though the latter had been broadened to include new groups on the left.[15]

Finally, we must recall that in 1986, given the need to resume social mobilizations, which had been losing steam and influence, the inability to reach political agreements between parties, and the need to reestablish a relation between the political and the social—a problem to which we will refer later—the opposition sought a new procedure for organizing. This time, the answer came in social organizations, including the communists, and was called the Civil Assembly. This organization showed a great capacity for mobilization not only when it organized nationwide demonstrations involving the whole country but also when it supported a national work stoppage in July 1986, an action that was harshly repressed. Nevertheless, despite the originality of overcoming political dissension through social organizations, where the whole opposition spectrum were represented without exclusions, the assembly inevitably had two fundamental deficiencies. First, there was a predominance of middle-sector organizations that left popular and leftist sectors in a relatively subordinate position. Second, they lacked a proper strategic political plan to channel social mobilization. An attempt was made to resolve this problem by uniting the social demands of the different sectors that made up the assembly, but it failed since unification was unable to reap the advantage that politics proper gives to collective action.[16] Thus, when the political wrangling resurfaced when the arsenals were discovered in 1986 and when the attempt on Pinochet's life was made, the assembly lost its unity and its ability to bring different groups together.

Political Opposition and Social Opposition

The original perception of the political actors was that the classical link between organizations and social actors on the national level and the political parties was being maintained. Thus it was assumed that what happened on the strictly political plane would be reflected immediately in the social plane, and, therefore, the agreements among ruling elites assured mass mobilization and action.

But we have pointed out that the military regime had transformed this classical relation, at least in three respects. First, the structural and institutional transformations introduced by the military regime had weakened the material and cultural spaces for the constitution of social actors, especially of their class bases, causing deep division and atomization in their ranks.[17] Second, the clandestine or semiclandestine survival of political parties and the emergence of the intermediate political class of sociopolitical activists and militants to which we alluded, intensified this crisis of representation. Finally, the absence of a state referent and the need to resolve pressing problems of material survival and threatened collective identities gave the mobilization of social sectors a rather incongruous direction, a role that on the whole was different from that produced by partisan political logic.

All this came into view when, at the beginning of the cycle of protests and mass mobilizations, political actors first and foremost had to confront the issue of their constitution and organization as such, after so many years of clandestine or semiclandestine politics. We have already discussed the initial process—inevitable in an opposition of this type in the Chilean case—of creating political blocs. Evidently this "partisan moment" caused a parting of the ways, with masses mobilized by a different logic, in which reconstituting their identities and satisfying urgent demands played a leading role, but in which they were still depending almost entirely on political party leadership. The whole subsequent period, which would show attrition in mass mobilizations, and the radicalization of the fringe of sociopolitical activists and militants was a bid to bring about a renewed articulation between the social and the political arenas. But this rearticulation, failing to rally around a strategic political formula for ending the regime, transferred the parties or bloc divisions to the social organizations themselves. Sectoral, organizational, or demand struggles, then, were subordinated to an ultimate political goal with no strategy or intermediate steps. This weakened the collective action that organizations, which lacked true autonomy, were able to undertake.

There were many attempts to rebuild sociopolitical articulations. First, on the level of the working class proper, there have been attempts since before 1980 at reorganizing on the national level, beyond grass-roots unionism. This local union activity had to reorganize along the lines of the restricted institutionalism created by the labor laws that the government imposed as part of its "modernizations." Reorganizations on the national level, in turn, were accomplished through general unions (*centrales*), which in part reproduced party divisions but also were original blocs arising from agreements or interparty splits.[18] In 1983, the Confederation of Copper Workers (CTC), which represented different facets of the Chilean trade union movement and its various political components, called the First National Protest, which had, as we said, huge political consequences. Shortly thereafter the National Workers Command (CNT) took the leadership and grouped nearly all the large labor unions, and organized several mobilizations and demonstrations. The Command took shape as the source of a new central labor union, which would solidify in August 1988, despite ongoing efforts in the PDC to preserve several ideological *centrales*.

The first democratic elections in the student federations revealed a unified opposition movement, which later changed as the student groups reproduced alliances and rifts occurring on the national level. Professional associations established a rearticulation between the political and the social that reproduced conflicts as well as breakthroughs on the political plane. Regardless, though new social actors had not been made autonomous from the parties, a greater tension between the political and the social undeniably had been building up, which hindered the simple mechanical reproduction of party-level processes.[19]

Toward the End of the Learning Process

With the discovery of weapons arsenals and the attempt on Pinochet's life in August and September 1983, both linked to the Manuel Rodríguez Patriotic Front, and the ensuing establishment of the state of siege by the government and the demobilization of the opposition, a new phase was ushered in. From the regime's standpoint, this new phase was characterized by institutionalism going into effect, which ensured the provisions stipulated in the constitution would be followed, specifically the plebiscite. This included a mild economic recovery, especially with respect to the foreign debt issue, and the enacting of political laws additional to the constitution (regarding political parties, electoral rolls, balloting, vote counts, and so forth), as well as the necessary steps to ensure Pinochet's nomination and his victory in the plebiscite.

From the opposition's point of view, this period represents a progressive step—to varying degrees—toward understanding transitions from this type of military regime to a democratic one. Opposition groups' experience with the mobilization cycle and the rearticulation of the regime after the discovery of the arsenals and the assassination attempt on Pinochet, as well as the learning experiences from other transitions in the Southern Cone, Europe, and Asia, were leading everyone to the same realization that the regime would not end through collapse or overthrow, but through a political process. Yet the opposition also realized that, given the lost time and its failure to have worked toward developing and enacting a formula for ending the regime, this political process inevitably would adjust to the institutional forms the regime had resorted to in order to perpetuate itself. As had happened in the aforementioned transitions, the opposition's objective would be expressly to change that institutional framework without creating power vacuums, as had happened with all the aforementioned transitions. Thus, debates on the illegitimacy of the constitution, given the perceived inevitability of the regime's agenda, gave way to much more realistic debates conducive to finding ways to initiate the transition process.

In response to the regime's plebiscite proposal, a group of well-known political figures (which came together similar to the National Agreement) produced the formula "Free Elections," which the parties supported through centrist and leftist committees.[20] These committees, at times overlapping with earlier ones and on whose existence they were predicated, meant a step forward in that they headed toward alternative transition formulas. But the appeal for free elections was a mere stepping-stone for other formulas, since there was no immediate possibility for them in Chile. By the same token, the debates over the idea of an opposition candidate or platform inevitably went nowhere because no competitive elections were on the horizon, as there were in the oft-cited Filipino case.[21] Nevertheless, both debates, later abandoned, did force the opposition to propose political and institutional alternatives. In effect, the "Free Elections" slogan led the Catholic Church and the political parties, with whom the Communist Party reluctantly joined ranks, to call for the people to register in the electoral rolls, a law which they had charged with being illegitimate.[22] This placed the regime and the opposition in the same camp (though at cross-purposes), which made them more of an institutional confrontation.

As for the legal registration of political parties, a precondition for taking part in a plebiscite or elections, the first debate centered on the illegitimacy of the law. In January 1987 the initial proposal from a sector of the socialist left to register a single opposition party to confront the regime in any election or plebiscite, was rejected because once the inevitability of the law was accepted, the issue of party identities held sway. So the centrist opposition parties and pro-regime right-wingers registered under their traditional names. One of the socialist parties, along with other nonpartisan sectors left, right, and center, entered as the Party for Democracy (PPD), which was defined as an instrument for contesting the regime in any kind of election.[23]

The 1988 Politico-Institutional Confrontation

This whole process of learning about the need to trigger a transition with a politico-institutional challenge, not an insurrectional one, played out by February 1988. At that time all the opposition parties, with the major exception of the Communists and some smaller groups, agreed to confront the government in the 1988 plebiscite, whose inevitability was accepted. The opposition saw it as the only chance to politically defeat the regime and its adherents.[24] Four months later, all opposition parties, including the PC, supported the same battle plan against the regime, for the first time during the whole military regime. This alienated the groups that were supporting armed forms of resistance against the dictatorship and doomed them to certain failure, as happened with all the other transitions.

From our point of view, it was important that the plebiscite offered the opposition different scenarios for initiating a process of transition, regardless of the outcome, and that the opposition had positioned itself on this path.[25] The lessons had been learned that transitions are accomplished from politico-institutional spaces that are won inside a military regime, and that, since a politico-military alternative neither existed nor was desirable as long as the opposition deepened its presence in those spaces, there would be hope for ending the regime and making a transition to democracy. This was the case even if the conditions imposed by the government had forced the opposition out of the plebiscite and, therefore, to seek out another institutional alternative to end the regime and initiate a process of transition.

In confronting the regime through the plebiscite in order to initiate a process of transition, the opposition faced several tasks and challenges. First, it had to turn a social majority, expressed as far back as 1983 in all the public opinion polls, into a political majority that hitherto had not been constituted.[26] This had already been partly achieved when the Party Agreement to Vote "No" (*Concertación por el No*) was constituted in February 1988 and when other opposition groups and parties later subscribed to this strategy. But they needed to spell out consensually what the plebiscite was going to mean, and communicate this meaning to the country at large. At the same time they had to ensure a single campaign organization and leadership, which in turn reflected the many and various sensibilities and tendencies that came together for the plebiscite under the "Vote No" banner.

The opposition managed to unite the two predominant elements in the majority opinion of the country, as all the polls showed: a desire for political change effected peacefully and orderly. This allowed the plebiscite to take on the twofold meaning of rejecting Pinochet and his institutional framework on the one hand and on the other replacing him without creating institutional power vacuums, in other words, a replacement arising from the regime's very institutions. An opposition victory in the plebiscite should mean not only Pinochet's ouster but also a negotiation or agreement process with the armed forces to reform or change the constitution in order to secure effective democratic elections and institutions in a reasonable time frame. This message united all opposition sectors and thus extended into the public campaign, though each group's rhetoric had different, apparently contradictory, implications. The different rhetorical stances, which came together at the end of the campaign, more than likely helped the opposition cause rather than hurting it.

Yet this single message or political line had to produce a unified opposition leadership and organization. History was against it, as we have shown. There were extremely complex problems to resolve, such as the disparity in political influence among the respective allied parties, the distinction between legal parties and de facto parties that had no access to legal prerogatives, the relationship of the Concertación parties to the Communist Party, infighting over campaign leadership spots that would have certain implications for the future, and the relation with the social organizations that joined the "No" campaign. All this could have split up the coalition. Unity seemed to be the coalition's great asset upon which it relied, the most valued aspect in public opinion polls, and the target at which the government campaign strategy was taking aim.

These problems were resolved, for the most part successfully, insofar as they kept up a united leadership, while at the same time there was a certain ambiguity that allowed them to resolve any problems promptly and pragmatically, avoiding ideological disputes over them that were irrelevant to the campaign itself.

Thus, a Command to Vote "No" (ACUSO) was formed, in which the Concertación party leaders held the highest decision-making authority. Yet a more restricted leadership circle brought together the truly important, legal and illegal leftist, parties. It also resolved the rifts caused by personalism in leadership, all the while ensuring a single, efficient direction through a secretariat that had all the means and technical capabilities at its disposal. Moreover, the illegal political parties supported the task of training delegates and monitoring elections, which only legal parties could do. Disputes over a potential nominee who could put a human face on the fight against Pinochet were solved by discarding the idea of a presidential candidate, which was completely unrealistic, and substituting it with a spokesperson who would be the head of the party that appeared strongest, the PDC. The leftist parties or groups that had not joined the Party for Democracy formed a subcoalition to represent them within the Command, the Socialist Command to Vote "No." This allowed them to not abandon the United Left coalition and to maintain indirect ties with the

Communist Party. The Communist Party was thus forced to subordinate itself to the Concertación strategy but without formally incorporating them, and without the former becoming isolated. Thus the most political sectors of the Concertación were strengthened, to the detriment of the more insurrectional ones.

Finally, a twofold movement emerged in the social organizations. In August 1988 the Chilean Unitary Workers Confederation (CUT) strengthened the labor union movement's autonomy and added a new actor to the democratic transition and consolidation process. Yet at the same time ACUSO became an heir to the Civil Assembly in order to mount the campaign. Moreover, representative groups of independent sectors, some elements of the business community, former backers of the regime, and others were organized, all of whom were staging their own mobilizations but were in fact subordinate to the political party leadership. Thus political parties and social organizations had a mutual support system in place, in contrast to the tensions and contrariness of previous periods.

Moreover, it was not enough to turn the social majority hostile to the Pinochet regime into a political majority. The latter also had to be turned into an electoral majority. In other words, it was a matter of winning an electoral campaign and ensuring that its returns were verified and recognized by the dictatorship. This was done under extremely trying circumstances.[27]

This process of generating and ensuring an electoral majority entailed several stages. First, the opposition needed to launch a campaign to register a high number of voters in order to legitimate the plebiscite. The main problem with this was overcoming the resistance and skepticism of social sectors hostile to the dictatorship, which did not believe in the possibility of ending it through this course of electoral action because they foresaw fraud as inevitable. The turnout at this campaign featured the highest number of registered voters in election history (slightly above 90 percent of the maximum eligible).

Second, once a high registration level was accomplished, the problem was conquering the fear and resistance of floating voters. This undecided group could tip the scales toward the regime if they perceived the opposition alternative as a return to the past or as a question mark in the future, a perception the military government nourished with their propaganda, which sought to combine the two great demands for change and security in order to repoliticize society in a positive sense. To that end they needed to set ideologies aside, to isolate the more radical and breakaway tendencies in the opposition and force them to subordinate themselves to the unitarian strategy. Also, it was important that individual and collective hopes for greater dignity be pinned on the act of voting "no" in an election. To that end the use of the media and the political class's direct contact with the people were vital. But this could only be accomplished in a climate with more freedom than the one that had prevailed throughout the previous fifteen years.

As the third element in the struggle for an electoral majority, the opposition had to attain certain minimal conditions for campaigning in the plebiscitarian period, which involved a struggle for various guarantees. These included the raising of states of exception, ending exiles, propriety and public disclosure in the registration process, and access to television, which played a rather important role in conveying the twofold message of change and security a "no" vote represented. Though this did not create a climate of total fairness—which was impossible in this type of event under a dictatorship—it at least thwarted the military government's attempts to manipulate the plebiscite, and allowed a repoliticization of society, which helped allay fears. Thus, without direct negotiations between the military government and the opposition, the government was forced to yield to pressure from the latter, the Church, and international opinion. Only thus could the government bring a modicum of credibility and legitimacy to the mechanism that it itself had created to perpetuate its power.

Third, recognition of a victory at the polls had to be guaranteed, and the opposition had to prevent not only fraud but also attempted coups that could happen in response to an imminent opposition win. In this regard, once again, the opposition's unity on practical issues and on the basic objective of winning an election ensured a proper, independent system— such as vote count—for monitoring elections (a system of polling station proxies designated by the legal parties). This allowed for them quickly to prove their victory and to counteract the government's uncoordinated efforts to resist. The opposition's credibility rested on the support of a vast contingent of international representatives and observers, all of which made unlikely a government disavowal of the results or recourse to an extrainstitutional loophole. It should be noted also that the government was never given a pretext for a recourse of this sort, since the allied parties to vote "no" enforced completely peaceful behavior in celebrating their victory, and were able to control those minoritarian groups who saw in this victory a chance for a mass uprising.

The Outcome of the Plebiscite and Its Implications

All the aforementioned elements were factors that helped the opposition to win in the plebiscite that was to decide the continuation or end of Pinochet's government. The official returns were: 43.01 percent voted "yes" for Pinochet, and 54.71 percent "no," with a registration upward of 90 percent, 2.39 percent abstaining. These last two statistics are records in Chilean history. Though conceived as a mechanism for reproducing the regime and for maintaining Pinochet in power, the opposition was able to convert the victory into an effective means of partial politicization and partial democratization of society, as well as a means of unifying blocs and historically warring tendencies. Moreover, winning the plebiscite unleashed an unprecedented process of transition. It also rewrote the responsibilities of an opposition that had worked *against* a dictatorial regime, in that it positioned it as the leading actor, not merely a reactive one, in a process whose outcome basically depended upon it.

The transition was not accomplished at that time but only set in motion, and thus the twofold task set before the opposition was, first, to achieve the constitutional transformations that would allow for general elections in the most democratic framework possible. Their second function was to secure a majoritarian democratic government that could complete the transition and initiate transformations toward a systemic democratization of Chile that the military regime had interrupted. The struggle for institutional transformations and especially to achieve a majoritarian democratic government, forced the existing opposition Concertación to stay united until truly democratic institutions were assured, and to undertake jointly the task of democratizing society, avoiding destabilizations and authoritarian regressions through two administrations during the decade, and electing a third as the new decade began. Clearly, both the center's (Christian Democratic Party's) isolationist tendencies and the left-wing sectors' temptation to capitalize on the dissatisfaction over an incomplete transition that did not resolve Chile's large socioeconomic problems, were factors that could split up the coalition. Yet the opposition's history shows that its experience under the dictatorship had strengthened the political class's accountability, whose earlier inability to form a majoritarian socio-political pact that could embrace democracy and social change played a large part in the democratic overthrow.

Conclusions

We have attempted to portray the evolution of the Chilean political opposition to the military regime as training that, given the nature of the opposition and the regime, we could call a prolonged learning process. This learning process was a matter of moving from a level of resistance or dissidence to one of true opposition, or to take the idea further, moving from a space of resistance, dissidence, and opposition to being a subject-actor of opposition. This in turn meant recognizing the difference between struggles against the dictatorship and struggles to end it and to make the transition to a new regime; it also meant being able to link the two goals, which is the true role of politics in such circumstances.

In the case of the Chilean opposition, this learning process took the form of overcoming three large obstacles, which arose from the fact that the opposition was made up of inheritances, and from the type of dictatorship and transformations undergone in society. These obstacles were, first, the absence of a consensual, consistent political strategy to end the military regime; second, the resultant fragmentation of political organizations that related the problem of their unity to ideological or organic matters and not to specific forms of struggle to end the regime; and third, the disarticulation of relations between the political and social spheres.

This learning process was obviously inconsistent, contradictory, but so far not reversible. This is because a solid core was constituted in the opposition whose education in the type of struggle and transition possible in these regimes planted the seeds of a sociopolitical majority that combined democratic support and social change in a new democratic regime.

✳ 11

Evaluation of and Prospects for
Chilean Political Democratization

This chapter goes beyond a description of the milestones and events in the so-called Chilean transition, which we redefine as a political "democratization"; it seeks to explore the principal issues at stake from the perspective of both debate and political struggle and of theoretical and analytical arguments.[1] First, we review a few concepts, revisiting material from the previous chapter. Then we assess the process in Chile that we term "incomplete democratization." Following this, we analyze the main issues that have arisen in recent years related to this incomplete nature of the democratization. Finally, we examine the prospects for political democratizations in the context of the presidential elections held in December 1999 and January 2000.

On the Autonomy of Political Processes

After the tremendous vogue that the literature on democratic transitions enjoyed, for several years now a challenge to this approach has been posed.[2] If the former coincided with what was mistakenly called the "new wave" of democratizations in the world—a term that hid, as we noted, the manifold forms these processes have taken in different contexts—the latter seems to coincide with the disenchantment over the outcome of these transitions or democratizations.

Behind the rise and fall of the topic of transitions or democratizations, there are two contrary views that merge theoretical and academic matters with political positions proper. One of them viewed the political transitions or democratizations as *the* new Latin American problématique, occupying the role that development, dependency, revolution, and structural reform each had occupied at a previous moment. The other view challenged the idea that a political phenomenon, such as democratization and its outcome—democracy—can be analyzed without at the same time considering or dealing with the system of power, the nature of the state, or the mode of production, of which it is a part.[3]

Without entering into a detailed discussion on the strengths and weaknesses of these perspectives, it should be acknowledged that both are rooted in a concept of democracy that totalizes one of the two dimensions of the concept and ignores or downplays the other. In fact, the transitions approach stresses principally though not exclusively the institutional dimension of democracy—the existence of free elections and the sociopolitical and legal conditions that guarantee them, which constitutes a so-called minimalist definition of "procedural democracy." Insofar as this basic core is guaranteed, democracies are present, and the transition, in the sense of a passage from an authoritarian regime to a democratic one, has ended. Conversely, in the view that deems democratic transitions to be part of a social transformation, there is a normative conception of democracy that considers it the ideal society type and not merely a political regime—in other words, what has been defined as "substantive democracy." If a certain type of state or mode of domination does not change, full democracy cannot exist, and therefore the object of political struggle and social analysis—democratic transitions—is illusory, lacking substance and meaning.

Although we are taking both visions to an extreme, doing so enables us to understand the heart of the matter at issue. The "transitologists" are left without an object of study once the transition ends—that is, once democracy has been ushered in. The normativists or idealists see no essential difference between a dictatorship and a democracy if the system of domination, such as what has been called neoliberalism, has not been replaced. In one case, the autonomy of political processes is carried to an extreme, and society is absorbed by them. In the other, this autonomy is denied, and they are absorbed into society.

We have stated that each of the approaches totalizes one of the two dimensions of democracy—the institutional and the normative, respectively. We have stressed that democracy is a specific political regime that can be distinguished from other political regimes as well as from other dimensions or levels of society. It can occur in conjunction with multiple forms of these dimensions or levels, that is, in multiple socioeconomic and cultural contexts. But it is also an ideal, an ethical principle, for the political organization of society. In other words, democracy is always a tension between an institutional dimension and a moral and ethical dimension that transcends institutions and refers to an ideal society. Thus the debate over a "minimalist" or "procedural" definition of democracy versus a "substantive" dimension—whether the latter is participatory, socioeconomic, or deliberative—is irrelevant.

The twofold dimension of democracy we described at once recovers the autonomy of the political system and regime, and its problematic imbrication or articulation with the other spheres of society. But this represents an attempt to steer clear of the determinism according to which a given configuration of these other levels or dimensions—such as the economy, the class structure, the symbolic order, and system of values—"corresponds" to a certain political system, and according to which there will only be "true" or "full" democracy if a certain economic, social, or cultural system emerges.

In the Chilean case, the determinist view of democracy has taken two directions that are opposed but that nonetheless both issue from democracy's relation to the market economy. Some on the right, and in part among the ruling coalition of center and left parties (the Concertación), believe democracy is only possible in the context of that economy, making it necessary to subordinate the democratization process to the demands and rhythms of that economic model. This is tantamount to defining the transition to democracy as part of a process of double transition to a market economy and to democracy. The so-called Chilean model has been lauded in international economic circles precisely for having completed the double transition, which makes it "successful" and "exemplary."

For others, from the most orthodox perspective of the left outside the Concertación, this very immersion of the transition process in what they call "the neoliberal system" makes the transition illusory and will render any "full democracy" impossible. In this view, there is no essential difference between the military dictatorship and the postauthoritarian regime.

In both cases, political democracy is identified with some socioeconomic system. Paradoxically, for the more orthodox or classical left, this type of political regime has only appeared in societies with capitalist economies. Thus, both views would assert the essential compatibility between capitalism and democracy, or between market economy and capitalism, and would only differ on the matter of what type of capitalism allows a democratic regime to exist. In the former view, a market economy is a necessary precondition, though not in everyone's view a sufficient one for democracy to exist. In the latter view, the type of market economy deemed neoliberal would be incompatible with democracy, and other types of capitalism would allow it. In this view, if a democratic regime were desirable in and of itself, one would need to struggle to make this form of capitalism win out over the neoliberal variety. The backward, deterministic, and hopelessly ideological nature of this argument is easily appreciated. Above all, it seems a step backward from the progress made in the social sciences, in political practice, and in the social life of the people, where democracy seems to be a good and an achievement in and of itself, representative of the collective historical will, rather than merely an expression of economic systems or types of domination, though those dimensions may be present.

This consideration only seeks to indicate our theoretical difference with both an institutionalist analysis that considers transitions and consolidations to be the end of a society's history, and a totalizing dialectical analysis that considers them a mere illusion or fantasy that hides society's "real" problems.

What we have asserted in this book is a perspective that makes it possible to study and analyze on the intellectual level, and formulate as a goal and task on the political level, the issue of the political regime as an object with its own validity, and thus the change of regime may be studied as a type of change independent of other transformations of society. Therein lies the study of democratizations, which are misnamed transitions, as we have seen in another chapter.

On Political Transitions

As we noted in the Chilean case, the shift from a military regime was accomplished in a specific type of political democratization that I have called a "transition." This, which in turn presupposes prior processes of opposition to and mobilization against the dictatorship, can be broken down into several subprocesses. These include the actual transition, which begins the moment the set of key actors orient their efforts toward changing the regime, and ends with the establishment of democratic institutions and governments, the inauguration or installation of the first democratic administration, the overcoming of authoritarian enclaves, and what has been termed democratic consolidation.

Let us recall that the idea of democratic consolidation has at least two different meanings.[4] First, there is "backward-looking" consolidation, which means the creation of conditions that hinder authoritarian regressions. Second, we have "forward-looking" consolidation, which entails a democratic deepening in order to head off situations in which democracy would be rendered irrelevant by de facto powers or crises that lead to new breakdowns or collapses of the regime. In this latter sense, unlike the former, one can say that consolidation is an ongoing and always-unfinished process for any democracy.

The results of political democratization understood as a change or passage from one political regime to another, especially in the case of transitions, which are generally processes with clearly defined objectives, can vary greatly in the characteristics and quality of the resulting democratic regime. The fact that a political democratization process or a transition has ended does not necessarily mean that its outcome is a complete democracy. In other words, a process of democratization or transition has a beginning and an end, independent of the result. If this were not the case and the deepening into a true, complete democratic regime were the parameter by which the end of a process were to be defined, a political transition or democratization could drag on for decades. In that event the concept would lose all meaning.

Political Democratization and Transition in Chile

Let us now attempt to apply this perspective to the Chilean case—not to enter into a detailed description of the democratization process but to evaluate it and examine prospects.

We can begin by stating the obvious. In Chile, there was a process of transition to democracy—in other words, a passage from a dictatorial regime to a democratic one. It makes sense to state the obvious because, although no one could claim Chile is under a dictatorship, there are those who maintain that the current regime is not essentially different from one, who do not accept that we are under another kind of regime, and claim that an actual transition never took place. In our view the existing regime is of a different sort than the dictatorship, though it is not a complete democracy: The whole point of changing from a dictatorship to this regime was the idea of establishing a democracy. Therefore we are seeing a process of transition, properly speaking—a process of change from one political regime to another—and it should be assessed as such.

Some are bothered by the concept of transition because they are still dreaming of the transition between modes of production (for example, from feudalism to capitalism, or from capitalism to socialism) and are stuck in a nostalgic, dogmatic use of terms. Consequently, they incur the error of calling this phenomenon of change or passage from one regime to another "transformism."[5] The concept of transformism, taken from a totally different kind of process, can only be set against the term "revolution." Even those who use the term certainly did not expect that, with the end of the dictatorship, the existing capitalism would automatically disappear, nor did they imagine or even dream of a revolution for Chile at the end of the 1980s.

In our view, this transition ended some time ago, and we are faced now with a regime that is consolidated in its democratic elements and its authoritarian elements, in other words, democratic administrations and parliaments in the framework of a regime of low-quality, incomplete democracy. However, that is qualitatively different from a military dictatorship, and there is no point in clouding our minds with terms like "transformism," which no one understands when applied to this kind of process.

Our basic contention on this matter is that the political transition in Chile was triggered by the outcome of the 1988 plebiscite, which ended all chance of an authoritarian regression, despite the clearly nondemocratic intentions of the civilian and military Pinochetism. It ended with the inauguration of the first democratic government in March 1990. Yet the end of the transition did not mean that the political regime and society had achieved full democracy. This was an incomplete transition that gave rise to a limited, low-quality democracy riddled with authoritarian enclaves. The task at hand was neither to continue with the already-concluded transition nor to consolidate the new postauthoritarian regime, which was already consolidated insofar as there was no chance of an authoritarian regression. The task was, rather, to carry out in-depth reforms of the regime and to generate an authentic political democracy in which de facto powers and political minorities were not the ones to fix limits on the popular will and sovereignty. In other words, the problems left unresolved by the transition needed to be resolved.

Thus, we disagree with the views that assert there was no transition at all, and with those that claim that Chile is still in transition and that the transition will only end when the authoritarian enclaves end. We also differ from the views that maintain that the transition ended at some point during the two first democratic governments. That means that the first democratic government cannot be defined as a transition government, as was done by many who later proclaimed that the transition had ended, and shortly thereafter, in the wake of the *boinazo* and military pressures, conceded that it had not really ended.[6] Where does that leave us? And why are the governments that followed not transition governments? Because they last six years rather than four?

In what follows, we attempt to develop the idea that Chilean political democratization was successful insofar as it forced out the dictatorship, prevented the breakdown of society by controlling economic variables, and safeguarded a government made up of the majoritarian democratic coalition. However, under no circumstances can it be considered exemplary or successful if the outcome of this process and the quality of the democratic regime are factored in: institutional weakness due to the presence of the de facto powers, representational weakness due to tensions between political actors and society, cultural weakness due to the absence of basic consensuses, and weakness of societal cohesion, unity, and direction due to the deterioration of state power.

Problems Resolved by the Chilean Political Democratization

In our view, the transition in Chile, or the transition from a dictatorial regime to a democratic regime, albeit incomplete, resolved three problems and paid a certain price: It left other problems unresolved and caused new ones.

The first problem that the political transition resolved was the end of the dictatorship. Not only was there a transition proper, there was also consolidation. In other words, an authoritarian regression has been highly unlikely, considering that we are talking about a relatively consolidated political regime. But herein lies the paradox. For the question is, What was consolidated? What we find is that the democratic elements of the new situation were consolidated (public liberties, constitutional state, free elections), but so were the authoritarian elements to which we refer below. In other words, the positive or successful aspects were consolidated as well as the negative or failing ones.

A second area in which the Chilean transition was successful—unlike virtually all the others in our region—is the government-led constitution of a majoritarian coalition. This was made up basically of the central axes, except for the communist left, of what formerly was the antidictatorial bloc. In other words, in no other country did a transition result in a majoritarian democratic government made up of a large number of the constituents from the antidictatorial bloc. But this has another implication. The bloc, with the above-mentioned qualification, had been the political expression of the middle-class and working-class sectors, and of the demand for social change throughout almost the entire twentieth century. And it was just this distance and confrontation between these two camps—center and left—that, as it polarized society, gave the right and the military the opportunity in 1973 to trigger the collapse of democracy.

Thus, the most positive result to come of the transition to democracy in Chile has been a majoritarian government made up of the majority of democratic and progressive forces. Naturally, we are talking about a majoritarian government in the social, the political, and the electoral arenas, but not in the institutional arena, due to the presence of authoritarian enclaves. Naturally, too, the internal equilibrium of this bloc and its exclusions will cause problems in the democratic or postauthoritarian regime, which we will discuss further on, but this second successful aspect of democratization is no less important because of it.

The third positive outcome, the third problem resolved, is the absence of a short-term economic crisis that would alter the correlation of prodemocratic forces, or be indicative of the presence of de facto powers' sites of destabilization or delegitimation, or the alienation of middle-class or working-class sectors. This was the case in most of the transitions in the region. Hyperinflation was the paradigmatic change in most people's daily lives, and the radical response to the neoliberal adjustments, which had extremely serious consequences for the dismantling of social actors, caused major cracks in the democratic bloc. We are not claiming that in the Chilean case there are no serious problems with the economic model of growth and the impossibility of its becoming a model of self-sustainable development. Nor are we ignoring that, though the growth rate had been high until 1997 and also thereafter, the economic crisis has been above the average of Latin American growth, and considerable relative gains have been made in overcoming poverty, the problems of equity and equality have not been resolved and in certain areas have worsened. We are simply saying that in the first six or seven years, the democratic, social, and political bloc has not had to pay the price of extremely regressive economic policies in order to face a moment of serious crisis inherited from the dictatorship. Instead, it has been able to focus on trying to rectify its most blatant flaws. Nevertheless, the resulting opportunity to address the political aspects per se and complete the transition by overcoming the authoritarian enclaves, regrettably, was not taken. Moreover, the downside of this positive aspect is that the absolute priority given to economic stability discouraged the formation and activity of social movements and actors, and the political reform aimed at overcoming the authoritarian enclaves, to which we will refer below.

The Critical Dimension of Political Democratization

Any honest assessment of the so-called political transition or democratization shows that the successes of the Chilean transition are not minor. Nevertheless, they all paid a price that can be seen in four broad unresolved aspects or problems. Moreover, if we speak of successes, we can now speak of failures, which do not negate the former but which compel a balanced appraisal. Obviously, we are not referring to society's more general problems but to specific aspects tied to the transition or to democratization itself, in other words, to the conversion of a military regime into a democratic one.

Some of these unresolved problems, or some of their aspects, are inherent to any transition and were unavoidable. More generally speaking, when we refer to political democratizations that do not involve revolutions or democratic foundations, but rather shifts from one regime to another within certain institutional frameworks and without an overthrow or top-pling of the dictatorial forces, there will always be some kind of inheri-tance, of presence of the military or authoritarian regime remaining in the new democratic regime. It is the latter's obligation to overcome it. This is the essence of transitions. When there is no other alternative for a change of regime—that is, when an overthrow, revolution, or democratic founda-tion are not possible or there is no consensus for them among the demo-cratic powers, or when the democratic opposition has not managed to negotiate an institutional proposal for a favorable exit, and that of the military regime is imposed—the recourse to transitions with inherent costs in their wake cannot be criticized. But this is different from that price to pay or those unresolved problems that do not depend on the nature of a change of regime in negotiated institutional frameworks, but on the qual-ity of negotiations and the political leadership of the democratic powers. Blaming the transition for everything is as misguided as blaming every-thing on the political leadership. Political analysis should make a distinc-tion between the two dimensions, which are present in some form in all the problems we discuss below.

The first of the unresolved problems or failures in Chilean political democratization is the issue of authoritarian enclaves, to which we referred in another chapter, that make for the quality and scope of the new demo-cratic regime. At first, their presence was inevitable, as we have shown, but not overcoming them under the democratic governments is the respon-sibility mainly of the sectors that identified themselves with the military regime and partly of the political leadership of the governments and the political actors that constitute them.[7] These enclaves refer to the power of the armed forces, the type of inherited courts and tribunals, the electoral system, the appointed senators, and all the nondemocratic constitutional and legal ties. They also refer to the ethical-symbolic problem of the viola-tion of human rights under the military dictatorship, which leaves the matter of "national reconciliation" unresolved.

Authoritarian enclaves still exist, and so, one must ask politically: Why have they not been overcome? The reply cannot be that they have not been overcome simply because their very existence prevents it. It is on this score that the criticism of the political leadership of the Concertación govern-ments becomes most apparent. During the first post-Pinochet government, under President Patricio Aylwin, due to an error in political judgment, the

government wasted its chance to face and overcome the institutional enclaves at the opportune time. It did so by setting only two priorities:
economic stability with social adjustment of the economic model, and
prevention of authoritarian regression, which, in our view, was already out
of the realm of possibility. The next democratic government, led by President Eduardo Frei Ruiz-Tagle, merely got caught up early on in an argument over the finished transition and the new phase of modernization, and
later gave up on the chance to overcome the inherited enclaves. They
produced constitutional reform bills more to solve an image problem
within the ruling coalition than out of any conviction that they were
necessary and viable.[8] After three years under President Ricardo Lagos, the
authoritarian enclaves are still there, especially those included in the Lagos
Constitution, with the exception of the reform that allowed elections at the
municipal level in 1992, and slow processes of negotiations in the Senate
herald some changes. Among the most controversial aspects are the appointed senators, the binomial electoral system that gives to the minority a
strong power of veto, and the irremovability of commanders in chief of the
armed forces.

However, from the mid-1990s, it became clear that the inherited enclaves
from the dictatorship were not the only limits to the expression of the
popular will and sovereignty. So, too, were many of the formulas and
institutions established as a result of the bargaining between the democratic opposition and the dictatorship in 1989 and, subsequently, between
the first democratic governments and rightist opposition. Without going
into a discussion of their appropriateness for their respective periods, these
agreements were not the expression of real consensus but of impositions
by the sectors tied to the military dictatorship and of misjudgments by the
Concertación leadership. Today, they are, if not an enclave, at least dead
weight.[9]

That there is a structural veto for a minority and for de facto powers,
and that the will of the social, political, and electoral majority cannot find
institutional expression, does not mean that there is no political democracy, but rather that it is poor or mediocre, that is, incomplete. Moreover,
this situation has a very important effect, to which we will return, namely,
that no other problem can be addressed directly without becoming embroiled in and contaminated by the presence of these enclaves and of the
past. Neither the defense policy the country needs, nor the in-depth re-

form of the judiciary, nor the issue of the redistributive model, to cite but a few examples, can be proposed as such without questioning the "settling scores" aspect or without pleading "revenge." This prevents true deliberation, without which democracy suffers, for it is the essence of all democracies.[10]

The second problem left unresolved by Chilean political democratization coincides with the counterpart of what we deemed its greatest success —the continuity of a majoritarian government coalition made up of the majority of the opposition bloc against the dictatorship and the central and leftist axes of Chilean society. This was possible because the party system in Chile—despite criticisms against it—is an entirely legitimized system in which political participation and extra- or antipartisan votes are minoritarian and on the decline, contrasted with the virtual majority of Latin American countries. Nevertheless, this legitimated party system is based on long-standing splits, dissension, and social projects, which of course have not gone away but do not tell the full story of the new problématiques and views of society. Moreover, the government coalition is made up of parties that historically expressed the main conflicts of Chilean society and the social sectors that embodied social change. Its responsibility for overseeing the transition and consolidation process leaves the social actors devoid of representation in matters that are not directly tied to the transition, or forces them to subordinate their dynamic to the requirements of the transition. In other words, the fundamental role the parties play in political democratization, and without which the latter would not have been accomplished in Chile, is accompanied by the difficulty of representing society under the democratic regime. Those who can represent this divisiveness are political actors that are not equipped politically to respond other than with an expression of sheer discontent, as in the case of the Communist Party or the alternativist political groups, which are generally short lived.

The third unresolved problem, which in part is linked to the previous one, is the lack of debate over the broad issues that define society and the foundational bases of democracy, and the consequent illusion of consensus, which actually only existed in order to end the dictatorship. Afterward there were circumstantial or isolated agreements between government and opposition. But no one anywhere in the world had dared to call these "consensual democracies" as did the political class.[11] The absence of this consensus can be explained, on the one hand, by the minority veto and the de facto powers, and, on the other hand, by the lack of debate on the crucial issues, or a debate that is drowned out by demands for economic or political stability. Last, there is still trauma over disagreement, conflict, and confrontation, which are demonized and pathologized. Yet conflict and debate must take place in order for a basic societal consensus to be reached.

The fourth problem has to do with the weakening and the difficulty of reconstructing the state's capacity for action, especially where control of economic forces is concerned. Here we are referring to problems that are tangential to the central question of political democratization but are an essential aspect of the democratic regime. Supposedly, in a political democracy all the various actors and forces are constituted as citizens and are therefore subject to the rules of the game concerning majorities and minorities, partisan representation, and other matters. Economics is not subjected to these rules. And this, as we noted previously—beyond the need to make autonomous an economy that at some point could have been overly subordinated to politics and to the state—suggests the need to reconstruct the relation between economy and politics. Failing that, there is no society, and without society the political regime is a delusion. The crucial problem for the future of democracy is the reconstruction of a political system and a ruling state that replace ideologies of the past and recent neoliberal versions alike.

Thus posttransition Chile reveals the flip side of Aníbal Pinto's classic theory that defined a basic contradiction between an atrophied economy and a developed institutional and cultural political system.[12] This weakness in the economic system at one point compelled a freeing of the economy from its political shackles. Today, the problem is exactly the opposite; this autonomization was accomplished barbarically, and not because of the intelligence or enterprising abilities of the economic ruling class but rather through an uncritical, brutal, and forced adaptation to the changes occurring in the world economy during the dictatorship.

A freed economy, true, but especially freed from the country and the society. The political, institutional, and cultural system was atrophied. One need only recall the authoritarian enclaves, the weakness of the system of decentralization and regionalization, the crisis in the educational system and the collapse of higher education, the tremendous weakness of social actors and of their powers of negotiation with economic powers, the abysmal backwardness of the institutionalism of family organization, and the difficulties in redefining a new role for the state as leader and protector. In other words, in whatever arena one considers, the new democratic regime suffers a freezing up and erosion of the institutional and cultural political system. Yet the nature of the socioeconomic model itself has kept the institutional resources needed to weather economic crises—such as those of 1998 and 1999—from being available.

In other words, the country's fundamental problems after the transition are related to the organization of the polis, the capacity for leadership, and seeing that cultural and social problems are expressed in politics. This means that there is not actually a crisis of the political and its legitimacy, not even among youth.[13] Rather, there is a crisis of political ability and activity in accounting for the political instead of revolving around itself. In the long run, there is a risk of this leading to a legitimacy crisis.

From False Consensus to Critical Debate

As early as 1997, it was clear that the apparent consensuses that had been attributed to the Chilean transition were reaching their end and that the much-vaunted Chilean model of "double transition, to the market economy and to democracy" showed weaknesses. In the opinion of some observers, it was an impasse; others deemed it a failure. Leftist intellectuals opposed to the Concertación had maintained a perplexed silence until then. The critical observations by the intellectuals sympathetic to the Concertación, including those of the author of this book, were silenced by the official political class, including the government and rightist opposition.

Among the critical elements that stood out much earlier than the best-sellers and open letters on contemporary Chile, there were at least two that we have already mentioned.[14] On the one hand, there was an interrogation of the notion that there really did exist a democracy of consensus, rather than merely adaptive and pragmatic agreements, where all the major topics were avoided or were not subject to debate: the constitutional issue; human rights; the policy toward the armed forces; authoritarian enclaves; the socioeconomic model and model of redistribution; the reduction of the leadership role of the state; the weakness of the processes of decentralization, regionalization, and local democratization; labor relations; and the sustainability of the development model. Therefore, one could hardly speak of consensus.

We have noted that in all these years there has only been debate around and apparent consensus on the end of the dictatorship, even when there was none with regard to the political reforms that would allow for a true democracy. One could add that such consensus and debate have existed over the need for and contents of reforms to basic and intermediate education, and over the formal prioritizing of the fight against poverty, although no agreements have been reached about the implementation of policies or about the redistributive aspect.

Moreover, there has been a questioning of the idea that we were still in transition. This was an idea that the opposition and the government have used to hinder a substantive debate on any topic, with the excuse that such a debate could upset the "stability" or "governability" of a transition that had not taken a single institutional step forward or backward since the election of the first democratic government and the reform that allowed municipal elections. This was an odd transition that, at the rate it was going, could wind up outlasting the very dictatorship it replaced. This idea of an unchanging transition with no end in sight allowed the leftist opposition to deny the difference between dictatorship and democracy, and reject the whole strategy to end the dictatorship, starting with the 1988 plebiscite, which they never liked.

From the beginning of the 1990s, some argued that if the pending problems were not resolved, they would be obstacles to facing the future and would take their revenge by lingering forever. What prevailed was the silence of the critics on the radical left, a climate of smugness among the right-wing opposition and, above all, albeit for different reasons, in the Concertación government. Thus, the above-mentioned challenges, articulated and published from the very first, could not ignite a national debate, which only became widespread in recent years.

Political Climates and "Heating Sensations"

Thus, it is as if the years 1997 and 1998 meant, parallel to the world economic crisis, the application to Chilean politics of actual weather patterns that have greatly impacted the country: a growing transformation of "heating sensations" beyond the actual temperature readings.

Three main "heating sensations" divided or polarized political actors and public opinion. First, right-wing opposition, which attributed the success of the "Chilean model" to the economic and political inheritances from the military regime, denounced the government's incapacity for leadership and direction, and its deviation from the "problems that beset the people." They further claimed the government did not respect the orthodoxy of the economic model and attempted to introduce political reforms that altered these institutional inheritances (among them, those referring to the so-called authoritarian enclaves, especially appointed senators, the electoral system, the makeup of the constitutional tribunal, the irremovability of the commanders in chief of the armed forces, and the National Security Council). The December 1997 parliamentary elections had the effect of bolstering this "heating sensation," without any connection to the actual facts, as we will see, and kindled presidential aspirations through a precandidacy of the sectors most linked to Pinochetism, as well as bolstering the vision that politics means "getting things done." Once the second half of 1998 was under way, the prenomination of Joaquín Lavín, the successful mayor of Las Condes running on the UDI ticket (Unión Democrática Independiente, or Independent Democratic Union), which was closer to Pinochetism, was made official. Meanwhile, National Renovation (Renovación Nacional, or RN), which was much diminished in its symbolic influence and its national leadership, desperately promoted former Senator Sebastián Piñera as a prenominee, but he subsequently withdrew in favor of Lavín.

There were also government sectors that were "satisfied" with both the economic model and the way the political democratization was progressing. These sectors felt that everything was on track, though they acknowledged shortcomings in the social sphere and a certain unrest. This sector likely fell in a kind of "postpolitics," in which one need only add some slight adjustment to the mix, but they felt things were better left to self-regulate, since they wanted the least possible government intervention and political debate. Another sector of government represented a divergent view. This group felt that some intervention was possible through "political operators" and top-down negotiations, which generally ended in failure in each of the transactions attempted.

It was from these government sectors and from the Concertación that a first proposal was made. Drafted in the middle of 1998, signed and promoted by several government ministers, it focuses on successes won and points out that the problems faced stem from characteristics inherent to all modernization. The paper finds fault with the disenchantment in the ranks of many Concertación sectors and calls for a closing of the ranks around the government and the future of the Concertación.[15]

The other major heating sensation that took center stage politically in 1997 is that of discontent. It was expressed both by a leftist intellectual in a best-seller that compiled metaphors, images, and trendy discourses from philosophy and sociology, and in the UNDP (United Nations Development Program) Human Development Report in Chile, which mixed serious empirical data with a very confusing, ambiguous theoretical interpretation.[16] It is popular in disillusioned government sectors, and especially in the leftist opposition.

Here, too, there are at least two visions. The moderate version, that of groups belonging to the Concertación, claims that the December 1997 parliamentary election returns reveal that people were distant from and disgruntled toward politics; also, it claims that an assessment of the transition had to be made, since it had not overcome the authoritarian enclaves, and had allowed the military, whose symbol was Pinochet's induction into Parliament as senator for life, to act with impunity. The transition had also prolonged an economic model whose social results were unrelated to the successes reflected in certain macroeconomic indicators. The progovernment sectors in this position got out of the fix of the more "officialist" document mentioned above, with another in which a more critical stance is taken. This indicated that these problems in part come from the very way the Concertación is run.[17] A third group, always within the world of the Concertación, issued a much more strongly worded document against the socioeconomic model inherited from the dictatorship and the failure to overcome the authoritarian enclaves.

In the radical versions coming from left-wing opposition sectors, there was no democratic transition as such, and there is no essential difference between the dictatorship and the current democracy. In this view, what we have is a simple case of "transformism," a vague concept to which we have already referred, one geared to uphold a neoliberal economic model born of the "merger" formed by the military, the transnational corporations, and the technocrats.[18] This was something akin to the new version of the old "oligarchy and imperialism" for the globalized world.

This whole climate prevented analysis and a satisfactory resolution to the many social conflicts that raged starting in 1996 and that in 1997 had their main outlet in the student movement launched at the Universidad de Chile. Above all, however, this climate threw up a barrier to understanding the nature of the most important political events of the previous two years, leading to real chaos and uneasiness in both the political class and in the observers and intellectuals in this field. The situation especially affected the Concertación of ruling parties.

The December 1997 Parliamentary Elections

The December 1997 parliamentary elections were the first since the democratic reinauguration that were not held jointly with the presidential elections. A widespread mistake that seems to have taken root in the country is that of trying to interpret them as a rejection of politics based on the drop-off in the electoral turnout due to low voter registration among youth, abstention, and the significant increase in null and blank votes. In fact, the registration phenomenon can be set right simply through automatic registration. This would lower the current voting costs, since youth are required to make an abstract act of registering before the electoral campaigns even start. The act of abstention per se was still quite low (between 11 and 13 percent). Its slight upturn in recent years coincides with the return to normal of an anomalous situation, in which, due to the postdictatorial democratic inauguration, abstention had been extremely low relative to the historical rate during the plebiscite and subsequent elections. Moreover, it is a serious error to count the unregistered, abstentions, and blank and null votes in order to claim a blanket rejection of the political class, and more so, of the government. Even so, voter turnout was 60 percent, which in comparative terms is high. Null votes rose substantially to 17 percent, which compels analysis of their meaning. Since there is neither research on the matter nor access to actual data, we can only speculate on the meaning of the null vote, which, we want to stress, has nothing to do with abstention or nonregistration, and only in one of its meanings coincides with the blank vote. Some of the possible meanings of a null vote are: the rejection of all choices offered if they do not match one's own, or if one has none; the conviction that though one has a choice represented by one of the candidates, the electoral and institutional system in place (inherited from the military regime) will not let that person be chosen; the rejection of specific policies (which are rather minimal and could not be taken together); and the classic voter nullification out of ignorance of how to vote. These cannot be subsumed under a single meaning, and each of them accounts for a very small percentage of votes, which would drastically diminish in the next elections.

By the same token, one should not interpret the 1997 political results as discontent or a protest vote against the government or political class as a whole, since allegedly the nonpolitical vote had been favored, giving the edge to candidates that "are doers" and are "close to the people." Surely there *is* discontent, and it is much more widespread than meets the eye. Yet that cannot be concluded from the results at the polls, especially if we take into account the enormous voluntary turnout achieved in the Concertación's 1999 presidential primaries and in the presidential elections of 1999. Discontent is manifested, rather, in the vast gulf between the political class and public opinion on certain key events or core issues, such as human rights and Pinochet's 1998 detention in London, to which we will return later. On the contrary, with important isolated exceptions, the elections were clearly political. Statistics from this and subsequent elections generally show that independents, the presence of the media, pragmatism or short-term concrete proposals (*cosismo*), and ambiguous political positions fared very poorly. Underlying this is a deep longing for ideas and real political debate, a need to which the political class seems not to be attuned.

The most significant political results were that the right-wing opposition remained at roughly 35 percent, and the National Renovation held its advantage over the UDI, but the defeat of the symbolic leaders of the RN against their UDI allies (with closer ties to Pinochetism) reveals how indistinct and short-sighted the more democratic right was. The December 1997 elections, as well as the political developments that ended with the UDI presidential candidate's final announcement in 1999, clearly illustrate that a right-wing democratic project was defeated indefinitely, and that the right revealed its essential makeup: Pinochetism. This was so even though the presidential candidate would distance himself from Pinochet during the 1999 campaign.

The Concertación parties, which support the government, won their share, except for the Christian Democratic Party, which fell four points, as did the Concertación, which for the first time finished under their PS-PPD (Socialist Party–Party for Democracy) allies. This cannot be interpreted, then, as a vote of no confidence against the government but rather as a vote only against the political line of the PDC, which was seen as overly hege-monizing within the government bloc. In this sense, the PDC's true defeat came in these elections, which was confirmed in the Concertación's 1999 primaries in which their prepresidential candidate was defeated by the Socialist-PPD-Radical candidate, Ricardo Lagos. These results only served to confirm the demand for a change of leadership in the Concertación. In 1997 in the heart of the PS-PPD bloc, the latter had a very slight edge, despite the major drop in socialist members of parliament as a result of the tactical error they made in their choice of candidates. This permanent stalemate only goes to show that, in the people's minds, this is a single political conglomerate that should be unified in order to solidify the center-left pole in the Concertación, though its leaders refuse to acknowledge it.

Predictably, the share attained by the Concertación did not let them increase their members of parliament enough to form a quorum, which would have let them carry out the political and constitutional reforms needed to end the authoritarian enclaves, especially the appointed senators. This situation was worsened by Pinochet's taking up a seat as senator-for-life under the current constitution. The Concertación was left without a strategy for overcoming the enclaves, and the prevailing mood was that the "transition," as the current process is erroneously termed, was obstructed, in the view of some observers, or had failed, according to others.

Change in the Army and Pinochet as Senator-for-Life

Pinochet's exit from his post as commander in chief of the armed forces after nearly twenty-five years had a twofold significance, the first of which was obscured by the second. This consisted, first, in the successful opera-tions carried out by the government so that at the end of his constitu-tionally sanctioned term, Pinochet would be replaced by a general with close ties neither to the Pinochetist inner circle nor to those who were strongly identified with the military regime, that is, someone relatively more independent on those points, as General Ricardo Izurieta seems to be. Only time will tell exactly what political cost this had for the govern-ment and what concessions had to be made to Pinochetism in order to attain it. The symbolic concessions, at least, though never stipulated or spelled out, were nevertheless manifest. They were illustrated by the gov-ernment's rejection of the constitutional accusation against Pinochet made in Chile by some Christian Democratic representatives, as in its defense of an alleged diplomatic immunity granted to Pinochet for his trip to London, and the persistent opposition to his being tried for crimes against humanity outside Chile when the former dictator was arrested in London in October 1998.

The second meaning was that Pinochet, by constitutional mandate, became senator-for-life, which was a symbol of supreme violence against a still-incomplete democratization process. That it was no surprise and that it was explicit in the constitution does not diminish this violence, whose inevitability was rather debatable, as we stated above. Inevitably, however, the Chilean political class had to give some sign of its disapproval of a situation that had been forced upon them. This was done through demonstrations when the former dictator was stepping into his new post, and especially through the constitutional accusation brought by some Christian Democratic delegates, after the government had opposed it, and with a fierce polarized debate inside the party, considering the party leadership's opposition to this initiative. The Socialist Party gave steady support to the accusation, and the PPD did as well, eventually. The governmental bloc suffered deep divisions on the fundamental principle around which it had formed: opposition to Pinochet. This conflict resurfaced at the end of the year when the former dictator was detained in London.

Those within the Concertación and the government who opposed the constitutional charge, which for legal reasons could only apply to Pinochet's behavior during the democratic period, advanced two types of reasons. The first type was legal, and the second, political, in the sense that this was to put the whole transition and the two democratic governments on trial. They fell into the right's same line of argumentation and did not understand that the main issue was to symbolically and politically demonstrate something unmistakable: the repudiation of Pinochet by both the country and world public opinion alike. The government made the mistake of intervening to prevent the indictment from being presented, and then pressuring for it to be dismissed, when a modicum of common sense would have obliged it to remove itself from an issue it had no call approving or rejecting institutionally. Rather, the government should have reserved judgment so it could arbitrate later on, if need be.

The initiative's defeat heightened the uncertainty over how to remove oneself from an institutional quandary that hinders democratization and permanently turns back the country's clock to a past that affects all present and future issues. Frei's government announced, with respect to the appointed senators, a constitutional reform designed to broaden the roles of the plebiscite or referendum so that the citizenry would resolve the matter of the authoritarian enclaves. But it was not implemented.

The government's mistake at this stage would have profound effects on the political event that exposed once and for all the unresolved problems with Chilean political democratization: Pinochet's arrest in London.

The Twenty-Fifth Anniversary and "National Reconciliation"

In some way the previous question, which took up the first six months of 1998, is tied to another that reached its crowning point in September. That month marked the symbolic twenty-five year anniversary of the September 1973 military coup that ended the Popular Unity's socialist government and the life of President Allende, destroyed Chilean democracy, and set up a military dictatorship headed by Pinochet for seventeen years.

The big issue, beyond the ideological debate over the Popular Unity, the 1973 coup, and Pinochet's military dictatorship, is whether or not the country has achieved its reconciliation or if it remains divided and split, as it was over these three watershed events.[19] The center and left sectors, at odds in 1973, now have built a solid social and political alliance, expressed in two successive coalition governments and in other ways. Thus the real issue is the reconciliation between the armed forces and the minority on the political right, on the one hand, and the whole of society, on the other.

Some relevant developments came to light in 1998. First, army leadership changed, which meant a new generation was taking power, one that was more concerned with institutional and professional matters than with political stance, though it always supported the military coup and military government and, in particular, Pinochet. Indeed, the real change would come about during the Lagos government when a new commander in chief of the army, General Cheyre, would keep the military government at a clear distance. Second, well-defined positions were taken by the Catholic Church authorities on human rights, especially regarding the need for information on the fate of the disappeared. Third, decisions were handed down by the courts to allow inquiries into certain civil rights violations cases that occurred under the dictatorship, even overruling the amnesty law. Finally, the debate around the bill to end the 11 September holiday, which after a tie vote in the Senate, ended with an agreement fostered by Pinochet himself and the president of the Senate to replace that commemoration in the future with one on another date in September designed as an observation of national unity.

All these considerations call to mind, in one way or another, the issue of national reconciliation. Two basic issues, if left unresolved, render the issue meaningless. First, information must be gotten from responsible parties— institutions and persons—on the whereabouts of the victims of human rights violations under the dictatorship, and there must be some type of sanctions to end impunity. Second, the armed forces must acknowledge their institutional responsibility for crimes and violations of human rights, starting with the very events of 11 September 1973.

In 1999, as a result of Pinochet's detention in London and amid fresh charges and open trials against the military, which also involved Pinochet and led to the arrest of several high-ranking officers from the era, and following an unexpected change of minister of defense, the Ministry of Defense proposed a roundtable (*mesa de diálogo*) to discuss the pending issue of human rights. It was rejected by the victims' families, but human rights lawyers participated, as did representatives of the armed forces and other sectors of national life. Over and above the strategy and intentions behind the initiative, the truth is that in the final report submitted to the new government in April 2000, the armed forces implicitly acknowledged responsibility, and a mechanism—albeit a weak one—to find the victims was voted into law. All this made for a general climate in which an unresolved problem was brought to the fore, and in which the reality of systematic, state-sponsored crimes against humanity was established beyond question. Though the armed forces have not admitted their own accountability, their representatives have changed their discourse. Pinochet's loss of immunity through his life-term seat in the Senate, and his having to stand trial in Chile after his return from London, bolstered this renewed chance for truth and justice to win out.

Real reconciliation seems a long way from materializing. Perhaps at some future date, once all the military officers implicated in these crimes and violations are permanently removed, the armed forces will officially seek pardon, as has happened in other countries. It seems harder for this step to be taken by the Pinochetist right, whose only historical foundation and seal of identity seem to be the heritage of the dictatorship, the preservation of its symbols, and the inherited institutionalism of the socioeconomic and political model.

Pinochet's Arrest in London

Pinochet's arrest in London—under accusation by the Spanish courts of crimes of state-sponsored genocide, torture, and terrorism—was an expression and catalyst of all the above-mentioned problems.[20]

First, it showed to what degree there was consensus neither on vital issues of human rights violations under the dictatorship, redress, justice, impunity, reconciliation, nor on the way they have been dealt with or can be in the future. It became evident that, due to an inability to solve them, the unresolved problems of the past are problems of the present and future. The Archbishop of Santiago's first reaction captured the situation: "These things happen because justice has not been served in Chile."

Second, it was shown that the political right is merely Pinochetism's faithful expression and that in it, every idea, project, or stance is subordinate to this essential truth. Its view of a crushed or distorted national sovereignty where practically the whole world lauded a chance for justice and civilization was supported by the economic de facto powers and the media, as well as the de jure powers, such as the judiciary.

Third, the government made every possible mistake, from granting to Pinochet a belated special mission that granted him no immunity; to the contradiction in asserting initially that it was not a matter of state nor did it affect the transition or democratic stability, nor was it political; and finally to organizing political operations to "let Pinochet return to Chile"—asserting that it was an issue of national sovereignty—and to falling out with traditionally friendly countries. Thus, the right's destabilizing discourse was legitimized, and military pressure on this score was accepted. This allowed—only where the Pinochet affair was concerned, naturally—a virtual joint rulership with the armed forces through the National Security Council. Their initial proposal that the reconciliation could be advanced through the courts was completely diluted by differentiating only in discourse the right's central position from civil and military Pinochetism: Let Pinochet return to Chile unconditionally. It thus lost all political autonomy and would remain powerless to choose future alternatives in this situation. As with the constitutional accusation to which we referred above —and it has not been stressed enough that had the government taken appropriate action then, it would have prevented the episode of the arrest and its aftermath—the regime failed to provide political guidance; detached itself from public opinion; pressured and strained the Concertación, forcing its position on them as dogma; and forbade debate over alternatives.

Fourth, these events produced the widest distance and largest gap between the political class, which responded self-referentially and backwardly to the situation, and a public that looked on perplexedly as the political class got entangled in the issues of national sovereignty, engaged in a double discourse, and failed to represent the demand for justice of the great majority of Chileans, and certainly, of all of humanity. It will be a tough sell explaining to public opinion—to Chilean society—why, when the majority of the country and the whole of humanity all express their will to resolve the situation in order to advance the cause of civilization, justice, and the dignity of the country, its political class falsely and arrogantly wields the argument that "we solve our own problems."

Fifth, one cannot fail to find extremely positive the effects the detainment of Pinochet had in pushing forward the unresolved issues of the transition. Among them let us point out the above-mentioned positive shifting positions in the judiciary, which continued with the proceedings on several human rights violations trials that were stalled, and began to investigate those in which Pinochet himself was implicated, finally stripping him of his rights under suspicion he was a party to those crimes. We have also referred to the setting up of a roundtable for discussions to be fostered by the government and supported by the military, probably with a mind to ending the lawsuits against them that were being processed in the judiciary. This meant, in effect, that the armed forces had changed their discourse and now at least admitted the existence of a human rights problem. It also meant, above all, that the idea was gaining currency that there could be no reconciliation or resolution of the problem without exposing the truth about the violations that occurred under the dictatorship and without justice for these crimes.

Even if the Pinochet trial proceedings were suspended because he was declared insane, nobody doubted now in Chile that he was the main party responsible for the crimes against humanity committed under his dictatorship. Concerning the results of the roundtable talks, President Lagos asked the armed forces to issue a report on the locations of the corpses of the missing. This information was very poor and deceptive. It served only to help find some mortal remains of very few people, while acknowledging that the rest were thrown into the sea, but at least it exposed the lies of the military, put the armed forces under severe scrutiny, and provoked distrust from public opinion. All this helped the armed forces to make some signs of recognition and especially to distance themselves from Pinochet and the military regime, even if so far an official act of pardon seeking remains to be seen, and in a vast majority of cases there is no truth or punishment because of the amnesty law decreed under Pinochet.

The Presidential Elections at the Turn of the Century

The presidential elections in December 1999 and January 2000 in Chile were held at the end of a decade of Concertación governments. This was the most stable coalition of the century and followed seventeen years of military dictatorship led by Pinochet. Let us remember that this coalition comprises the Christian Democratic Party (center), the Social-Democratic Radical Party (center-left), the Party for Democracy (the most recently formed, during the 1988 plebiscite), and the Socialist Party ("renovated" left).

Compared to the two previous presidential contests since the democratic recovery (that of 1989, in which Patricio Aylwin was elected, and the 1993 elections, which Eduardo Frei Ruiz-Tagle won), this election featured three major firsts. For the first time these elections were not held jointly with parliamentary elections. For the first time the Concertación nominee, Ricardo Lagos, did not belong to the PDC but to the Socialist Party, Party for Democracy, and Radical Party bloc, having defeated by a healthy margin the Christian Democratic precandidate in the primaries. For the first time, the Concertación candidate faced a single right-wing candidate, Joaquín Lavín. The election returns would add a fourth first, unprecedented in Chilean history: for the first time there was a runoff between the two candidates with the largest majority.

Clearly, the 1999 elections were downplayed, which contrasted with other similar events in the country's history. The electoral climate was not as tense, since some thought that this country had already entered the "new era." In their view this new era was characterized by democracy, market economy, and globalization. However, they thought Chile had made its entrance belatedly and not forcefully enough, thus it would have to remove the obstacles that still tied it to twentieth-century society and that hindered the full development of globalization and the market economy. Many of them held that politics should facilitate this process and that, therefore, the presidential elections made sense only to ensure that Chile did not "lag behind." Others did not feel that the changes in government, presidencies, or politics could play any key role in social transformations, as they did before, and thought it better that the governments govern as little as possible: politics is irrelevant. Both views were shared, to varying degrees, by the world of the right and the business community.

Another view of this issue arose in left-wing sectors outside the ruling coalition. It mainly revolved around the Communist Party positions and other alternativist stances, and gave rise to three presidential candidates. This view, though it posited a radical change in what it terms the "neo-liberal model" administered by the Concertación, maintained that this coalition was unable to implement these changes in any of its more right-wing or left-wing versions. Thus, it was only possible to make use of this election for rallying a public opinion sector to express discontent over what they considered the "Concertación administration of Pinochet's inheritance."

Lastly, two main moods emerged in the intellectual climate and in the Concertación's views, which changed somewhat as the last stage of the campaign heated up. First, there were those who shared the point of view that there should be no large government programs or ambitious ideas that would necessitate historic changes. This was not because they did not believe in the importance of politics but because they thought that this would be a return to the past with its sweeping or foundational projects that polarized societies and that, in the Chilean case particularly, caused the fall of democracy; the trauma of the 1960s and 1970s seemed to linger. This trauma, for some, was manifested also in a certain fear of a change of leadership in the Concertación from the PDC hegemony during the first two governments to the leadership of presidential candidate Ricardo Lagos. The latter largely addressed the sectors on the left within the Concertación (Socialist Party, Party for Democracy, and sectors of the Radical Party). Finally, left-wing sectors in the Concertación saw the next Concertación government as a chance for a transformation that, while preserving the successes achieved by the first two Concertación governments, would allow the historic changes needed to enter the next century. However, the prevailing discourse centered on economic continuity mixed with a change of sociocultural climate, and on the question of how long the political institutional framework inherited from Pinochet would endure.

The presidential campaign unfolded in this intellectual and cultural climate, culminating in the first round in December 1999, and in the second, between the two first relative majorities, Ricardo Lagos and Joaquín Lavín, in January 2000. The predominant characteristic of this campaign was the right-wing candidate's imposition of style and issues, especially in the use of the media, which, with the single exception of a few radio stations and, to some extent, a television channel, gave their unqualified support.

Let us recall that Lavín was the candidate for an alliance in which, for the first time in the postauthoritarian period, the whole right-wing spectrum was represented under the unopposed predominance of the more hardline and Pinochetist sector headed by the Independent Democratic Union party. Nevertheless, the candidate, backed by the iron discipline of his supporting parties, sought to depoliticize the election at all costs and to shed his image as a rightist and a Pinochetist. He criticized traditional politics and spoke much more about change, though without clarifying what that entailed, and much less about upholding the military regime's work, as his political sector had done up until then. Moreover, his campaign pledged to further and deepen the market economy model by criticizing state and political intervention as it promised to "solve the people's problems."

The importance of this new style lay less in its success at the polls, as the figures show, than in its ability to force the opposing candidate—especially his spokespeople—to step into the realm of depoliticization and of concrete offers and counteroffers, despite efforts by their own candidate, Ricardo Lagos, who was aware he drew his strength from the sociological and political substrate of the electorate. Moreover, it was obvious that the Frei government had shown exceedingly poor judgment in political leadership, despite their economic and social successes—which were tarnished the previous year due to the crisis in Asia and certain mistakes made in handling it. All this made Ricardo Lagos's double role as the expression of new Concertación leadership that had to portray itself as both continuity and change, a somewhat more complex image than Lavín's simple, generic statement about change.

In the December 1999 elections, out of a total of slightly more than 7 million votes, with a very low abstention of 10 percent, Ricardo Lagos earned 47.9 percent of the vote, Joaquín Lavín, 47.5 percent, and the remainder of the field, 4.5 percent. The Communist candidate's drop in this election from the previous ones was noteworthy. Lagos won 50.81 percent of the male vote and Lavín, 45.3 percent; Lavín won with 50.9 percent of the female vote against Lagos's 44.1 percent.

Predictably, in the second round in January 2000, there were no substantive changes to the outcome of the first, and Lagos increased his lead with votes from voters who in December had favored alternative candidates. Thus, in the second-round runoff selections, abstentions dropped off slightly, Ricardo Lagos earned 51.3 percent of the vote, 54.3 percent among men and 48.7 percent among women. Lavín earned 48.7 percent, 45.7 percent, and 51.3 percent, respectively, winning the female vote once again, though by a slimmer margin. The vote difference between the two candidates increased by roughly 30,000 to 190,000. In our view, these figures show a diametrically opposite situation from the one that Lavín supporters, some of Lagos's campaign strategists, and almost all the media outlets portray. They declared that this was a breakthrough election that tested in the political realm how much the country had changed since its return to democracy.

In fact, in the elections on 12 December 1999 and in the second-round runoff in January 2000, we saw the same basic patterns of electoral behavior established in the 1988 plebiscite, which ended with Pinochet's military dictatorship supported unconditionally by the Chilean right, now with a nearly four-point jump for the right-wing candidate. We are probably talking about a shifting electorate of no more than 10 percent, which would coincide with a nonmodern vote, variable according to circumstance, publicity, and media campaigns. The overwhelming majority of the electorate is still basically modern since it votes for political alternatives and projects that clearly distinguish right, center, and left, and in this case the right and center-left presidential candidates.

The electorate gave new support to the Concertación to run the country, this time under different and reformed leadership in the person of Ricardo

Lagos. Lagos's and the Concertación's great success was changing leadership while maintaining a suitable relationship between continuity and change in the Concertación, though this was not well expressed in its communication campaign. The critical aspect of this was the inability to repoliticize that small segment of the electorate that has changed its voting patterns. Though small, this voter constituency is significant for deciding one way or the other in two-party elections.

The vote for the right was the highest since 1938, primarily on the strength of Joaquín Lavín's success in divorcing the right from its Pinochetist past, thereby bolstering its parliamentary and municipal support by slightly more than a third. It remained to be seen if, once the campaign was over, the rightist parties would be able to take up the mantle of this campaign and bring about a true democratic shift, or revert to their role as "keepers of the military regime's inheritance." The critical aspect of his candidacy lay in his having written off politics, reducing it to resolving individual, particular problems and demands from the state, thus cheapening its wider meaning, which is to build a desirable society.

Challenges Faced by the Lagos Government: A Brief Overview

It has been said that the Lagos government is the last government of the twentieth century, but also the first one of the twenty-first. For the government that took power on 11 March 2000 would not be able to face problems in the future if it did not successfully address issues that essentially are legacies of the past: trials and justice regarding human rights violations under the dictatorship, without which there is no true recovery for the country; constitutional reform that safeguards a truly democratic regime; regulation and societal control of the economy without changing its growth dynamic; the redirection of this growth to serve the needs of the people while ensuring environmental development; the reduction of inequalities that force a redistribution process; the strengthening of the ruling capacity of the state and of its role as protector while ensuring the strengthening of society and citizen participation; and the overcoming of cultural and media banality by promoting diversity, thus generating new outlets for creativity and promoting ethical values of solidarity. This is to name but a few of the topics that were not addressed in the presidential campaign, in light of the heated competition among proposals regarding what were called "concrete problems."

Once the new government took hold, the country realized that media spin does not show the reality, and that governing is not the same as marketing or running an ad campaign. The real problems involved in running a country are much more complex than what were called "people's concrete concerns," which, moreover, cannot be addressed without sound, coherent ideological-political projects. In his first congressional address, President Lagos defined Chile's prospects for becoming a developed country by the bicentennial year of its independence (2010). Nevertheless, the focus of this goal has been clouded by two factors. First, the world economic crisis forced Chile's growth rate down from an average of approximately 7 percent in the first half of the 1990s to approximately 3 percent in recent years, despite its growth rate remaining higher than the Latin American average. This shows that the Chilean economy was well run. Even so, this goes beyond a growth-rate problem to a deeper issue: the point to which growth in this globalized economic model involves the growth of each country, and if in 2010 what we call a developed country will mean the same thing as it does today. Second, this goal did not have the same clarity in its concrete policies in all arenas, and the main issue during the first round of Lagos's presidential campaign—social reform—became less and less central.

Once again, by not prioritizing political and state reform, including the new constitutional reforms that overcome authoritarian enclaves, the government was burdened with immediate problems that hindered its formulation of a coherent plan. Nevertheless, in the first three years the government has shown significant work in four areas: first, the clear submission of the military to enlightened political power, among other things, in imposing tasks on the military on the issue of human rights violations after the roundtable discussions, in naming a socialist woman—a daughter of a general murdered by the Pinochet dictatorship—as minister of defense, and in the statements and actions themselves of the commander in chief of the army, although the constitution has not been changed with respect to the irremovability of commanders in chief; second, Chile's insertion in the globalized world, especially through the signing of economic agreements with the United States, the European Union, and Asian and Latin American countries; third, the vast plan to transform the infrastructure of the country and the cities for the bicentennial; and finally, the priority assigned to cultural development on the regional and state levels.

The largest problems in constructing a national project stem, in part, from the highly inadequate institutionalism inherited from the military regime, which has not been changed, leaving the government bound to negotiations with entrepreneurial de facto powers that do not have a national project and with opposition on the right that sacrifices all notions of country for the chance to gain power in the upcoming presidential elections. They also arise from the absence in the Concertación of a clear vision of the future now that the great successes of the 1990s have been achieved. This leaves it at the mercy of a single-minded struggle for shares in power that divide it, in which the Christian Democrats seek above all to return to their hegemonic position, and the parties closest to Lagos fail to define a project to give direction to the bloc.

The two elections held during Lagos's government—municipal in 2001 and parliamentary in 2002—consolidated an opposition right at 44 percent, four points below the presidential one, and a coalition fluctuating between approximately 49 and 52 percent. For its part, the opposition was marked by the clear predominance of the more radical right in its bloc and the near disappearance of the right-center, and the dominance of the PPD-PRSD (Party for Democracy and Radical Party) over the Christian Democratic Party in the Concertación. Hence the triumph of the right in the future only depends on what may happen inside the Concertación.

At the end of 2002 a series of specific problems related to bribes and compensation issues in high government posts reintroduced the issue of state reform, around which a consensus between government and opposition was established to draft several bills, which has never happened until now. The fundamental question is if this is the time to review institutionalism as a whole, and to make the leap forward that the country needs in order to face all its other problems, or if once again partial solutions will be sought that perpetuate the incomplete nature of Chilean democracy.

An Opportunity for Chile

In Chile, as in other countries in the region, the symbolism of a turn of the century coincides with the end of a sociopolitical model. If in the 1980s and 1990s a model or project existed in Latin America, or at least an imaginary or a myth in that regard, it was what was called "the double transition to democracy and the market economy." This model replaced the national-popular or populist, developmentalist, revolutionary, or authoritarian projects of other ages. This very model or myth of "double transition" has run its course.

In fact, one cannot maintain that a transition to democracy is under way, given that the institutional system is moving neither forward nor backward—which would be characteristic of a transition—but rather it is consolidated. Yet, as we have seen, what is consolidated is an incomplete democracy or a semidemocracy, so what is needed is a very in-depth political reform to turn it into a true political democracy, one that translates the ethical principles of democracy into legitimate, stable, and dynamic institutions.

Moreover, the neoliberal market economy model—or "privatizing model"—has worn out as the basis for integrated, self-sustainable national development, here and everywhere in the world. If there was any doubt of this on the world stage and in the Chilean case, the economic crisis in Asia, in the first case, and the energy crisis in Chile, demonstrate how the free play of the market not only breaks up societies but also is totally inefficient in meeting its own goals. Since the last years of the 1990s, this economic model has shown its failure.

If it is true that what is involved is not a return to a model of total subordination of the economy to the state and to politics, neither is it right to persist with the tired old lecture that there is no alternative model and that we should go on with more of the same. The alternative model, which is different for each country, consists of giving to the state, on the levels of national and supranational blocs, a leading role in development; establishing regulatory and normative frameworks on market forces; and guaranteeing citizen control over these frameworks and forces. In other words, in recognizing that politics and economics are different, independent arenas, we also need to bring the ethical principles of democracy into market performance, obviously with mechanisms and institutions other than politics.

This image or myth that we have made of ourselves of simultaneously undergoing a transition to democracy and entering modernity through the market economy, has been a recurring scenario in all political proposals, though varying according to ideology. Faced with the crisis, there are those who think that the model must be protected at all costs and, therefore, that no variation should be introduced; rather, all ideas or actions that appear unorthodox should be written off, and a hands-off approach to both political institutions and the economic model should be taken.

Nevertheless, there is a majoritarian social sector aware of the shortcomings of the double transition model. Some, at a loss for how to change it or convinced it is not possible, simply propose that it be adjusted more or less deeply on a case-by-case basis. Yet there is a very widespread demand for a change of course, for a thorough transformation. A small sector among these proponents believes that no gains have been made since the dictatorship, and, thus, they do not concern themselves with the costs or chances for setbacks, nor with the real possibility of generating new consensuses to introduce these transformations. A vast majority that wants significant changes, by contrast, knows that these transformations cannot jeopardize gains won to date. This is why the only political actor to head the alternative for transformation, for the time being, is the Concertación.

The main issue is to answer the question of whether it is possible to think about a national project or task—such as the national-popular project and development since the second quarter of the twentieth century, structural reforms of the 1960s and 1970s, or the democratic recovery in the 1980s and early 1990s—independent of whatever assessment we may have of these projects or their outcomes.

Patricio Aylwin's first democratic government defined the national task in terms of "transition to democracy" and hinted at the idea of "growth with equity," maintaining macroeconomic equilibrium, and seeking to correct the social effects of the economic model. Moreover, it defined a method of isolated negotiations and agreements that it called "democracy of consensuses," which, as we have already noted, seems mistaken to us, in that it did not institutionally forge any basic consensus. But at all events, whatever criticisms may be leveled at these definitions for not going far enough, one should recognize that the government *did* have goals and orientations, and that, judging by them, they made some crucial progress. By contrast, one should also recognize that during the second Concertación government—despite a very strong economic performance up to 1997—the country was rudderless, lacking a shared direction, and, therefore, political guidance in projects and orientations, and in goals that mobilized social and cultural energy.

Thus, the task before the new government is to forge a new pact or a national consensus to carry out the transformation and reconstruction of the country at the turn of the century. If this is not accomplished, perhaps disaster still may be averted, but the country will simply be increasingly a pure space intersected by the globalized world and ruled by the de facto powers within and without. To phrase this another way, what is at stake in the coming years is forming the country into a community worth living in, rather than a territory and a space for individual and family consumption.

Merely by way of illustrating this point, some areas should be pointed out in which new consensuses should be defined in the prospect of a national project that leads to simultaneously completing the pending tasks of the transition and assuring democratic deepening. The first area is related to the problem of the reconciliation and resolution of matters pending since the dictatorship, and which the transition and the first democratic governments' negotiations failed to solve. As we have stated, the experience of more than a decade of democracy shows that these problems of the past are problems of the future; in other words, even though they are not the only ones, they define coexistence and the ethical legacy of the future. There are at least three issues here. The first deals with the tasks of completing the truth—to make justice in order to end the prevailing climate of impunity and to improve the means of reparations to victims and families. The state should lead the search for truth, punishment, and reparations by generating new formulas, since those used to date have been inadequate for making progress toward an effective reconciliation. The second refers to overcoming the authoritarian enclaves, which are manifested mainly in the constitutional limitations on the popular will, in the excessive influence of the de facto powers, and in the very negotiations in which the transition was involved. It does not suffice to say at this point that we need to overcome them and that there should be a constitutional change. Instead, we need concrete formulas on how to achieve that end.

A second area has to do with the socioeconomic model, where there are at least three issues that need to be drastically redefined. The first issue is social inequality and the need to ensure formulas for redistribution, beyond simply overcoming poverty, which in itself is indispensable. The second is ending the prevalence of the market model and the refoundation of the institutional system and the role of the state in areas such as labor relations, higher education, public communication, the environment, social security, and health care. The third issue is ensuring the state's leadership role, kept in check by the political system and the citizenry, through a state reform that goes beyond modernization and streamlining.

A third area deals with the model of coexistence and the formulation of freedoms and solidarities. A first aspect involves the expansion of outlets for participation, which requires a thorough review of the current forms of local and regional government in order to grant them greater autonomy and decision-making power, and better opportunities for deliberation and participation. This is all the more imperative in the case of indigenous peoples, where it is fitting to develop the plurinational nature of the state. Moreover, formulations must be sought that institutionalize the equality of representational duties between genders and youth involvement at the level of municipalities, regions, and national agencies. A second aspect reflects the increased secularization of institutions such as family, the elimination of different forms of censure, and the generation of mechanisms to establish effective equality in the ability to create and innovate in the new information and communication technologies.

A fourth area that a national project should address is that of the country's insertion into the globalization process. This requires a clear-cut definition of its Latin American trajectory, along with formulas for permanent incorporation into the spaces for economic integration and for generating supranational government levels of jurisdiction. No one in Chile is more qualified to take on this task than President Lagos and the Concertación. But he should assert his leadership very clearly by privileging those topics, and the Concertación must carry out a refoundation of its programmatic and ideological bases, salvaging all that is of value from what was built during these years but also overcoming all its limitations.

A special responsibility is incumbent upon the opposition, whose power of political veto is exacerbated by the current institutional and electoral system. If, as Lavín showed in his campaign speech, the right is able to forsake its stubbornly blind ideological link to the military regime legacy, then it will be able to hold onto the electorate it managed to win over. Otherwise, it will go back to being a minority whose only meaning will be the one given it by a political system inherited from a dictatorship. There is no better opportunity for the right to show that it is a political force with a democratic project.

In sum, we are facing the possibility of a change of scene, of a considerable shift in the socioeconomic, political, and cultural model to mobilize and harness the social energies of this country. Without these forces, the erosion, banality, and irrelevance of politics will become inevitable, which surely will affect the legitimacy of the country's democracy. President Lagos's government is the chance to ask what kind of country can be—and is being—built. And the answer in part will affect the life of at least two or three generations to come.

Conclusion

What we have attempted to show is that the problems Chile faces today are not economic, but basically political and institutional. This assertion inverts the famous theory of strong political development contrasted with scant, weak economic development. What the country needs today is no longer an economic miracle but a giant political and institutional leap forward in all areas of social life. This should be focused on the reformulation and recreation of institutions, the strengthening of the state and the political party representation system, and the generation of social actors and the autonomous will of the citizens. Will the political class dare go against the fashionable ideology that sees society only as the sum of individuals or as a market, and understand that absolute priority must be given today to the reconstruction of the polis, in other words, of the political and sociocultural system?

Epilogue: What Future for Politics in Chile and Latin America?

Will countries be able to confront globalization with their own projects and through larger blocs, in order to avoid a fragmented emergence of national-state communities in which some are globalized and others are left out, as well as the unilateral hegemony of a superpower that character-izes current globalization? This is the great question today and in coming decades.

Latin America and the Globalized World

For most of the twentieth century, Latin America was characterized by the national popular model of modernity. It is leaving that model behind through globalization, authoritarianisms and democratizations, and re-forms that have led to a new development model. The region is entering the globalized world without a true industrial state society ever having been constituted in any of its countries, and without having experienced true democracy rooted in its societies.

The question today is whether these are real societies with relevant democracies in which it makes sense to speak of a national project. For the first time in Latin America—after civil wars, cycles of democracy and authoritarianism, brutally repressive military regimes, and democratic foundation processes as in Central America, transitions as in the Southern

Cone, and reforms as in Mexico—there appears to be the consolidation of regimes of a democratic stripe and the institutionalization of political processes that facilitate the resolution of conflicts and the constitution of party coalitions that overcome the classic centrifugal polarization of political forces. Paradoxically, in many cases these democracies, although consolidated—that is, without the risk of a return to the military dictatorships of the past—are pervaded by institutional and ethical legacies of the dictatorships (human rights violations and crimes that have eluded truth and justice). In every case the democracies have failed to take root in the whole of social life. The latter has been torn apart by economic transformations to the point of making effective state action impossible, increasing poverty and inequalities, seriously restricting minimal rights to a dignified life even in the absence of repression by the state apparatus, and practically eliminating the possibility of organized collective action. There are a few cases of postauthoritarian regimes that are still unconsolidated. Mexico and Chile are examples of incomplete transitions and reforms; Colombia is a case of the decomposition of the state itself; Venezuela is marked by the search for a new relationship between the state and the people, disintermediating politics through the formula of a *caudillo*; and Brazil seems to have achieved a true party system mediating between regions and the state but has one of the world's highest levels of economic and social inequality. Argentina is an example of a society in which political democracy has been regained and has achieved immense legitimacy in spite of the economic and social crisis, but it has not been able to reconstruct a political and entrepreneurial class equal to the new economic realities. Instead, that class secludes itself in the often mafialike political game and in economic speculation and corruption. The Argentine crisis demonstrates civil society's importance in mobilizing reactively and curbing the independent activity of the political class and the world of speculation, but it also shows its weakness and limitations in contributing to the content of solutions. In every case—and this is absolutely new in Latin America—the military solution has either been absent or, in some instances, subordinated to political power. But also in every case the predominance of de facto powers shows the erosion of the one basic condition for any political regime, and especially for democracy: the existence of a political society or polis society.

The idea of democracy always assumed the existence of a society—a territory with a population in which economy and social, cultural, and political structure corresponded or were coextensive in space and there was a center of decision making. More precisely, there was a polis—that is, the power concerning the general direction of society was found in the state, an object of struggle and cooperation in which inhabitants-turned-citizens represented themselves. There is no democracy, nor is there any other type of political regime, where there is no polis.

Thus, the weakening of the polis is the central problem for these countries and their democracies today, once authoritarian structures and nondemocratic regimes are overcome through transitions and democratizations—that is, once democracy exists as the single legitimate political regime. In essence, there is no space of correspondence among economy, culture, and politics, and consequently there is no center of decision making. More simply, power lies outside of a society or, within it, is not controlled by the society. For example, if the Tokyo Stock Exchange decides what happens to employment in a country, or a group of foreign investors determines through the country-risk rating which candidate should be elected or forces candidates to change their platform, we do not have a polis in the classic sense: a space where the people who live there make the decisions that affect them.

In many cases this explosion of the polis makes democracy illusory, taking away the foundation for democracy or any other political regime. That is happening in the current era because of the unrestricted predominance in social life, overflowing territorial space, of the very element that many considered the condition sine qua non of democracy: the existence of an economic space that is not controlled by the state and politics—the market. The existence of globalized markets independent of states—that is, the freeing of economic space from its territorial base and from state control and regulation—is incompatible with the democratic idea because it contradicts the existence of political societies or polis societies, or simply countries. In theoretical terms, the globalized market economy and democracy are incompatible. In practical terms, that incompatibility results in a coexistence in which democracy and the idea of the country can be made irrelevant.

This allows us to explain the paradox of Latin America: Never before have there been democratic regimes in practically every country in the region, and that is the case precisely in the period of the prevalence of the economic model of transnational markets—or more accurately, of economic powers that pass through national spaces and reorganize economies by starting with their always fragmentary insertion into the world economy.

Indeed, as the polis society—that is, the space where citizens, through their systems of representation, make the key decisions that affect them—is diminished, the political regime is made irrelevant and consequently can coexist with the national and transnational de facto powers that actually make the decisions. Granted, we are speaking in absolute terms about a phenomenon that is relative, since neither the polis nor the state has completely disappeared. Therefore, democracy is not entirely irrelevant either. For making the decisions that are not made by the de facto powers, restraining the arbitrariness of those powers, and allowing a minimal space of liberty, popular sovereignty, and citizen expression, there ultimately is no other regime than democracy. In other words, a national dimension still exists and will continue to exist, but it is very much reduced by the above-mentioned restriction of the spheres in which the community can make decisions and by the narrowing of the citizen base itself due to exclusion and poverty. Thus, the legitimacy enjoyed by democracies in Latin America in recent years bears no relation to its incapacity to take on and resolve the issues it is supposed to resolve as a political regime, which is the fault not of democracy but of the type of society being constructed under this modality of development.

Currently, Latin American democracies are characterized by two types of deficit. The first comes from the so-called democratic transitions themselves, whether from oligarchic regimes, civilian authoritarianisms, traditional military dictatorships, modern military regimes, or cases of civil war. The second is a result of the socioeconomic, political, and cultural transformations of contemporary society that have profoundly transformed the character of politics and have overturned the classic foundation of democratic theory and practice, which was the polis society. These are distinct issues, but they have become intertwined and have combined to deepen the crisis of politics in the past decade.

The first deficit has to do with imperfections and corruptions inherited from the predominant institutional forms of the authoritarian regimes and, at times, of the transitions. The latter, for their part, also reproduce preauthoritarian political problems that characterized the imperfect democracies, populisms, and traditional dictatorships that prevailed until the 1960s.

Some aspects of this deficit are the authoritarian enclaves inherited from the military regimes and from certain high-level negotiations among the actors involved in the transitions, exemplified primarily by the Chilean case; classic weaknesses of the presidentialist system or party system, aggravated in the posttransition, as in Argentina and Peru; remnants of clientelism as in Brazil and corruption as in Mexico, to cite some of the most striking but not the only examples; and the generalized absence of renewal of the political class and of adequate mechanisms of representation and participation, replaced by the predominance of de facto corporatist and media powers.

This type of deficit reaches an ambivalent verdict on the outcome of the democratizations. On the one hand, it is undeniable that for the first time in Latin American history there is an almost complete panorama of democratic regimes—even if some countries have not yet finished their transitions—and that the crises that have occurred up to now fortunately have not been resolved with regressions to militarism or to authoritarian regimes. From this point of view, in comparison with earlier periods, politics has been revalorized, strengthened, and legitimized, even though that may seem paradoxical given the current situation of enormous and dire crises. On the other hand, the deficiencies and problems mentioned above are contributing to a growing dissatisfaction with the results of democratizations—and thus to a devalorization not only of democracy but of politics itself and of its agents and actors.

The political deficits of the transitions are not the only culprits in Latin America's crisis of politics and the problems its democracies face. It should not be forgotten that—parallel to the military regimes in some cases and to the processes of transition or the establishment of new, imperfect democracies in others—these societies experienced profound structural and cultural transformations, some similar to those that occurred in other regions and others of a unique character. The national-state industrial society, which was the societal basis for modern political phenomena and for democracy as the principal form of government, has been disarticulated by a number of factors: the processes of selective globalization hegemonized by the United States through the neoliberal model (which is not the same as globalization, but rather is one way of realizing it); the new productive models based on information and networks; the interpenetration of markets and the expansion of communications; the emergence of national and supranational identitarian movements; and the overpowering role of transnational de facto powers. The weakening of the national-state industrial society is particularly significant in countries like ours in which it was the architect and constituent of society, the principal agent of development and the privileged referent for any collective action, which gave politics a central role. If, as some have said, the national state and democracy never became deeply rooted in Latin American societies and left some zones unaffected, societies were left even more disarticulated as these unique, precarious referents weakened or disappeared. As we have noted, what is at stake is the viability of these societies as countries.

Politics had been the principal means of access to the goods and services that the state provided to vast sectors of the middle and popular classes, and the main source of meaning for projects and collective action. With all their imperfections and inequalities, these two functions are losing their relevance today, which moves the question of the meaning of politics to center stage. To fill this void, the neoliberal ideologies and media trivializations and the political actors linked to them propose a new political project: Let us replace the state with markets—that is, with the forces that operate in the latter—and replace politics as a form of organizing society with the promise of solving the "most concrete problems of the people," which is nothing but the sum of individual needs.

In the new democratic space opened by the transitions, instead of political projects and actors the electoral market is established, distorting the classic tradition of citizen choice. In the electoral market, incoherent promises of impossible solutions to the "problems of the people" compete through the media, with enormous sums of money leading easily to corruption. The entire political class is forced to compete in this new market and abandon its essential, unique, and indispensable duty of political deliberation and decision making concerning projects for a better society. Obviously, this is a slippery slope because of corruption and the decisive role of money in politics. Society is no longer necessary. In this schema politics is dissociated from the idea of the good society and from change oriented toward it. That is, traditional or classical politics and political activity have become detached from their relation with "the political" as the field in which the people determine the major issues of the country. As a result the political class appears to be revolving around itself.

Many of the problems of current politics, distinct from but combined with those of the political democratizations and transitions, stem from the way this situation has impacted different countries. These problems include the excessive role that marketing and the media have come to play in electoral campaigns, the utilitarianism and deideologization of the political class, the lack of accountability, the population's withdrawing in the face of the near certainty that they cannot control the forces that govern their lives and their seeking refuge in apathy or intensified individualism, the new widespread forms of corruption, and the inordinate power of national and international de facto powers.

While the first deficit involves the transitions, the second is a deficit of the polis. Any overcoming of the defects and the current irrelevance of politics, any necessary reform of politics, above all requires the strengthening of the polis—that is, the space of debate, conflict, consensus, and decision making concerning the general issues on the part of the people, or rather, of citizens. The deficit of politics today can only be overcome by restoring the leadership role of states, the representative role of parties or agents of representation, and the real participation of autonomous social actors in social life. That entails regulating and controlling the economy and the powers that dominate it.

While Latin America historically was characterized by a suffocating predominance of the political over the economic, the latter gained autonomy with the change in the development model. Today the situation has been reversed. Without returning to discarded formulas, it is indeed appropriate to return to the fundamental principle of any democracy: Politics should direct social life in the space we call society or the country.

The fundamental problématique of our society therefore is no longer to construct a democratic regime starting from a situation of civil war, authoritarianism, or a military regime, as it was in the 1980s. Rather, it is to construct a new social base in which democracy has meaning and relevance. This reconstruction of the polis, the political community, is what a national project means today.

This task of reconstruction, which varies according to the realities of the different countries of the region, has at least three dimensions. The first dimension is the reconstruction of the country as a historical and moral community. These societies have suffered fissures and upheavals in their history that they have not faced and overcome in order to move toward the future as a moral unit. Practically every society in the region has experienced some time of division and upheaval, causing the various sectors and their heirs simply to coexist in the same space without feeling themselves part of a single historical and moral community. At different times this took on various forms, including hidden or open civil war; massive crimes against humanity perpetrated by military dictatorships; and the subjugation of indigenous populations. That is, in each society there is a stigma by which some negate others. That has not been the object of a true reconciliation, nor have we known very well what is entailed by such a reconciliation. Consequently, some people have remained closed off in the past while others are ignorant of it; history and shared undertakings disappear. It must be added that in other eras the antagonistic historical and ideological visions concerning the country shared a common object—the idea of the national project—even if they argued over the meaning, content, or direction of that project. Today it is the very idea of the national project that is in question. The will for a common destiny is disappearing.

The second dimension is the reconstruction of the socioeconomic community. That involves, on the one hand, overcoming the exclusions that today appear not only as instances of exploitation and domination but also as the simple, massive expulsion of vast sectors. It is a basic question of belonging to the polis through a stable, minimum standard of living and minimal rights, which due to these exclusions are sometimes limited to half the population. On the other hand, there is a question that goes beyond overcoming poverty and exclusions, which has to do with socioeconomic equality. If poverty and exclusion affect people's lives, inequalities or extreme differences in wealth and power affect the existence of a country as such and make it into various countries within a single space, without common interests and aspirations. Finally, there is no economic community if there is no capacity for collective action to control and regulate the economy and if those who make economic decisions reside outside of the country, escape from these controls and regulations, or render them impossible.

The third dimension, related to the second, is the reconstruction of the political community—in other words, making the state assume its role as guarantor of social unity and cohesion and as manager of development, over and above the de facto powers and transnationalized markets, and making politics the arena where the great issues of society are actually determined. Ethical and historical reconciliation and the change of the development model are the expressions of the two above-mentioned dimensions of the reconstruction of society, the basis for any regime. Political reform is the principal expression of the third dimension. When we speak of political reform we are assuming that it covers all the components of what we call politics: the state, where it means assuring the principle of "stateness," or the capacity to direct development and be the referent of collective action; the democratic regime, where it means improving that regime's quality and making it relevant; the political actors, which should be representative; and civil society or the citizenry, where it means guaranteeing participation.

The reconstruction of the polis society means its expansion both "downward" and "upward." In other words, there must be the incorporation of large sectors that are excluded not only from the national state community but also from local space, be that the municipality or the region. But there also must be the expansion of supranational-state space. Just as Europeans have understood this to mean at once strengthening their own national states and strengthening the European Union, in our case it means the construction and strengthening of the Latin American political community. This construction of the Latin American polis—in a sense in its inception through such matters as the Democratic Clause of Mercosur—is a task for today and not for tomorrow. We will return to this later.

The state, society, and social and political actors must be reinforced while recognizing the autonomy of each of them in the framework of a new world context characterized by globalization. As we have said, however, globalization should not be confused with the current form it is taking in the geopolitical dimension (hegemony of the United States) and the economico-ideological dimension (neoliberalism).

In the birth of industrial society there was no known model for society other than capitalism, so the reaction against the perverse effects of liberal capitalism was necessarily confused with the struggle against what was actually part of industrial society. From this identification of industrialization and capitalism, there arose initial reactions against industrialization itself. Some time later—this would be one of the contributions of Marxism —the two dimensions would become dissociated. The workers' movement would claim the industrial condition as the mode of social life to develop, but they demand the reform and radical transformation of capitalism. Socialism would show, beyond its historic perversions in some societies, how an industrial society with a different form of economic and social organization is possible. Social movements for social and political democracy would force the recognition of rights among those impacted by industrial capitalism—workers, the poor, the excluded—as well as societal participation in the public decisions in a particular society, which is known as citizenship.

Globalization—understood as the interpenetration on a global scale of economies, cultures, and political decisions that intersect national states—would seem to be an irreversible phenomenon, in the same way that industrialism was initially viewed. Again, though, it appears associated with a particular type of capitalist domination hegemonized by the United States. Consequently, the struggles against imperialism and neoliberalism are confused with the struggles against globalization.

These two dimensions—globalization and its contemporary form—must be separated in order to not remain outside of history. That implies, in the first place, strengthening national states and democracies, with their local and regional dimension, and the supranational forms of political organization on a continental and world scale. Justice on the international level is evidence of that. Without strong representative and participatory governments on all these levels, globalization will continue to advance, but in its unequalizing and destructive dimension. Only with organized local communities and solid states integrated into blocs can democratic governments and citizenries on a world scale be considered. That is what is lacking in the globalization dominated by the United States and neoliberalism, which leaves the entire process at the mercy of de facto powers. The democratic struggle at every level is precisely what can make it possible to restrain the de facto powers. Therefore, what is known as the antiglobalization movement should be politicized on the various levels (local, national, regional bloc, world), which means giving a general orientation to the different social identities and movements while respecting their diversity, and which also means participating in the institutional realm.

In sum, the great question faced by Latin American countries in today's globalized world has two parts: Will they be able to constitute a national project with which to be inserted into this world? And will they be able to do it together with other countries, constituting a bloc—a Latin American cultural and political space? To be able to control the economy and technology, which is external to them and unfortunately does not belong to them, Latin American countries will have to recompose and impact politics and culture.

Thus, beyond the economic question, a new, more complex vision of globalization must be developed in which the social, political, and cultural factors and the idea of geo-economic-political-cultural blocs in the globalized world are put into play. Most likely the insertion of countries will not take place in an isolated way—which only a great power could achieve, and even then with difficulty—but through the formation of large blocs that are not only economic but above all political and cultural. Latin America should be one of those, which means thinking with a logic of integration on every level and aspiring to be one of the models of modernity for the world that is being created. That process will be gradual and will necessarily take place in pieces, through subblocs and subspaces.

If one wishes Latin America to constitute a large bloc in the process of globalization—that is, a space not only of common economic development but of scientific and technological development and cultural industries, of citizenship and strong civil society, of participation and diversity, of interculturality, of shared labor and environmental institutionalism, and so on—then one must think of subspaces in which each of these aspects may be partially realized and in which links with other subspaces may be established.

The construction of a large Latin American economic-political-cultural bloc will probably take place around three great axes, looking beyond the crises that can be observed today. One axis is formed by Mexico and Central America. Another is made up of the Andean countries, which face the most problematic situation today. The third is constituted by the countries of Mercosur, where Brazil occupies the strongest position. It makes no sense to think of this bloc without including Mercosur.

Chile and the Possibility of a National Project

In the twentieth century Chile was constituted as a historical society and political community around what we could call the democratic-state, national-popular, or political-party matrix or project. This process, in bloom since the 1920s and really coming of age in the 1930s, took on a variety of forms until the 1970s.

One of the main characteristics of this society was that economy, culture, and social organization in a sense were fused into politics. The latter constituted the principal mark of collective identities, and from it the principal orientations of individual and group subjectivities arose. The basic cement of the Chilean society consisted of politics and—unlike in other Latin American societies—party politics. Politics allowed access to the goods or services that the state directly or indirectly administered, such as health care, education, employment, and credits. Yet, especially since the 1960s, politics was also the principal source of meaning for individual and collective projects. This form of structuring the country was not without its problems, such as economic instability and dependency, the structural exclusion of peasants and the urban poor until the 1960s, the polarization of political life, and the weakness of the civil society's organizations and cultural manifestations.

This type of society, and of Latin American and Chilean modernity, was dismantled and transformed, and in a sense ceased to exist. That was a result of the most generic processes of globalization and of the implementation of a counterproject that sought nothing less than the destruction of the national-popular project and its replacement by a different type of matrix, attempted by the military dictatorship starting in 1973. The enemy against which this regime directed all of its force and violence was the national-popular world in any of its political, cultural, or social expressions, and in its democratic institutionalism.

In a first, specifically political dimension, the authoritarian neoliberal project maintained the idea of the nation and of society, except that this nation was made up of both friends and enemies. This is a national or societal vision that could not but be repressive, insofar as it pointed to internal enemies that had to be eliminated. Along with this essentially military and authoritarian dimension, however, there arose another, from the economy, which impacted the society, culture, and politics, and went in the opposite direction from the idea of the national community. This latter dimension saw society as a purely economic space, a market that one approaches according to the resources at one's disposal, the population being merely an aggregate of consuming individuals. In this vision society does not exist; the country is a fiction. There was an effort to impose a double equation against the national, popular, and democratic matrix: State plus politics equals repression; society equals market.

This project was a complete failure in terms of establishing a new, coherent, and stable matrix to replace the previous one, but it did achieve the dismantling of the national-popular matrix and left the country without a unifying and structuring principle. At the same time, in the symbolic and ethical dimension, the military and neoliberal current imposed the principle of impunity that "as power increases, explanations decrease." Hence, the enormous moral significance of Pinochet's arrest in London and his being stripped of diplomatic immunity and indicted in Chile, showing that impunity must have its limits if a society is to exist at all. Meanwhile, from the economic realm prevailed the idea that everything is a competition—that everything is measured by the market and that life consists of earning in any way possible, even at the expense of others. The generalization of these perverse criteria, found today in advertising, the media, calls for achievement, and behavior on both the micro and the macro levels of society has had as its worst consequences not only the destruction of a certain form of coexistence and institutionalism, a certain national project, but also the delegitimation of the very idea of a national project, of reconstruction of a community or society starting from certain principles around which the society and its debates, struggles, and conflicts are organized.

The process of political democratization, begun with the defeat of the dictatorship in the 1988 plebiscite and consolidated with the inauguration of the first democratic government in 1990, brought back the free election of politicians and brought public liberties back into effect. However, this took place in the context of strong institutional and ethical-symbolic legacies of the dictatorship, along with military and civilian de facto powers that limit the expression of the popular will. In spite of that, the country has maintained economic stability and growth and has been able to correct some of the perversions of the inherited socioeconomic model—above all in the reduction of poverty—but without being able to reduce inequalities.

In the last few years we have witnessed contradictory processes. On the one hand, there has been the erosion of the remaining components of the national, popular, and democratic project (for example, the disappearance of what sociologists call the middle class and its replacement by an aggregate of strata or segments, or the replacement of social movements by the public opinion, de facto powers, and corporatist lobby groups). At the same time, there has been the rejoining of the shreds that still keep alive the idea of national community—for example, the recovery of democracy, although with an institutionalism that takes away its relevance and quality and in the long run may transform it into a mere formality. Some embrace this change as modernization and greater liberty for individuals, failing to consider that a demodernization of what has been the Chilean modernity —and at times its simple replacement by the survival of the fittest and the most opportunist—is also taking place.

The major issue, then, is how to reconstitute the idea of a political community or society, given the structural and cultural changes arising from the phenomena of globalization and the legacies of the military and neoliberal project, which the return to an incomplete democracy has not yet resolved. On the political level, four questions must be faced in order to resolve Chiles's central problem as it enters the twenty-first century: the reconstruction of a national community or, in classic terms, of a polis or political society; historical and moral reconciliation; socioeconomic equality; and the role of the state, politics, and the insertion in Latin American space in response to globalization.

The issue of national reconciliation involves the reconstruction of the basic unity of a society, the fracturing of which has transformed it into a sum of enemies or of individuals and groups who do not really recognize one another as part of a single country. It is not possible to reconstruct this minimal unity, an issue not of the past but of the future, without ending impunity and the survival of the fittest, whether the fittest be an individual or de facto powers. Consequently, the issue of justice, punishment, and reparation for the crimes and human rights violations committed by the military dictatorship with the support of civilians—that is, the institutional act by which it is recognized that certain things should never happen and will not occur again—is a condition sine qua non for the country to have any future. In discussing historical reconciliation, it is also appropriate to deal with the issue of the integration of the Mapuche as an autonomous people in a multinational state.

The second issue that must be faced in order to reconstruct a national community is that of socioeconomic equality and sociocultural diversity. The concept of equality should not be confused with that of equity; the latter—and this is not to deny its own validity and legitimacy—has been utilized lately rather as an ideological substitute for the former. While equity refers to an equality of individual opportunities, when we speak of equality we are referring to the minimum reasonable, ethical, and possible distance between social categories. This means that the distance between rich and poor, between weak and strong, does not entail the existence of more than one country within the same territorial space, as is the case today. For there to be a national community, there must be minimal socio-economic equality accompanied by maximal cultural diversity. Just as economic policy needs measurable indicators of macroeconomic growth and equilibria, social policy requires goals of socioeconomic equality that can be measured from year to year. In other words, the issue of socioeconomic equality and cultural diversity is the cornerstone of any social policy with the purpose not of producing goods but of producing society and social relations. Yet equality assumes redistribution, which cannot be accomplished by coercive or revolutionary methods. Rather, redistribution must take place through political majorities and a relegitimation and deep transformation of the state and of politics. That leads us to the third issue.

The state cannot cease to be the principal agent of unity, regulation, and redistribution. That means abandoning the nonsense of antistatism and of state reform purely in terms of size, efficiency, and competitiveness. These issues are certainly important but are entirely secondary in relation to the central issue, that of returning to the state its leadership role, which will require that in many dimensions the state's resources and size be increased. Certainly the state should be kept in check by systems of representation, by party systems, and by citizen participation. But this is not merely a question of the size of the state apparatus. The topics of national unity, social equality, cultural diversity, and the restoration of the state's leadership role suggest reversing the classic thesis of Aníbal Pinto, who claimed that Chile had an atrophied economy and very weak economic development accompanied by highly developed sociopolitical institutions. We have stated in this book that today we find the reverse situation: a dynamic economy that seeks to be modern and competitive but has been loosened from and is too independent of society, and an extremely poor system of political institutions, beginning with a constitution that was imposed and is full of nondemocratic enclaves, but also encompassing decentralization and such dimensions as labor, the environment, culture, higher education, and communications. On the political-institutional level, with respect to norms and organization, a profound democratizing and modernizing transformation is needed, in technocratic terms as well as in the sense of a true modernity that allows the constitution of subjects and actors in each realm.

Underlying these issues is the important topic of the relegitimation of politics and the improvement of its quality. With respect to the past this involves constitutional reform and the elimination of authoritarian enclaves. With respect to the future it requires that the society invest in politics: for example, automatic voting registration and compulsory voting, financing parties and campaigns and curbing expenses, and primary elections. The revalorization and relegitimation of politics is a condition sine qua non for the country to no longer be an assemblage of self-interested individual and de facto powers who do not recognize one another in a past and as a result do not have a future as a community in a globalized world.

The final point is that a national project is only possible in the framework of building a space composed of different countries that move as a group into the globalized world. This is Latin America's calling. In this construction, as we have said, Mercosur plays a fundamental role. Regardless of immediate economic calculations and estimations of the benefits of other alliances and negotiations with other blocs, there is no destiny for Chile if it does not construct its national project in this framework. Chile has no choice but to join the set of countries in which Brazil seems to be the central pillar. As things stand at present, this is Mercosur. Chile's role will never be that of leader, as some naively seek, but it can be modestly indispensable: bringing Mexico closer to South America; being the interlocutor with the Andean countries, with which it has had ties historically; and joining Argentina and other countries in playing the necessary role of counterpart in the space led by Brazil. Chile's own contribution will be what historically has always been its unique comparative advantage: a democratic political institutionalism that still remains to be constructed.

Notes

Chapter 1

1. These ideas are spread throughout several of my works, particularly "A New Socio-historical 'Problématique' and Sociological Perspective," *Sociologie et Sociétes* 30, no. 1 (Spring 1998); *Hacia una nueva era política: Estudio sobre las democratizaciones* (Mexico City: Fondo de Cultura Económica, 1995); and "¿En qué sociedad vivi(re)mos? Tipos societales y desarrollo en el cambio de siglo," in *Democracia para una nueva sociedad: Modelo para armar*, ed. Helena González and Heidulf Schmidt (Caracas: Editorial Nueva Sociedad, 1997): 65–75.

2. A critique of the "minimalist or processualist definition" of democracy is in Guillermo O'Donnell, "Democratic Theory and Comparative Politics," Department of Government and International Studies, Working Paper 99–7 (Notre Dame, Ind.: University of Notre Dame Press, 1999).

3. In the following pages I draw on my article, "Democratización, desarrollo, modernidad: ¿Una nueva problemática para América Latina?" *Revista Paraguaya de Sociología* 31, no. 91 (September–December 1994): 243–54.

4. On the general problématique of Latin America in the 1990s, see José Luis Reyna, ed., *América Latina a fines de siglo* (Mexico City: Fondo de Cultura Económica, 1995), and Peter H. Smith, ed., *Latin America in Comparative Perspective: New Approaches to Methods and Analysis* (Boulder, Colo.: Westview Press, 1995). For another perspective, see Raquel Sosa Elízaga, *América Latina y el Caribe: Perspectivas de su reconstrucción* (Mexico City: ALAS, UNAM, 1996). One of the most notable works in the effort to overcome determinist paradigms and, at the same time, to show general trends in what we could call the Latin American sociopolitical model, is Alain Touraine, *Política y sociedad en América Latina* (Barcelona: Espasa, 1989).

5. On economic transformations, see William C. Smith, Carlos H. Acuña, and Eduardo A. Gamarra, eds., *Latin American Political Economy in the Age of Neoliberal Reform: Theoretical and Comparative Perspectives for the 1990s* (Coral Gables, Fla.: North-South Center, University of Miami; New Brunswick, N.J.: Transaction Publishers, 1994); Ricardo French-Davis, *Macroeconomía, comercio y finanzas para reformar las reformas en América Latina* (Santiago: CEPAL–McGraw Hill, 2000). CEPAL, *Transformación productiva con equidad: Un enfoque integrado* (Santiago: CEPAL, 1992).

6. Josetxo Beriain, ed., *Las consecuencias perversas de la modernidad* (Barcelona: Anthropos, 1996); Alain Touraine, *Critique of Modernity* (Cambridge, Mass.: Blackwell, 1995). On Latin America, see "Identidad y modernidad en América Latina," *Revista Persona y Sociedad* 10, no. 1 (April 1996); Néstor García Canclini, *Hybrid Cultures: Strategies for Entering and Leaving Modernity* (Minneapolis: University of

Minnesota Press, 1995). For a more catholic perspective, see Pedro Morandé, *Cultura y modernización en América Latina: Ensayo sociológico acerca de la crisis del desarrollismo y de su superación* Cuadernos del Instituto de Sociología (Santiago: Edit. Pontificia Universidad Católica de Chile, 1984).

7. Manuel Antonio Garretón, ed., *América Latina: Un espacio cultural en el mundo globalizado* (Bogotá: Convenio Andrés Bello, 1999); Rubens Bayardo and Mónica Lacarrieu, eds., *La dinámica global/local: Cultura y comunicación: Nuevos desafíos* (Buenos Aires: Ediciones Ciccus/La Crujía, 1999).

8. The term "national-popular" comes from Gino Germani, *Política y sociedad en una época de transición: De la sociedad tradicional a la sociedad de masas* (Buenos Aires: Paidós, 1965), and is taken up in Touraine, *Política y sociedad*. The concept of state-centric matrix is found in Marcelo Cavarozzi, *El capitalismo político tardío y sus crisis en América Latina* (Rosario, Argentina: Homo Sapiens Ediciones, 1996).

9. Touraine, *Política y sociedad*; Cavarozzi, *El capitalismo político tardío*; Nuria Cunill Grau, *Repensando lo público a través de la sociedad: Nuevas formas de gestión pública y representación social* (Caracas: Editorial Nueva Sociedad, 1997).

10. Different authors have used this concept to refer to the idea of a situation wherein there is no longer absolute hegemony by one social sector of the interior of the state, as there was in the oligarchic era, but unstable arrangements, naturally asymmetrical, among the included sectors: various factions of the bourgeoisie, middle sectors, and industrial workers. See Francisco Weffort, "Classes populares e desenvolvimento social" (Ilpes, manuscript, 1968).

11. Among others, see Alain Touraine, "Los problemas de una sociología propia en América Latina," *Revista Mexicana de Sociología* 51, no. 3 (July–September 1989): 4–22; Immanuel Wallerstein, *El legado de la sociología, la promesa de la ciencia social*, ed. Roberto Briceño-León and Heinz Sonntag (Caracas: Editorial Nueva Sociedad, 1999); Fernando Henrique Cardoso, "El pensamiento socio-económico latinoamericano: Las últimas cuatro décadas," *Nueva Sociedad* 139 (September–October 1995): 19–25; "América Latina: La visión de los cientistas sociales," *Nueva Sociedad* 139 (September–October 1995): 61–164.

Chapter 2

1. An earlier version of this chapter was presented at the I Congreso Iberoamericano de Filosofía, Cáceres, September 1998, and at the seminar entitled "Desafíos de la sociedad latinoamericana frente a las transformaciones contemporáneas," Department of Sociology, School of Social Sciences, Universidad de la República, Montevideo, 3–4 December 1998. I also revisit hypotheses developed in the following seminars: "Escenarios futuros: Agendas de gobierno y desafíos socio-políticos en América Latina," Centro de Investigaciones Interdisciplinarias en Ciencias y Humanidades and Instituto de Investigaciones Sociales, UNAM, Cuernavaca, México, 2–4 March 1998; and "Los nuevos mecanismos: Estado, mercado y sociedad

civil," Universidad Nacional General San Martín, Buenos Aires, May 1998; as well as articles published in *Revista Universitaria* and *Mensaje*, and especially "Transformaciones sociales y reconstrucción de los estados nacionales: Hacia una nueva matriz socio-política," in *La dinámica global/local: Cultura y comunicación: Nuevos desafíos*, ed. Rubens Bayardo and Mónica Lacarrieu (Buenos Aires: Ediciones Ciccus/La Crujía, 1999): 135–44.

2. In the vast literature on the topic, from the most favorable stances to the most critical, see Manuel Castells, *The Information Age: Economy, Society and Culture*, 3 vols. (Cambridge, Mass.: Blackwell, 1996–98); Jordi Borja and Manuel Castells, *Local y global: La gestión de las ciudades en la era de la información* (Madrid: Taurus, 1997). For a perspective from Latin America, see Jacques Chonchol, *¿Hacia dónde nos lleva la globalización? Reflexiones para Chile* (Santiago: Ediciones LOM, 2000); Victor Flores Olea and Abelardo Mariña Flores, *Crítica de la globalidad: Dominación y liberación en nuestro tiempo* (Mexico City: Fondo de Cultura Económica, 1999); Néstor García Canclini, *La globalización imaginada* (Buenos Aires: Paidós, 1999); Manuel Castells, *Globalización, identidad y estado en América Latina* (Santiago: PNUD, 1999); Bayardo and Lacarrieu, *La dinámica global/local*; Rubens Bayardo and Mónica Lacarrieu, eds., *Globalización e identidad cultural* (Buenos Aires: Ediciones Ciccus, 1997); Manuel Antonio Garretón, ed., *América Latina: Un espacio cultural en el mundo globalizado* (Bogotá: Convenio Andrés Bello, 1999).

3. See Juan Rial and Daniel Zovatto, eds., *Urnas y desencanto político: Elecciones y democracia en América Latina (1992–1996)* (San José: IIDH-CAPEL, 1998).

4. Castells, *The Information Age*; Alain Touraine, *¿Podremos vivir juntos? Iguales y diferentes* (Mexico City: Fondo de Cultura Económica, 1997); Josetxo Beriain, ed., *Las consecuencias perversas de la modernidad* (Barcelona: Anthropos, 1996); Anthony Giddens, *The Consequences of Modernity* (Stanford: Stanford University Press, 1980); Ulrich Beck, *Risk Society: Towards a New Modernity* (London: Sage, 1992).

5. Thomas H. Marshall, *Class, Citizenship and Social Development* (Garden City, N.Y.: Doubleday, 1964). An excellent study of a Latin American case is Sinesio López, *Ciudadanos reales e imaginarios: Concepciones, desarrollo y mapas de la ciudadanía en el Perú* (Lima: Instituto de Diálogo y Propuestas, 1997). I am indebted to Hilda Sábato for the distinction between the "rights" dimension and the "subject" dimension of citizenship to which I allude below.

Chapter 3

1. This chapter is based on a talk given in the Proyecto Formación de Conceptos en Ciencias y Humanidades, Centro de Investigaciones Interdisciplinarias en Ciencias y Humanidades, UNAM, and its publication, Manuel Antonio Garretón, *Democracia y democratización* (Mexico City: Videoteca de Ciencias y Humanidades, Colección Conceptos, Centro de Investigaciones Interdisciplinarias en Ciencias y Humanidades, Universidad Nacional Autónoma de México, 1999).

2. On the theoretical debate on democracy, see Alain Touraine, *What Is Democracy?* (Boulder, Colo.: Westview Press, 1997); Norberto Bobbio, *The Future of Democracy: A Defense of the Rules of the Game* (Minneapolis: University of Minnesota Press, 1987). On democracy in Latin America, see Aldo Solari, Rolando Franco, and Joel Jutkowitz, *Teoría, acción social y desarrollo en América Latina* (Mexico City: Siglo XXI, 1976); Larry Diamond, Juan J. Linz, and Seymour Martin Lipset, *Democracy in Developing Countries: Latin America* (Boulder, Colo.: Lynne Rienner Publishers, 1996); and Edgardo Lander, *La democracia en las ciencias sociales latinoamericanas contemporáneas* (Caracas: Ediciones Faces UCV, 1996). On transitions and democratizations in general and concerning Latin America in particular, see Juan J. Linz and Alfred Stepan, *Problems of Democratic Transition and Consolidation: Southern Europe, South America, and Post-Communist Europe* (Baltimore: Johns Hopkins University Press, 1996); Carlos Barba Solano, José Luis Barros, and Javier Hurtado, eds., *Transiciones a la democracia en Europa y América Latina*, 2 vols. (Mexico City: Editorial Miguel Angel Porrúa, FLACSO, 1991); Guillermo O'Donnell, Phillipe C. Schmitter, and Laurence Whitehead, eds., *Transitions from Authoritarian Rule*, 4 vols. (Baltimore: Johns Hopkins University Press, 1986); Scott Mainwaring, Guillermo O'Donnell, and J. Samuel Valenzuela, eds., *Issues in Democratic Consolidation: The New South American Democracies in Comparative Perspective* (Notre Dame, Ind.: University of Notre Dame Press, 1992). For an updated assessment and reexamination, see Jonathan Hartlyn, "Contemporary Latin America, Democracy and Consolidation: Unexpected Patterns, Re-elaborated Concepts, Multiple Components" (forthcoming in a volume edited by the Latin American Program, Wilson Center, Washington, D.C.). My own views are in Manuel Antonio Garretón, *Hacia una nueva era política: Estudio sobre las democratizaciones* (Mexico City: Fondo de Cultura Económica, 1995) and "Revisando las transiciones democráticas en América Latina," *Nueva Sociedad* 148 (March–April 1997): 20–29.

3. Seymour Martin Lipset, *Political Man: The Social Bases of Politics*, revised and expanded edition (Baltimore: Johns Hopkins University Press, 1981).

4. David Apter, *The Politics of Modernization* (Chicago: University of Chicago Press, 1965).

5. Guillermo O'Donnell, *Modernización y autoritarismo* (Buenos Aires: Paidós, 1972). Clearly, O'Donnell's thought is much more complex than is shown by this work, which fulfilled a demystifying purpose, as is borne out by his excellent anthology *Counterpoints: Selected Essays on Authoritarianism and Democratization* (Notre Dame, Ind.: University of Notre Dame Press, 1999).

6. The classic text is Gabriel A. Almond and Sidney Verba, *The Civic Culture: Political Attitudes and Democracy in Five Nations* (Princeton: Princeton University Press, 1962). Regarding Latin America, see Claudio Véliz, *The Centralist Tradition of Latin America* (Princeton: Princeton University Press, 1980).

7. Barrington Moore, *The Social Origins of Dictatorship and Democracy* (Boston:

Beacon Press, 1966); José Medina Echavarría, *Consideraciones sociológicas sobre el desarrollo económico en América Latina* (Santiago: CEPAL, 1963).

8. Pablo González Casanova, *Democracy in Mexico* (New York: Oxford University Press, 1970); Gino Germani, *Política y sociedad en una época de transición: De la sociedad tradicional a la sociedad de masas* (Buenos Aires: Paidós, 1965).

9. Francisco Weffort, *¿Cuál democracia?* (San José: FLACSO, 1993).

10. General Juan José Torres came to power in the wake of the October 1970 coup; the Popular Assembly comprised mainly labor and peasant organizations on the radical left.—Trans.

11. René Zavaleta Mercado, *El poder dual en América Latina: Estudios de los casos de Bolivia y Chile* (Mexico City: Siglo XXI, 1974).

12. Tomás Moulián and Manuel Antonio Garretón, *La Unidad Popular y el conflicto político en Chile* (Santiago: Ediciones CESOC, 1993).

13. For a recent critique of democratization processes and the studies of these in Latin America, based on the impossibility of real democracies owing to this type of regime's lack of social roots in the region, see Carlos Franco, *Acerca del modo de pensar la democracia en América Latina* (Lima: Friedrich Ebert Stiftung, 1998).

14. See the works cited in n. 2 of this chapter.

15. Moore, *The Social Origins*; Dankwart Rustow, "Transitions to Democracy: Towards a Dynamic Model," *Comparative Politics* 2, no. 3 (April 1970): 337–63.

16. My view is in the texts cited in n. 2 of this chapter.

17. For more on the Chilean case, see Part II of this book.

18. A different view is found in Hartlyn, "Contemporary Latin America."

19. See *Encuentro Académico sobre Reconciliación y Democracia* (Santiago: Consejo de Rectores de las Universidades Chilenas, 1996) and my own work in that volume, "Democratización incompleta, enclaves autoritarios y reconciliación (im)posible?"

20. On authoritarian enclaves, democratic relevance, and de facto powers, see my *La posibilidad democrática en Chile* (Santiago: FLACSO, 1988); *Hacia una nueva era política*; and "Situación actual y nuevas cuestiones de la democratización política en América Latina," in *Sociedad civil en América Latina: Representación de intereses y gobernabilidad*, ed. Peter Hengstenberg, Karl Kohut, and Günther Maihold (Caracas: Editorial Nueva Sociedad, 1999), 59–74.

Chapter 4

1. Partial versions of this article, completely revised and expanded here, appeared in "New State-Society Relations in Latin America," in *Redefining the State in Latin America*, ed. Colin I. Bradford (Paris: OECD, 1994): 239–49; "Las nuevas relaciones entre Estado y Sociedad y el desafío democrático en América Latina," *Revista Internacional de Filosofía Política* 4 (November 1994): 61–72; and "Transformación

del Estado en América Latina," *Espacios: Revista Centroamericana de Cultura Política* 6 (October–December 1995): 4–16.

2. CEPAL, *Equidad, Desarrollo y Ciudadanía* (Santiago: CEPAL, 2000); Dagmar Raczynski, ed., *Estrategias para combatir la pobreza en América Latina: Programas, instituciones y recursos* (Santiago: Cieplan-BID, 1995); Nora Lustig, ed., *Coping with Austerity: Poverty and Inequality in Latin America* (Washington, D.C.: Brookings Institution, 1995).

3. See, among others, the materials collected by the BID (Banco Interamericano de Desarrollo [Inter-American Development Bank, or IDB]), the PNUD (Programa de las Naciones Unidas para el Desarrollo [United Nations Development Program, or UNDP]), and the OECD (Organization for Economic Cooperation and Development) in Colin I. Bradford, ed., *Redefining the State in Latin America* (Paris: OECD, 1994); BID and PNUD, *Reforma social y pobreza: Hacia una agenda integrada de desarrollo* (Washington, D.C.: BID, PNUD, 1993); Fernando Calderón and Mario R. Dos Santos, *Hacia un nuevo orden estatal en América Latina: Veinte tesis sociopolíticas y un corolario* (Buenos Aires: CLACSO; Santiago: Fondo de Cultura Económica, 1991); and Nuria Cunill Grau, *Repensando lo público a través de la sociedad: Nuevas formas de gestión pública y representación social* (Caracas: Editorial Nueva Sociedad, 1997).

4. The idea expressed by Guillermo O'Donnell on the need to extend and deepen the nonexistent or precarious "rule of law" in different spheres of society, or in whole societies, takes this general tack. See "Some Reflections on Redefining the Role of the State," in Bradford, *Redefining the State*, 251–60; Cunill Grau, *Repensando lo público*.

5. Stephan Haggard and Robert R. Kaufman, "Democratic Institutions, Economic Policy and Performance in Latin America," in Bradford, *Redefining the State*, 69–90.

6. Here I return to aspects explained with Malva Espinosa in the report prepared for the Independent Committee for Population and Quality of Life, *From Adjustment Policies to the New Relations between the State and Society* (Paris, 1994).

Chapter 5

1. This chapter is based on a paper delivered at the Conferencia Internacional de Política Social, San José, Costa Rica, 8–10 September 1998, organized by the Red de Estudios Sociales Centro America-Caribe-Europa (RESCE) and UNICEF.

2. Raúl Urzúa, ed., *Cambio social y políticas públicas* (Santiago: CAPP, Universidad de Chile, PROLAP, 1997); Sonia M. Draibe, "Neoliberalismo y políticas sociales: Reflexiones a partir de las experiencias latinoamericanas," *Desarrollo Económico: Revista de Ciencias Sociales* 34, no. 134 (July–September 1994): 181–96; Nuria Cunill Grau, *Repensando lo público a través de la sociedad: Nuevas formas de gestión pública y representación social* (Caracas: Editorial Nueva Sociedad, 1997);

Carlos M. Vilas, ed., *Estado y políticas sociales después del ajuste: Debates y alternativas* (Mexico City: Universidad Autónoma de México; Caracas: Nueva Sociedad, 1995).

3. CEPAL, *Equidad y transformación productiva: Un enfoque integrado* (Santiago: CEPAL, 1992).

4. CEPAL, *Panorama social de América Latina 1998* (Santiago: CEPAL, 1999), and *Panorama social de América Latina 1999* (Santiago: CEPAL, 2000).

5. Dagmar Raczynski, ed., *Estrategias para combatir la pobreza en América Latina: Programas, instituciones y recursos* (Santiago: Cieplan-BID, 1995); *Focalización y Pobreza*, Cuadernos de la CEPAL 71 (Santiago: CEPAL, 1995).

6. Alain Touraine, *¿Podremos vivir juntos? Iguales y diferentes* (Mexico City: Fondo de Cultura Económica, 1997).

7. See Peter Hengstenberg, Karl Kohut, and Gunther Maihold, eds., *Sociedad civil en América Latina: Representación de intereses y gobernabilidad* (Caracas: Editorial Nueva Sociedad, 1999); Sinesio López, *Ciudadanos reales e imaginarios: Concepciones, desarrollo y mapas de la ciudadanía en el Perú* (Lima: Instituto de Diálogo y Propuestas, 1997).

8. Alain Touraine, *Política y sociedad en América Latina* (Barcelona: Espasa, 1989).

9. In what follows I revisit references and arguments introduced and developed in Manuel Antonio Garretón and Malva Espinosa, *From Adjustment Policies to the New Relations between the State and Society* (Paris, 1994). A summary can be found in Manuel Antonio Garretón and Malva Espinosa, "El marco de las políticas sociales: Del ajuste a las nuevas relaciones entre Estado y sociedad," *Revista Persona y Sociedad* 9, no. 2 (September 1995).

10. CEPAL, *Equidad, Desarrollo y Ciudadanía* (Santiago: CEPAL, 2000); CEPAL, *Panorama social de América Latina 1998, 1999*.

11. Mario dos Santos, *Las estrategias de gobernabilidad en la crisis*, Informe comparative del Proyecto RLA 90/011 (Buenos Aires: PNUD, UNESCO, CLACSO, 1994).

Chapter 6

1. This chapter is based on my participation in the seminar "Partidos políticos y problemas de representatividad," organized by Fundación Ebert/ILDIS, La Paz, December 1996, published as "Representividad y partidos políticos: Los problemas actuales," in *Partidos políticos y representación en América Latina*, ed. Thomas Manz and Moira Zuazo (Caracas: Editorial Nueva Sociedad, 1998), and "Representividad y partidos políticos: Los problemas actuales," *Revista Argentina de Ciencia Política* 2 (December 1998).

2. Scott Mainwaring and Timothy R. Scully, *Building Democratic Institutions: Party Systems in Latin America* (Stanford: Stanford University Press, 1995); Thomas Manz and Moira Zuazo, eds., *Partidos políticos y representación en América Latina*

(Caracas: Editorial Nueva Sociedad, 1998); Marcos Novaro, *Representación y liderazgo en las democracias contemporáneas* (Rosario, Argentina: Homo Sapiens Ediciones, 2000).

3. Alain Touraine, *¿Podremos vivir juntos? Iguales y diferentes* (Mexico City: Fondo de Cultura Económica, 1997); Manuel Castells, *The Power of Identity*, vol. 2 of *The Information Age: Economy, Society and Culture* (Cambridge, Mass.: Blackwell, 1997).

4. See Frederick Turner, "Reassessing Political Culture," in *Latin America in Comparative Perspective: New Approaches to Methods and Analysis*, ed. Peter H. Smith (Boulder, Colo.: Westview Press, 1995), 195–224.

5. See UNDP, *Human Development Report* (New York: Oxford University Press, 1998, 1999).

Chapter 7

1. The first part of this chapter is based on the article "La sociedad civil: Sola, no puede traer abajo las dictaduras," *Ideele: Revista del Instituto de Defensa Legal* 129 (July 2000).

2. The conceptual discussion behind the civil society topic can be found, for example, in Jean Cohen and Andrew Arato, *Civil Society and Political Theory* (Cambridge, Mass.: MIT Press, 1992), and Víctor Pérez Díaz, *La primacía de la sociedad civil* (Madrid: Alianza Editorial, 1994). Concerning Latin America, see Alain Touraine, *Política y sociedad en América Latina* (Barcelona: Espasa, 1989), and Peter Hengstenberg, Karl Kohut, and Günther Maihold, eds., *Sociedad civil en América Latina: Representación de intereses y gobernabilidad* (Caracas: Editorial Nueva Sociedad, 1999).

3. Manuel Antonio Garretón, "Popular Mobilization and the Military Regime in Chile: The Complexities of the Invisible Transition," in *Power and Popular Protest: Latin American Social Movements*, ed. Susan Eckstein (Berkeley: University of California Press, 1988), 259–77.

4. The Contadora Group (Mexico, Venezuela, Colombia, Panama) formed to broker regional peace negotiations in Central America.—Trans.

5. I am reintroducing elements of my article, "Social Movements and the Process of Democratization: A General Framework," *Revue Internationale de Sociologie* 6, no. 1 (1996): 39–50.

6. Alain Touraine, *Política y sociedad en América Latina* (Barcelona: Espasa, 1989).

Chapter 8

1. This chapter is based on the conference paper, "Cambio en la cultura política latinoamericana," delivered at the III Congreso Nacional sobre Democracia, "De la

gobernabilidad democrática al cambio institucional," Centro de Estudiantes de Ciencia Política, Universidad de Rosario, 24–25 August 1998, on the panel "Cultura, política, instituciones y procedimientos democráticos" (published in *Escenarios Alternativos: Revista de Análisis Político* 3, no. 5 [Summer 1999]). On these topics, see Rubens Bayardo and Mónica Lacarrieu, eds., *La dinámica global/local: Cultura y comunicación: Nuevos desafíos* (Buenos Aires: Ediciones Ciccus/La Crujía, 1999); and Frederick Turner, "Reassessing Political Culture," in *Latin America in Comparative Perspective: New Approaches to Methods and Analysis*, ed. Peter H. Smith (Boulder, Colo.: Westview Press, 1995), 195–224.

2. See Juan Rial and Daniel Zovatto, eds., *Urnas y desencanto político: Elecciones y democracia en América Latina (1992–1996)* (San José: IIDH-CAPEL, 1998).

3. Giovanni Sartori, *Homo videns: La sociedad teledirigida* (Madrid: Taurus, 1998).

Chapter 9

1. This part is based on my article "Chile," in vol. 1 of *The Encyclopedia of Democracy*, ed. Seymour Martin Lipset (Washington, D.C.: Congressional Quarterly Press, 1995), 200–202.

2. The National Intelligence Directorate (Dirección Nacional de Inteligencia) was Pinochet's secret police.—Trans.

Chapter 10

1. Two books on the military regime that complement each other in the periods they cover are J. Samuel Valenzuela and Arturo Valenzuela, eds., *Military Rule in Chile: Dictatorship and Oppositions* (Baltimore: Johns Hopkins University Press, 1987), and Paul W. Drake and Iván Jaksic, eds., *The Struggle for Democracy in Chile, 1982–1990* (Lincoln: University of Nebraska Press, 1995).

2. Juan J. Linz, "Opposition to and under an Authoritarian Regime: The Case of Spain," in *Regimes and Oppositions*, ed. Robert A. Dahl (New Haven: Yale University Press, 1973), 171–259.

3. I am referring to the MIR (Movimiento de Izquierda Revolucionaria, or Movement of the Revolutionary Left). This group has been classified as insurrectional since the 1960s. Many of its main leaders and midlevel cadres, as well as rank and file, were killed, arrested, or thrown out of the country. At all events their armed resistance was never really significant, and it was only with the emergence of the Manuel Rodríguez Patriotic Front, which at first had ties to the Communist Party, that the ideas of armed struggle became more important. They quickly failed, however, and continued on in isolated, desperate fighting through splinter groups of the Front, such as the United Popular Action Movement–Lautaro (MAPU-L), which arose in the mid-1980s.

4. See Arturo Valenzuela and J. Samuel Valenzuela, "Party Oppositions under the Chilean Authoritarian Regime," in Valenzuela and Valenzuela, *Military Rule in Chile*, 184–229; Alex E. Fernández Jilberto, *Dictadura militar y oposición política en Chile 1973–1981*, Latin American Studies 31 (Amsterdam: Center for Latin American Research and Development, 1981).

5. At the beginning of the military regime, the government officially eliminated left-wing parties and imposed a "recess" on the right-wing parties, which complied. The PDC did not comply and continued to be active. In 1977, a new decree called for the "dissolution" of all political parties. This did not hinder activities by the PDC or those of the parties on the left.

6. See "La crisis en el socialismo chileno," *Chile-América* 54–55 (June–July 1979): 81–137.

7. Javier Martínez and Eugenio Tironi, "La clase obrera en el nuevo estilo de desarrollo: Un enfoque estructural," in *Chile 1973–198?*, ed. FLACSO (Santiago: FLACSO, Revista Mexicana de Sociología, 1983); Guillermo Campero and José A. Venezuela, *El movimiento sindical en el régimen militar chileno, 1973–1981* (Santiago: ILET, 1984).

8. See CESOC, *Constitución de 1980: Comentarios de Juristas Internacionales* (Santiago: CESOC, 1984). On the political significance, see the works cited in chap. 1.

9. This change was announced by their secretary general in September 1980, but it would have its greatest impact from 1983 onward.

10. Movement for Unified Popular Action (Movimiento de Acción Popular Unitaria)—Trans.

11. Pilar Vergara, *Auge y caída del neoliberalismo en Chile* (Santiago: FLACSO, 1985).

12. Carlos M. Huneeus, "La política de apertura y sus implicancias para la inauguración de la democracia en Chile," *Revista de Ciencia Política* 7, no. 1 (1985).

13. Gonzalo de la Maza and Mario Garcés, *La explosión de las mayorías: Protesta Nacional 1983–1984* (Santiago: ECO, 1985). I have analyzed the protest movement in chap. 4 of Manuel Antonio Garretón, *Reconstruir la política: Transición y consolidación democrática en Chile* (Santiago: Editorial Andante, 1987).

14. Garretón, *Reconstruir la política*, chap. 4.

15. In 1986, the National Union Party (right) and the Christian Left (left) pulled out of the National Agreement, and some socialist groups, along with the Movement for Unified Popular Action (MAPU), were brought in.

16. Asamblea de la Civilidad, *La demanda de Chile* (Santiago: April 1986).

17. Javier Martínez and Eugenio Tironi, *Las clases sociales en Chile: Cambio y estratificación 1970–1980* (Santiago: Ediciones SUR, 1985).

18. Campero and Venezuela, *El movimiento sindical*.

19. Clearly, the most significant opposition effort to rearticulate the political and the social realms was the Civil Assembly, but with the drawbacks we mentioned. An overview of the social movements in Chile in this period can be found in CLACSO-

ILET, *Los movimientos sociales y la lucha democrática en Chile* (Santiago: CLACSO-ILET, 1986).

20. See the manifesto of the Council for Free Elections, "Convocatoria a una tarea nacional," 13 March 1987. Later the committee of parties for the Democratic Alliance and that of the Left for Free Elections were formed.

21. The candidate initiative as well as a government program were especially supported by the Democratic Alliance in 1987, now without the socialist sectors in it, and rejected by the left as a whole.

22. In September–October 1986, the Law of Electoral Registries was enacted, and in February 1987 the registering process began. The government had destroyed the registries extant to 1973.

23. This process of registering political parties (National Advance, National Renewal, National Party, and Radical Democracy, the latter on the regional level, on the right; Christian Democratic Party, Radical Party, and Social Democracy in the center; Humanist Party and Party for Democracy, mainly with leftist tendencies) was a key moment for the repoliticization of society, insofar as the parties had to launch national campaigns to gain signatures to register. The Political Parties Law was enacted in March 1987, and only the parties inscribed under that law could have representatives at the voting tables and television exposure.

24. On 2 February 1988, thirteen opposition parties signed the "Concertación por el 'No,'" to which other small parties were later added, making a total of seventeen parties by the end of 1988. After the plebiscite, the agreement became the Concertación of Parties for Democracy. The main member parties that expressed their will to become a government coalition with a single presidential candidate were the Christian Democratic Party (CDP), the Radical Party, the Social Democrats, the Núñez Socialist Party, the Almeyda Socialist Party, the Party for Democracy (PPD), the Humanist Party (PH), the Radical Socialist Democratic Party, the MAPU, the Christian Left, and several small center and right socialist groups. Actually, the key parties of the CPD were the Christian Democratic Party, the Núñez-PPD Socialist Party, and the Almeyda Socialist Party. Subsequent to the 1989 presidential and parliamentary elections, the two socialist parties merged, and the PPD became an independent party, whereby the two basic axes of the agreement in Patricio Aylwin's government, which formed electoral subagreements, were the CPD, around which rallied the Radical Party, and the Socialist-PPD alliance.

25. I have analyzed the importance of the plebiscite for triggering a process of transition in *El Plebiscito de 1988 y la transición a la democracia* (Santiago: FLACSO, 1988).

26. A general summary of the opinion polls from recent years vis-à-vis the plebiscite is Manuel Antonio Garretón and Sergio Contreras, "Sociedad, política y plebiscito: Lo que revelan las encuestas," *Mensaje* 373 (October 1988).

27. In the campaign the military government used the whole state machinery, including regional and municipal authorities, direct intervention by the high com-

mand of the armed forces, monitoring of television until the last month in which the opposition had a daily allotment of fifteen minutes, scare tactics, and direct repression. We should add that neither the date nor the candidate was determined until one month prior to the plebiscite, which hampered the opposition campaign.

Chapter 11

1. There is an abundant descriptive and analytical literature on the so-called Chilean transition. On this topic we recommend Alexander Wilde's exhaustive survey, "Irruptions of Memory: Expressive Politics in Chile's Transition to Democracy," *Journal of Latin American Studies* 31, no. 2 (May 1999): 473–500. My own view is in Manuel Antonio Garretón, *Hacia una nueva era política: Estudio sobre las democratizaciones* (Mexico City: Fondo de Cultura Económica, 1995).

2. See n. 2 in Chapter 2 above. On the limitations of and questioning of this field of study, especially for Latin America, see Carlos Franco, *Acerca del modo de pensar la democracia en América Latina* (Lima: Friedrich Ebert Stiftung, 1998). Excellent examples of various approaches can be found in Guillermo O'Donnell, *Counterpoints: Selected Essays on Authoritarianism and Democratization* (Notre Dame, Ind.: University of Notre Dame Press, 1999). For my own perspective, see Chapter 3 of this book.

3. A good example of this position in the Chilean case is found in Tomás Moulián, *Chile actual: Anatomía de un mito* (Santiago: Ediciones LOM, 1997).

4. One should not confuse the two meanings of "forward-looking" and "backward-looking" consolidation with the allusions Di Palma makes to two types of legitimation with the same names of "forward-looking" and "backward-looking." Cited by Juan J. Linz and Alfred Stepan, *Problems of Democratic Transition and Consolidation: Southern Europe, South America, and Post-Communist Europe* (Baltimore: Johns Hopkins University Press, 1996).

5. Moulián, *Chile actual.*

6. Protests by Chilean military personnel on 28 May 1993 in the streets of Santiago, over prosecutions of members of the army for alleged human rights violations.—Trans.

7. See the debate on this score in *Revista de Ciencia Política* 16, nos. 1–2 (1994). Also see Manuel Antonio Garretón, *Hacia una nueva era política: Estudio sobre las democratizaciones* (Mexico City: Fondo de Cultura Económica, 1995); Oscar Godoy, "La transición chilena a la democracia pactada," *Estudios Públicos* 74 (Fall 1999): 79–106.

8. Manuel Antonio Garretón, "El segundo gobierno democrático en Chile. ¿De la transición y consolidación a la profundización democrática?" *Revista Mexicana de Sociología* 58, no. 1 (January–March 1996): 121–32.

9. I should point out examples of this type of obstacle or restriction, not only those aspects that were poorly negotiated during the 1989 constitutional reforms

(municipal authorities, presidential terms, electoral system, etc.) but also certain normative ones under the democratic governments (television, municipalization and regionalization, labor laws, regulatory frameworks for privatized public service firms, defense policy, military spending, etc.).

10. Senator Carlos Ominami, among others, has submitted a very detailed list of substantive bills that have not been able to pass due to the presence of appointed senators.

11. Probably those who generalized naively and mistakenly the concept of "consensus democracies" for Chile, on the more democratic right and especially coalition sectors tied to government leadership, slightly adapted this idea from the literature on "consociational or consensual democracy," developed mainly by Arend Lijphart. She seeks to draw a distinction between majoritarian democracy and the type that resolves certain fundamental aspects through consensus. But here we are talking about "agreements on fundamentals" and not particular political arrangements on specific aspects in which the majority *should* decide. In other words, there was a naive and mistaken reading of theories developed for other kinds of situations.

12. See Aníbal Pinto, *Tres ensayos sobre Chile y América Latina* (Buenos Aires: Ediciones Solar, 1971).

13. Manuel Antonio Garretón and T. Villanueva, *Política y jóvenes en Chile: Una reformulación* (Santiago: Corporación PARTICIPA and Fundación Ebert, 1999).

14. A complete review of this literature is in Alexander Wilde, "Irruptions of Memory: Expressive Politics in Chile's Transition to Democracy," *Journal of Latin American Studies* 31, no. 2 (May 1999): 473–500.

15. "La fuerza de nuestras ideas," *El Mercurio*, 17 May 1998.

16. Moulián, *Chile actual*; PNUD, *Desarrollo humano en Chile 1998: Las paradojas de la modernización* (Santiago: PNUD, 1998).

17. "La gente tiene razón," Santiago, June 1998 (unpublished manuscript).

18. Moulián, *Chile actual*.

19. On the issue of reconciliation, see, among others, Consejo de Rectores de Universidades Chilenas, *Encuentro Académico sobre reconciliación y democracia* (Santiago, 1995), and Manuel Antonio Garretón, "Crucial but Limited: Reflections on the Chilean Truth Commission and the (Im)possible Reconciliation," presented at the International Seminar on Justice, Truth and Reconciliation: The Role of Truth Commissions in Transitional Societies. Geneva, Switzerland, 9–12 December 1998.

20. On this topic, see the studies included in *Entre la II Cumbre y la detención de Pinochet, Chile 1998* (Santiago: FLACSO). Also see *International Affairs* 75, no. 2 (April 1999).

Index